Pentecostal Theology and
the Theological Vision of N.T. Wright
A Conversation

Pentecostal Theology and the Theological Vision of
N.T. Wright

A Conversation

Edited By
Janet Meyer Everts
Jeffrey S. Lamp

CPT Press
Cleveland, Tennessee

Pentecostal Theology and the Theological Vision of N.T. Wright
A Conversation

Published by CPT Press
900 Walker ST NE
Cleveland, TN 37311
USA
email: cptpress@pentecostaltheology.org
website: www.cptpress.com

Copyright © 2015 CPT Press

All rights reserved. No part of this book may be reproduced or translated in any form, by print, photoprint, microfilm, microfiche, electronic database, internet database, or any other means without written permission from the publisher.

Library of Congress Control Number: 2015949786

ISBN-10: 1935931547
ISBN-13: 9781935931546

To a new generation of Pentecostal scholars,
for the glory of God

Contents

Preface
Amos Yong ix

Introduction
Janet Meyer Everts 1

Chapter 1
N.T. Wright – Right or Wrong for Pentecostals? A Survey of His Thought and Its Implications for Pentecostals
Jeffrey S. Lamp 7

Chapter 2
'Who Do I Say I Am?' A Constructive Critique of N.T. Wright's View of Jesus' Self-Understanding
Chris Green 27

Chapter 3
A Pneumatological Addition to N.T. Wright's Hermeneutic Done in the Pentecostal Tradition
Timothy Senapatiratne 44

Chapter 4
N.T. Wright's 'Justification' and the Cry of the Spirit
Rick Wadholm Jr. 60

Chapter 5
Justification and the Spirit: An Appreciative Interaction with N.T. Wright
Frank D. Macchia 76

Chapter 6
Assessing N.T. Wright's Reading of Paul through the Lens of Dispensationalism
Glen W. Menzies 85

Chapter 7
Faith, Hope, and Love: The Communion of Saints Seen from N.T. Wright's Eschatological Perspective
Janet Meyer Everts 107

Chapter 8
Realized Eschatology or Eschatology in the Process of Realization? A Pentecostal Engagement with N.T. Wright's View of the Present Mission of the Church in the World
Jeffrey S. Lamp 124

Chapter 9
The Word and the Wind: A Response
N.T. Wright 141

Bibliography 179
Index of Biblical (and Other Ancient) References 187
Index of Authors 190

Preface

Amos Yong[*]

I am a relative latecomer to the work of N.T. Wright. My initial exposure came in late 2007 when I was researching on the topic of political theology and I began to observe his contributions to the emerging field of what is called 'empire studies' in the New Testament. I was irresistibly drawn into the three volumes of the magisterial *Christian Origins and the Question of God* and was hooked. As a constructive and systematic theologian rather than a New Testament scholar, my reading Wright raised all kinds of theological implications and possible applications. As I was also then writing a book on Pentecostalism and political theology, I kept asking about the public theological significance – which includes the political, economic, social, and civil arenas – of Wright's hypothesis. It was then that I emailed some of my friends and New Testament colleagues in the Society for Pentecostal Studies asking if they were aware of published Pentecostal responses to Wright.

That email precipitated a brief exchange with Frank Macchia, one of the contributors to this volume, about his own discovery of Wright (separate from me but at about the same time). Some of the results of Macchia's own wrestling with Wright's work can be seen in his article later in this book. Nor is Macchia the only Pentecostal grappling with the implications of Wright's theology, as Rick Wadholm's contribution shows. Clearly Wright has been a catalyst for Pentecostal theologians like Macchia, Wadholm, and me.

All this presses the question: What about Pentecostal biblical studies in general and Pentecostal readings of the New Testament in particular? What are the implications of Wright's 'new perspec-

---

[*] Amos Yong (PhD, Boston University) is Director of the Center for Missiological Research and Professor of Theology and Mission at Fuller Theological Seminary, Pasadena, California. He is the author and editor of more than two dozen books, including co-editor of the *Pentecostal Manifestos* series published by Wm. B. Eerdmans.

tive' for Pentecostal biblical interpretation and biblical scholarship? In working through some of the Wright corpus, I identified five possible lines of conversation between Pentecostal scholars and the work of N.T. Wright. I am delighted that the contributors to this volume have taken up these topics (and much more).

First, Wright's is a fully-human Jesus who yet fulfills through his life, death, resurrection, and ascension into heaven God's plans to restore Israel and redeem the world. This theme about the restoration of Israel is one that has been largely neglected by Pentecostal scholars, with one or two exceptions. What are the implications for New Testament soteriology and Pentecostal theologies of salvation when revisited in conversation with the main theses coming out of Wright's version of the 'new perspective' on Paul and Jesus? How might the Lukan and Pauline materials be understood afresh within this framework? Glen Menzies' chapter in this volume addresses some of these issues, in particular the restoration of Israel motif, and indicates how a more classically Pentecostal perspective might compare and contrast with Wright's offerings. What is delightful about Menzies' analysis is his situating Wright's proposal centrally amid a currently ambiguous Pentecostal dialogue with dispensational eschatology. In this context, the restoration of Israel may mean more than one thing – whether for dispensational theology, Pentecostal eschatology, or even N.T. Wright – which is precisely why such a dialogue between Wright and Pentecostal scholars has the potential to spark conversation in multiple directions.

The second dialogical possibility builds on the preceding and is admirably and critically navigated by Chris Green in this volume as he examines Wright's contribution to what is now known as the Third Quest for the historical Jesus. Green's chapter is most forthright about registering questions regarding Wright's project, although this is done both appropriately and appreciatively. The Green–Wright discussion prompts further questions about the identity of the Galilean Jew often occluded by the theological tradition. I think Wright's Christology, while resolutely orthodox according to Nicene standards, leads to important and neglected questions about Jesus the Christ that do not arise within the dominant theological tradition's creedal frame of reference. Green also recognizes this, although he is more concerned to ask if Wright's revision can be clearly shown to be consistent with the creeds. While I think this is an important matter that ought to be pursued, the other side of the Pentecostal coin, the one that features the Oneness tradition and its more-Jewish oriented theology of the Godhead and Christology, is neglected in this volume. I wonder what might ensue in a conversation about Jesus, about God, and about God's saving purposes when, for instance, Oneness Pentecostals engage with the work of N.T. Wright? Both Oneness and Trinitarian Pentecostals love Jesus; it is evident that N.T. Wright does as well. How might a reconsideration of the person and work of Christ unfold in a dialogue between Pentecostals on both sides of this Christological divide and Wright's understanding of Jesus? More precisely, how might Green's chapter mediate a Wright-Oneness conversation? That is something that only the future can unfold, but we are in a better position to see this happening in light of the concerns and possible resources articulated by Green.

Third, Pentecostals are eschatologically oriented, focused as they are on Jesus the coming king. Wright's Jesus is the eschatological king who inaugurates God's final plans to save the world, and Wright's Paul proclaims this eschatological gospel while inviting the people of God to inhabit, embrace, and work out its meaning in the world. Here then is a vision of the coming reign of God that does not get hung up with elaborate 'end-time' charts but is nevertheless deeply and palpably motivated by what the Spirit of Jesus is doing in these 'last days' to save the world. Isn't this something that Pentecostals can and ought to get excited about? What emerges is a partially realized or inaugurated (Wright's preferred nomenclature) eschatology, but one that is replete with ecclesiological, discipling, ethical, and missional implications. Similar to the invitation to revisit New Testament Christology and Pneumatology by getting behind the fourth-century achievements, what about reconsidering the eschatologies of St. Paul and the evangelists apart from Darbyian or other Dispensationalist lenses? I am happy to report that a number of the chapters in this book – including Menzies, Everts, and Lamp most substantively – take up these matters and helpfully chart important and constructive paths forward for Pentecostal eschatology. What is so crucial about this engagement is that thinking about eschatology with Wright is irreducible to a futuristic or other-worldly horizon; instead eschatological matters are interwoven with so many other theological and practical themes, which all of the Pentecostal interlocutors who take up these matters in the pages to come recognize and confront squarely. The result, unless dialogue is squelched, is a revitalization of Pentecostal eschatology not just for the purposes of speculating about what might happen but also for the task of what it means to live *presently* as people full of the Holy Spirit in the last days (Acts 2.17).

This leads, fourth, to the fact that Pentecostal self-identity is bound up with missiology: Pentecostals are no more or less than people of mission. What shows forth plainly in Wright's scholarship is not only that Jesus was a person on a divinely ordained mission, but also that those who embrace his name – beginning with St. Paul, for example – are also called and empowered to engage with that same mission, one that involves the renewal of Israel and the redemption of the world. Pentecostal missiologies, however, can receive a major boost in light of Wright's insistence that the salvation intended by Jesus involves not only individual hearts and lives but also has sociopolitical and economic dimensions. I am inclined to say that even Pentecostals who proclaim a 'five-fold' or 'full' gospel often still are not as holistic as they might be. N.T. Wright shows how the basic thrust of the gospel involves these domains as well. In conversation with Wright, Pentecostal missiologies not only can affirm at least some versions of the prosperity theology (those emphasizing the difference God makes in the material aspects of our lives) without embracing its greed, consumerism, and materialism, but also can be emboldened to bear the kind of prophetic witness to the powers of this world that characterized the ministry of Jesus and the message of Paul. In turn, might Pentecostal scholars also show that the full gospel includes the charismatic and empowering work of the Holy Spirit that transforms even the ends of the earth? Jeff Lamp's second article in this volume reveals how Pentecostals can engage with many of these themes and trajectories. It is suggestive not only for the present and future of Pentecostal missiological praxis, but also for a holistic Pentecostal spirituality, soteriology, and theology of mission underwritten by explicitly theological rather than merely pragmatic warrants. In the big scheme of things, however, the dialogical promise of a Pentecostal–Wright discussion will be fulfilled when Pentecostal biblical and systematic-constructive theologians finally suggest how Pentecostal intuitions and insights might complement or even correct Wright's eschatological ideas. While this task remains, the groundwork is more than adequately laid in this volume.

And this leads to my final conversational plank (for now): How might Wright's approach to Scripture compare to, contrast with, or complement a Pentecostal understanding of the Bible and of hermeneutics? When I read N.T. Wright, I am driven back consistently to the sacred texts that he carefully attends to. Wright is no bibliolater; but he is committed to the apostolic testimony as preserved in the biblical canon. Pentecostals are also people of the book, although their 'this-is-that' hermeneutic oftentimes collapses the distance between the scriptural and the present day horizons. Wright's critical and historical realism is a solid reminder to us that 'what happened back then' is fundamentally important for Christian life today. But Pentecostals can also contribute to Wright's accomplishments the testimony that what happened back then continues to happen today. They hereby provide concrete witness to the possibilities inherent in Wright's own emphatic claim that the drama of Scripture needs to be critically and realistically improvised by each generation as they live into and out of the apostolic script and narrative of the book of Acts. The point is that the Bible is a living book, and Wright's writings and Pentecostal testimonies both bear complementary witness to that fact. All of these issues, plus a number of others, are capably handled in Tim Senapatiratne's chapter in this volume. He also proposes a constructive way forward for Wright's hermeneutics when he suggests that Wright needs to take more seriously the pneumatological dimension not only of Scripture as inspired but of the community of faith as receiving the Spirit's witness to the living Christ. Such a pneumatological theology of revelation, Scripture, and hermeneutics is unfolded in a distinctive Pentecostal manner in Senapatiratne's article, due in no small part to Senapatiratne's mastery both of the former bishop of Durham's wide-ranging writings and of Pentecostal biblical, hermeneutical, and theological scholarship.

In each of these ways, I as a Pentecostal theologian am challenged by Tom Wright. Reading Wright invites me to love Jesus more, to be more emboldened in testifying to the risen Christ, to long for the coming of the ascended one finally to redeem our world, indeed all of creation, and to return again and again to the wellsprings of the gospel message of Jesus Christ as mediated through the apostolic testimony. When I was a child I went to the altar regularly to give my heart to Jesus. N.T. Wright invites me not to stop converting to Jesus even as an adult.

I am therefore grateful to Jenny Everts and Jeff Lamp for responding with enthusiasm to my initial prompt and to the other authors for their contribution to this book. The rest of these pages take up important matters that will be of concern to Pentecostal biblical scholars, theologians, and all interested in the gospel and its proclamation and embodiment in the twenty-first century. I am eager to follow the conversation that will undoubtedly follow from this exploratory dialogue.

INTRODUCTION

According to that great fount of American wisdom, *Poor Richard's Almanac*, 'The wise Man draws more Advantage from his Enemies than the Fool from his Friends'.[1] Using this criterion N.T. Wright is a wise man indeed. When the popular American Evangelical pastor and author John Piper published his scathing critique of Wright's theology in November 2007, Wright was already well known in American scholarly circles and welcomed by Evangelical biblical scholars. I remember hearing N.T. Wright's presentations at the Institute of Biblical Research during the AAR/SBL meeting in November 2007. They were well attended, but quite normal, academic presentations. (My co-editor, Jeff Lamp, remembers this as well.) People were asking questions, spending time after sessions with Wright, and generally engaging in formal and informal academic discussion with Wright and others about the topics presented.

However when I attended the Wheaton theology conference on 'Jesus, Paul and the People of God: A Theological Dialogue with N.T. Wright',[2] two and a half years later in April 2010, the scene and the atmosphere had changed entirely. The Wheaton campus was mobbed with students from as far away as Toronto and Texas. The gymnasium and chapel were packed to overflowing and for evening sessions open to the public, overflow seating with big screen television monitors was available. It was obvious that Wright had achieved rock star status with most of these young Evangelical college and seminary students and more than a little hero worship was going on. In conversation with these students, it emerged that

---

[1] This quotation is attributed to both Benjamin Franklin (*Poor Richard's Almanac*, 1749) and Thomas Fuller (*Gnomologia*, 1732).

[2] The proceedings of the Conference are available as a book: Nicholas Perrin and Richard B. Hays (eds.), *Jesus, Paul, and the People of God: A Theological Dialogue with N.T. Wright* (Downers Grove: IVP Academic, 2011).

Piper's book and the controversy it generated is what had made Wright a star. Most had not liked the tone of Piper's book and had read Wright's book, *Justification: God's Plan & Paul's Vision*,³ which had come out almost exactly a year before the Wheaton conference. After reading the book, many had sided with Wright in the debate. Others had come to hear Wright on a variety of theological issues so they could come to a balanced view on the wider theological debate. Almost none of the younger generation of evangelicals who attended the conference thought Piper spoke for them. They wanted to hear Wright for themselves and come to their own conclusions on the matter.

Even though Pentecostals and Charismatics are not usually identified with the sort of hyper-Reformed theology claimed by John Piper, they too were affected by the controversy Piper's book generated. In March of 2008, Amos Yong, then the President of the Society for Pentecostal Studies (SPS), approached the Biblical Studies section of the Society and asked them to consider doing a volume on N.T. Wright. At the following SPS meeting, Jeffrey Lamp presented the paper that is included as the overview essay for this volume. The Biblical Studies section, chaired by Lee Roy Martin, agreed to do a volume on Wright and decided that all proceeds from the volume would be used to provide scholarships for young biblical scholars to attend SPS. I agreed to chair the paper sessions for the following two meetings and Jeffrey Lamp and I were appointed co-editors.

By a happy or unhappy chance, the 2010 SPS meeting was scheduled to be held in Minneapolis, only a few blocks from Bethlehem Baptist Church, where John Piper was the preaching pastor. The theme of that year's session on Wright was Wright's eschatology and *Surprised by Hope: Rethinking Heaven, the Resurrection, and the Mission of the Church*.⁴ (At the time the session topic was decided the book on justification had not yet been published.) The session was standing room only and actually had hecklers in attendance. By SPS standards it was pretty exciting. The big issue for the hecklers seemed to be whether or not Wright was a 'universalist'. They were

---

³ N.T. Wright, *Justification: God's Plan & Paul's Vision* (Downers Grove: IVP Academic, 2009).

⁴ N.T. Wright, *Surprised by Hope: Rethinking Heaven, the Resurrection, and the Mission of the Church* (New York: Harper One, 2008).

out to prove that he was and not even direct quotations from Wright could convince them otherwise.⁵ The outcome of this heated discussion was that several young scholars offered to do papers the following year when the session topic was the debate about justification, hermeneutics, and *Justification: God's Plan & Paul's Vision*. This session was equally well attended and the discussion was lively, but there were no hecklers. Papers from both sessions have been selected for this volume.

Although Pentecostals and Charismatics are hardly unthinking or uncritical in their assessments of N.T. Wright, the authors of these essays in general find themselves in sympathy with Wright's approach. There are several reasons for this. One of the most important is the globalization of twenty-first-century Christianity, a phenomenon that has deeply affected both the Anglican Communion and the Pentecostal movement.⁶ N.T. Wright's sensitivity to the effects of this cultural shift and his willingness to incorporate new cultural paradigms into his biblical exegesis and theological understanding of traditional doctrines is very appealing to Pentecostal scholars. Pentecostal scholars are also practitioners of their faith, not just theoretical theologians. Many of the authors represented in this volume are ordained ministers and pastors; all are involved in ministry in their local churches. They sense Wright's deep commitment to pastoral ministry and respect his role as a priest and former bishop in the Anglican Church. As many of these essays point out, Wright's thinking leaves a great deal of room for the Spirit. No Pentecostal is going to be happy with a rigid system that leaves no room for the movement of the Spirit, and any Pentecostal is going to embrace a theology that welcomes the presence of the Spirit (either implicitly or explicitly) in the interpretation of Scripture and is open to the presence of the Spirit in other aspects of Christian life and theology. Steven Land, the former president of Pentecostal Theological Seminary, characterizes Pentecostal spirituality as 'a

---

⁵ For those who would like to read what N.T. Wright has to say on the subject of universalism and hell, see N.T. Wright, *For All the Saints? Remembering the Christian Departed* (Harrisburg, PA: Morehouse, 2003), pp. 42-46.

⁶ Pentecostal scholars have been aware of this trend for some time and have been responsive to it. See Murray W. Dempster *et al.* (eds.), *The Globalization of Pentecostalism: A Religion Made to Travel* (Oxford: Regnum Books, 1999) for examples of representative issues and authors.

passion for the Kingdom'. There is no question that in almost every article and book of N.T. Wright, this 'passion for the Kingdom' comes through. It may be this 'passion for the Kingdom' that is most appealing of all to Pentecostal and Charismatic scholars who recognize in N.T. Wright 'a man of like passions' – for the global Church, for the care of souls, for the Spirit, and for the Kingdom of God. In the essays that follow this sense of common passions comes through.

The first essay in this volume is the amazingly comprehensive overview essay by Jeffrey Lamp. As editor of this volume I am convinced that armed with this essay and the two volumes by N.T. Wright our sessions addressed, *Surprised by Hope: Rethinking Heaven, the Resurrection, and the Mission of the Church* and *Justification: God's Plan & Paul's Vision*, most biblically literate readers should be able to make sense of the essays which follow. For those who want or need further reading suggestions, they are found at the beginning of the essay.

The next group of four essays comes from the session on *Justification: God's Plan & Paul's Vision*. All but one of these essays are by younger scholars, reflecting the tremendous interest the debate over justification and hermeneutics has generated in the emerging generation of biblical scholars and theologians. In more conservative Protestant circles the question of whether theological tradition should control the interpretation of the biblical text and to what extent has become an important concern. The debate between John Piper and N.T. Wright is merely an overheated example of an ongoing discussion in American Evangelical circles. So it is hardly surprising that two newly minted PhDs would want to write essays on hermeneutics. The first essay is by a theologian, Chris Green, who suggests that Wright should allow the theological tradition more control in his biblical interpretation. The biblical scholar, Timothy Senapatiratne, is far more supportive of Wright's methods, although he makes some thoroughly Pentecostal suggestions. These two essays are followed by a very interesting essay by Rick Wadholm, a pastor and (at the time the paper was written) seminary student from northwestern Minnesota. When the justification controversy reached his congregation, he decided to examine Wright's view of justification from a biblical perspective for one of his seminary courses. He wrote and presented this paper as a result of his research. Frank Macchia is a Pentecostal theologian who has himself written a book on justification.[7] This section concludes with his observations on the contributions and limitations of Wright's theology of justification to his own theology. It is a must read essay for anyone who wants to understand a Pentecostal perspective on justification or a Pentecostal perspective on Wright's view of justification.

The last group of essays deals with issues that are raised in Wright's book *Surprised by Hope: Rethinking Heaven, the Resurrection, and the Mission of the Church*. The first essay, by Glen Menzies, compares Wright's view of the end with the Dispensationalism in which Menzies was raised as a classical Pentecostal. It gives a thorough review of both views and comes to some rather surprising conclusions. Wright's view of heaven and the communion of saints is the subject of the next essay, by Janet Meyer Everts. Since it was written as an aid to ecumenical discussion between Pentecostals and Catholics on the sometimes divisive issue of the 'Communion of Saints', it was somewhat ironic that it was this paper that generated most of the controversy about Wright's universalism and view of hell. (For those who want a quick summary, please see footnote 22.) The final essay on the mission of the Church is again by Jeffrey Lamp, who suggests that it is best to see Wright's view of the mission of the Church as 'eschatology in the process of realization'. God has begun 'setting the world to rights' in Jesus' resurrection and continues to do so through the Church in the present world. In these three essays the eschatological foundation of so much of Wright's theology becomes evident, as does the natural appeal of this eschatological perspective to Pentecostals and Charismatics.

Last, but certainly not least, is the response essay by N.T. Wright. In it he describes his own 'Pentecostal' experience and asks, 'Does that make me a Pentecostal?' Most recent experts on global Pentecostalism would say, 'Yes'. Today Pentecostalism is being defined in phenomenological terms as a global movement that emphasizes the working of the gifts of the Holy Spirit. Global Pentecostalism, then, is found in churches and individuals in those churches that emphasize the experience of the empowering Holy

---

[7] Frank D. Macchia, *Justified in the Spirit: Creation, Redemption, and the Triune God* (Grand Rapids: Eerdmans, 2010).

Spirit and the practice of spiritual gifts.[8] So not only does N.T. Wright's perspective appeal to Pentecostals, like so many other Christians around the globe, Wright has been touched by the appeal of Pentecostalism, even if he would not call himself a Pentecostal. Wright has taken the time to respond at length to each individual essay in the book. This is especially helpful to anyone who reads this book, as they will have a detailed response from Wright as they read each essay. His essay stands as a fitting conclusion to the entire volume.

No introduction would be complete without expressions of gratitude. I truly appreciate my co-editor Jeffrey Lamp. I think Jeffrey has read everything N.T. Wright has written – twice! Jeffrey Lamp and I must together extend great gratitude to Lee Roy Martin and the Centre for Pentecostal Theology. Lee Roy supported this project from the beginning; the Centre has offered me a home away from home for several research projects, including this one; the Centre (read Lee Roy Martin and John Christopher Thomas) agreed to publish this volume; and Lee Roy answered all of my stupid editorial questions. We could not have done this without you, Lee Roy!

By the time this volume is published, Lee Roy Martin will have completed his term as president and past-president of the Society of Pentecostal Studies. We would like to dedicate this volume to him as a token of our appreciation for his support of this project and the encouragement he offers to all the biblical scholars of the Society of Pentecostal Studies.

Janet Meyer Everts
Hope College
March 2015

---

[8] Allan Heaton Anderson, *Introduction to Pentecostalism* (Cambridge: Cambridge University Press, 2nd edn, 2014), p. 6.

1

N.T. WRIGHT – RIGHT OR WRONG FOR PENTECOSTALS? A SURVEY OF HIS THOUGHT AND ITS IMPLICATIONS FOR PENTECOSTALS

JEFFREY S. LAMP[*]

Introduction

N.T. Wright is one of the most prominent and provocative New Testament scholars in the world, and his former ecclesiastical role as Bishop of Durham in the Church of England gave him additional access to the mainstream for his ideas. Given the popularity and scrutiny of his work, particularly in the area of Christian origins and early Christianity, an informed assessment from a Pentecostal perspective is vital, both for credibility in the field of New Testament studies and for engagement with his ideas in Pentecostalism's own theological project.

This discussion will survey the big picture of Wright's understanding of God's plan to set the world to rights. To keep the topic manageable, it will focus on Wright's articulation of Paul's theology, particularly as it finds expression in Galatians and Romans. Wright's project covers much more ground than just the Apostle Paul's contributions. Even given this rather restricted focus, there is ample

---

[*] Jeffrey Lamp (PhD, Trinity Evangelical Divinity School) is Professor of New Testament at Oral Roberts University, Tulsa, Oklahoma. He has served as a pastor in the United Methodist Church.

fodder for Pentecostals both to discern the contours of Wright's thought and to observe how the distinctive concerns of Pentecostal traditions fit neatly within this scheme as integral to it rather than as a sort of troublesome 'tack-on' component of a systematic theology.

The bulk of this discussion will consist of the construction of a pictorial representation of Wright's framework. The diagram is my own rendering of Wright's framework, and may not be as Wright would draw it. However, I believe it accurately represents the substance of Wright's conceptualization of Pauline theology. The final section of the paper will make some observations as to how Wright's framework might cohere with and further inform Pentecostals in the articulation of their own mission in the academy and in the world.

Paul's Theological Framework according to Wright

This section of the discussion will be a step-by-step construction of the following diagram:

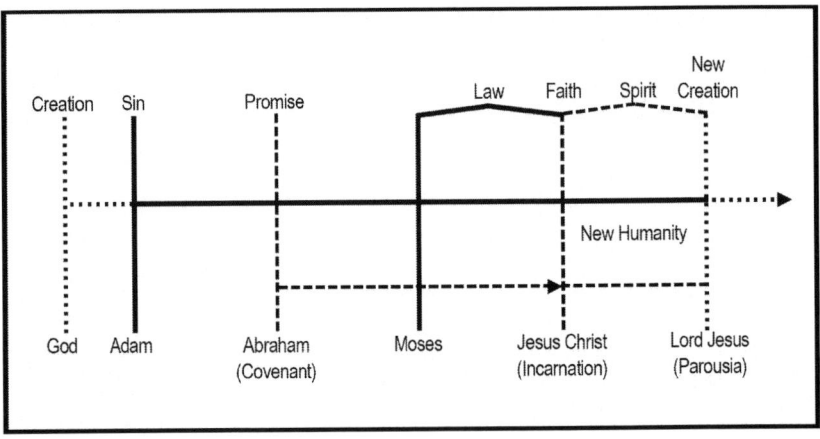

A few comments on the layout of the diagram are in order. First, regarding the line coding, the dotted lines represent the theological concepts of creation and new creation, unmarred by fallenness; the solid lines represent aspects of fallenness; and the dashed lines represent the elements of God's promise to set the world to rights. The legend across the top of the diagram lists pertinent theological categories, while the legend across the bottom of the diagram identifies the key biblical figures associated with the categories.

Another word is necessary regarding sources for this discussion. One could simply say, 'Read everything Wright has written', because his thought is cumulative on these matters. At a more practical level, there is a sort of 'canon within the canon' that is most helpful. One could get an overview by reading one of his synthetic articles on Paul's theology,[1] his briefer volumes on Paul,[2] his more substantive volumes on the matter,[3] his commentary on Romans,[4] or his 'Christian Origins and the Question of God' series.[5] For the present discussion, the majority of citations from Wright will come from among these sources. At that, representative rather than exhaustive references are given to avoid the clutter of endless footnotes. Such reference will occur at the beginning of each section to

---

[1] Wright, 'Romans and the Theology of Paul', in David M. Hay and E. Elizabeth Johnson (eds.), *Romans* (vol. 3 of *Pauline Theology*; Minneapolis: Fortress, 1995), pp. 30-67; Wright, 'New Exodus, New Inheritance: The Narrative Structure of Romans 3–8', in Sven K. Soderlund and N.T. Wright (eds.), *Romans and the People of God: Essays in Honor of Gordon D. Fee on the Occasion of His 65th Birthday* (Grand Rapids: Eerdmans, 1999), pp. 26-35.

[2] Wright, *What Saint Paul Really Said: Was Paul of Tarsus the Real Founder of Christianity?* (Grand Rapids: Eerdmans, 1997); Wright, *Paul: In Fresh Perspective* (Minneapolis: Fortress, 2005). Cited hereafter as *WSPRS* and *Paul*, respectively.

[3] Wright, *Climax of the Covenant: Christ and the Law in Pauline Theology* (Minneapolis: Fortress, 1992); Wright, *Surprised by Hope: Rethinking Heaven, the Resurrection, and the Mission of the Church* (New York: HarperCollins, 2008); Wright, *Justification: God's Plan & Paul's Vision* (Downers Grove: IVP Academic, 2009). Cited hereafter as *Climax*, *SH*, and *Justification*, respectively.

[4] Wright, *Romans* (New Interpreter's Bible 10; Nashville: Abingdon Press, 2002).

[5] Wright, *The New Testament and the People of God* (Christian Origins and the Question of God 1; Minneapolis: Fortress, 1992); Wright, *Jesus and the Victory of God* (Christian Origins and the Question of God 2; Minneapolis: Fortress, 1996); Wright, *The Resurrection of the Son of God* (Christian Origins and the Question of God 3; Minneapolis: Fortress, 2003). Cited hereafter as *NTPG*, *JVG*, and *RSG*, respectively.

reduce clutter, with limited footnotes occurring elsewhere in the text.

God's Good Creation[6]

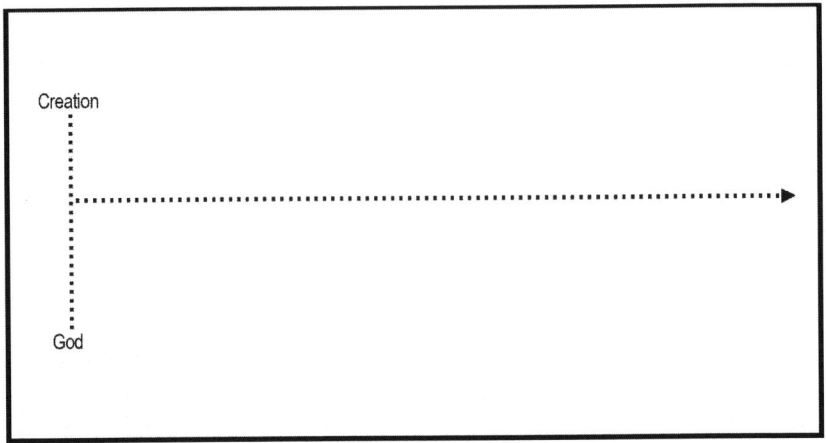

Paul is in agreement with the creation accounts in Genesis that God created the universe good. Paul, however, adds a feature that enhances the traditional Jewish picture of God's creative activity. Whereas Genesis 1 pictures God in consultation in the creative act ('us', v. 26) and the wisdom traditions depict Lady Wisdom as the agency of creation (e.g. Prov. 3.19; Wisd. 7.22–8.1), Paul ascribes creative agency to Christ (1 Cor. 8.6; Col. 1.16). Paul does not engage in speculation regarding the event of creation beyond ascribing creative agency to Christ, but this ascription has foundational importance for what follows in Paul's theological reflection. The original creation was good and is itself connected with Christ. God's redemption in Christ, accordingly, should involve all that finds its origin and being in Christ. Indeed, in Col. 1.16, the verse in which creative agency is attributed to Christ, creation's *telos* is Christ himself. As Wright reads Paul, creation is not to be obliterated at the end of the age, but is rather to be 'set to rights', as Wright phrases it. The destiny of creation is inextricably bound to the destiny of both humanity and Christ. Creation is both the object and the stage

---

[6] Wright, *Climax*, ch. 5; Wright, *Paul*, pp. 26-34; Wright, *SH*, p. 94; Wright, *Colossians and Philemon* (Tyndale New Testament Commentary; Grand Rapids: Eerdmans, 1986), pp. 70-73.

of God's redemption in Christ, all because of its origin in the Christ who redeems all things through the blood of his cross (Col. 1.20).

Wright also makes a connection between creation and covenant. The creator God is also the covenant God. These two themes are drawn together in Psalms 19 and 74 and Paul teases out the implications of these psalms in such passages as Col. 1.15-20, 1 Corinthians 15, and Romans 1–11, where the problem with creation is dealt with in terms of covenant. As Wright casts it, the covenant is there to solve the problems with creation, while creation is invoked to solve the problems within the covenant. Of course, this presupposes that there is a problem with creation that results in a covenant necessary to deal with it.

The Problem of Sin[7]

Part of the reason Paul does not dwell much on the original state of the creation is because rather early in the Genesis narrative the problem of sin is introduced into the human drama. According to Paul, sin appears through the disobedience of the man Adam (Rom. 5.12). Paul's interest in Adam is not primarily for purposes of delineating the etiology of sin, but rather to concretize it in human history and then contrast it and its effects with Christ and his redemptive work. In Wright's terms, Adam's sin brings about the world gone

---

[7] Wright, *Romans*, pp. 428-64, 523-32; Wright, *Paul*, pp. 34-38; Wright, *SH*, pp. 94-95.

wrong, the exigency for God's program of setting the world to rights.

God's Promised Restoration[8]

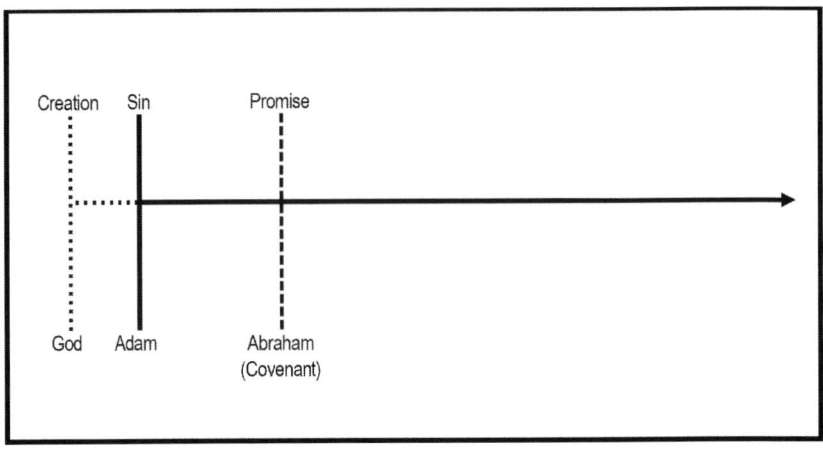

In Genesis 15, God establishes a covenant with Abram in fulfillment of the call of Abram recorded in Gen. 12.1-3. This is the point where God initiates setting the world to rights. Here God begins the process of creating a people through whom he will bring about the restoration of the cosmos. This people is called to be a blessing to all the families of the world. The direction is forward looking, as God declares that through Abram's offspring the promised restoration will take place. The Old Testament manifestation of the promise is the people of Israel, the chosen, royal, and priestly nation. Virtually instantly upon the establishment of the covenant, however, a problem arises. This covenant people, Israel, is itself a part of the problem. In Wright's terms, the people of Abraham are also in Adam. So the people through whom the solution is to come are also part of the people for whom they are the solution.

But for Paul, Abraham is focal to God's promise of restoration. In much traditional exegesis of Romans 4 and Gal. 3.6-18, Abraham is relegated to the role of a case study of faith, the clinching example that proves the truthfulness of Paul's doctrine of justification by faith. As Wright sees it, Abraham is much more than an example;

---

[8] Wright, *NTPG*, pp. 260-68; Wright, *Romans*, pp. 487-507; Wright, *Justification*, pp. 66-68.

he is integral to the entire process, and so Paul enters Abraham into his own exposition of what it is that God is doing to set the world to rights. The point of emphasis is not so much Abraham's faith, important as that is to the overall picture, but that Christ is the true seed of Abraham. This is how Paul handles the issue of how it is that the people of Israel, who were elected to bring God's salvation to the world, could do so while being part of the Adamic problem. But before we get to this, there is another crucial intervening component to Paul's framework that will help develop the notion of Christ as the seed of Abraham.

Moses and the Law[9]

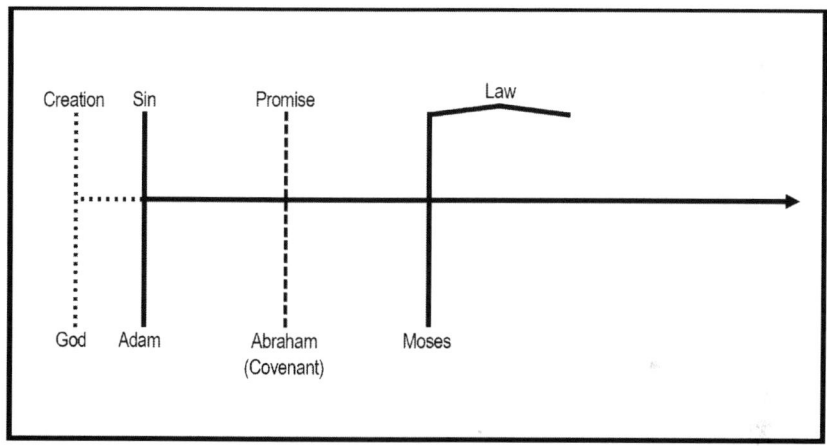

The place of the Mosaic Law in God's plan of salvation in Christ has long been and continues to be a topic of much discussion. Did God truly intend for Israel to obey the Law perfectly and thus come into salvation through this perfect obedience, only to see Israel fail and thus necessitate Christ as the solution to the problem of sin? This appears to make Christ a sort of 'Plan B' in God's dealings with human beings. But if Christ was always 'Plan A' for God, then what role does the Law play in God's plan? Here Wright offers a creative, albeit controversial, solution.

As noted earlier, Israel was both the covenant people of God through whom salvation would come to the world as well as a peo-

---

[9] Wright, 'Romans and the Theology of Paul', pp. 49-54; Wright, *Romans*, pp. 523-32, 549-72.

ple in Adam who suffer both the susceptibility to and consequences of sin. So why does God give such a people the Law? After all, says Paul, there is no Law that could make alive and bring righteousness (Gal. 3.21), but rather sin takes opportunity through the commandment to work death in human beings (Rom. 7.9-11, 13). Surely God knew this would happen. And indeed, according to Wright, this is precisely the point. Here Rom. 7.13 is most instructive:

> Did what is good [Law], then, bring death to me? By no means! It was sin, working death in me through what is good, in order that sin might be shown to be sin, and through the commandment might become sinful beyond measure.

God gives the Law to Israel, not that Israel would live by it and through perfect adherence bring righteousness to the world, but rather quite the opposite. God gave Israel the Law so that where the Law is, sin would be made known abundantly and concentrated in one place. Throughout the early part of Romans 7 Paul asserts that without Law there is no knowledge of sin (v. 7), that sin lay dormant apart from Law but revived with the introduction of Law (vv. 8b-9). It was with the giving of Law that sin became known and localized in Israel.

Wright sees this strand of Paul's thought originating from a reading of Deut. 29.10–30.6. In this passage, where Moses is reaffirming the covenant with the people of Israel, the prospect of exile on account of disobedience is put forth as nearly a foregone conclusion. Putting aside for the moment the source-critical questions relating to the dating of the passage, in terms of the narrative logic of the Old Testament, this declaration predates the actual exile of the people for disobedience. It appears as if the sin of Israel and the exile are included in the calculus of God's redemptive purpose. Paul's thinking in Romans and Galatians appears to read the Deuteronomic passage in this way.

So the Law was not given as 'Plan A' to be jettisoned for Christ the 'Plan B'. Nor is the Law, in this reading, given primarily as an act of God's grace to reveal the divine will to the covenant people. Rather, Law is given so that sin might gravitate toward Israel, to be gathered into one place, so that Israel might bear the sin of the world.

Abraham's Promised Seed: Jesus Christ[10]

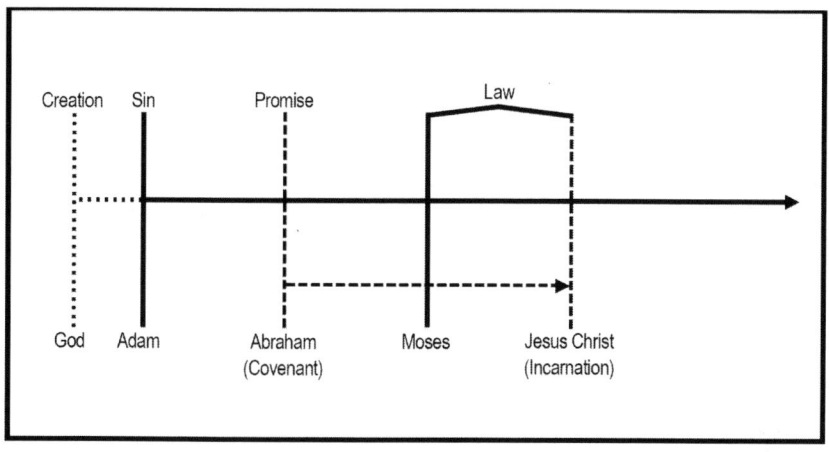

Israel, being part of Adam, could do nothing to procure forgiveness of sins. However, one acting on behalf of Israel as her kingly representative, one who was not infected with Adam's sin but who was of another order of humanity, could bear sin and its destructive effects on the cosmos and begin to set the world to rights. Here the notion of the seed of Abraham, the heir of the promise of Abraham, becomes focal to Paul's logic. In Gal. 3.16, Paul stresses that the promise to Abraham was for a singular seed, not seeds. Whatever one makes of Paul's exegesis on this point, theologically it carries huge freight. Israel was never intended as a collective nation to deliver the world from sin. Rather, Israel was to localize sin by receiving Law, while one would arise within Israel as her kingly representative to bear the sin Israel carried and deal with it through his own death. In the vein of Isaiah's Suffering Servant song in Isa. 52.13–53.12, Paul asserts that Jesus, the Son of God who knew no sin, came in the likeness of sinful human flesh to deal with sin (Rom. 8.3). How did this occur? Sin was condemned in the flesh. To use the language of Galatians, Christ became a curse in order to redeem us from the curse (Gal. 3.13). In short, the sinless Christ

---

[10] Wright, *NTPG*, pp. 268-71, ch. 10; Wright, *JVG*, pp. xvii-xviii, ch. 13; Wright, 'New Exodus, New Inheritance'; Wright, *Romans*, pp. 468-86; Wright, *RSG*, Part II; Wright, *Paul*, pp. 135-45. A helpful summary of the ideas presented here is found in Wright, *Romans*, pp. 396-496.

bore the sin heaped upon Israel and cursed the curse by dying on the cross.

One of the most controversial of Wright's proposals is that at the time of Jesus, Israel saw herself as still in Exile. In the incarnation, death, and resurrection of Jesus, God had fulfilled his promise to bring his people back from exile after the curse. Paul's most explicit treatment of this idea occurs in Rom. 10.5-13, in which Paul exegetes Deuteronomy 30 to the effect that the time of Israel's rebellion begins not with the Babylonian exile, but rather with the giving of Torah at Sinai. Israel's history of breaking Torah simply further identifies its status as a people in Adam, a people under curse, eventuating in the geographical exile in Babylon. So in Jesus, God effects the end of the exile of his people, and in Jesus, God enacts his own return to Zion.

Another image Wright employs in describing God's redemption in Christ is that of the Exodus. Wright understands Paul's discussion in Romans 6–8 as employing the framework of the Exodus to describe Christ's redemption as a New Exodus: Romans 6 describes the deliverance of the people from slavery to freedom via their passing through the waters; Rom. 7.1–8.11 describes how the people come to Sinai only to discover both that the Torah is unable to give the life it promised and that God has provided it; Rom. 8.12-30 describes how the promise of resurrection before them and the gift of the Spirit to guide them leads them through the present life toward the promised land, the renewal of all creation. Exodus and Exile provide powerful images that are reimaged in Paul's telling of the story of God's dealings with the world.

So the promise of Abraham is fulfilled in Christ. The whole complex from promise to fulfillment entailed the formation of the covenant people Israel, her reception of Law, and her inability to live by Law. There was no 'Plan B', only 'Plan A' that always contained within its contours everything from Abraham to Christ. 'God had a single plan all along through which he intended to rescue the world and the human race, and that single plan was centered upon the call of Israel, a call which Paul saw coming to fruition in Israel's representative, the Messiah'.[11]

---

[11] Wright, *Justification*, p. 35.

But the death of Jesus is only one part of his efficacious work of setting the world to rights. Both the resurrection and ascension of Jesus are crucial to righting the world. Wright's treatment of the resurrection finds two significant expressions, one a highly scholarly treatment of the resurrection of Jesus in its historical and theological contexts (*The Resurrection of the Son of God*) and a more popularized presentation of some of the key themes of this scholarly work (*Surprised by Hope*). At the risk of oversimplification, the resurrection completes the reversal of Adam's sin by conquering death. But more than this, it is an affirmation of the whole creation, not simply that by which human beings procure the blessing of life-after-death. For Christ's resurrection is bodily, though glorified. In Wright's terminology, Christ's resurrection is a 'transformed physicality'. It is not simply a precursor for the type of physicality to be experienced by human beings in the eschaton, it also prefigures the transformed cosmos in which transformed human beings will dwell. So the resurrection marks the incursion of the new creation into the world. In like manner, the ascension, in which the bodily Christ enters heaven, stands as testimony that human beings have a place in God's presence. If the resurrection marks the incursion of heaven into earth, then the ascension marks the incursion of humanity into heaven, all anticipatory of the eschaton when heaven and earth will come together into one.

This discussion anticipates a later stage of our survey, but what we see at this point is that Christ has broken the power of the old order by defeating sin and death and ushering in the new creation that will be consummated in the eschaton. We turn our attention now to what Paul understands God to be doing in the interim.

People of the Spirit: The New Humanity in Christ[12]

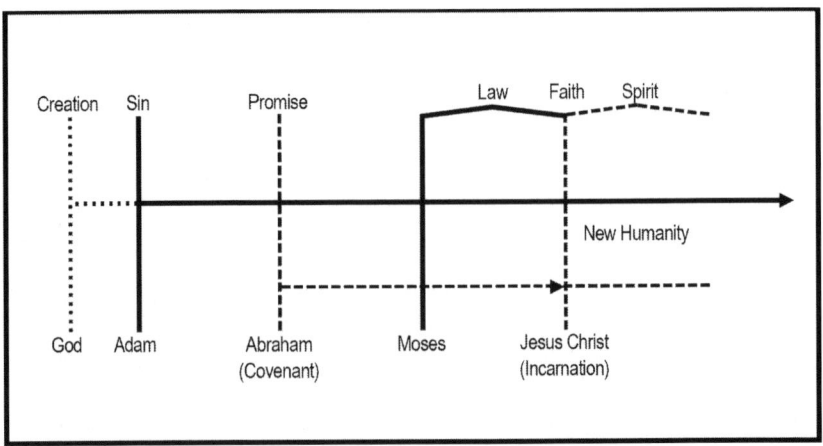

With Christ came a new reality. The fulfillment of the Abrahamic promise in Christ brought with it faith as that which identifies one as a member of the covenant people. However one construes the hotly debated construction πίστις Χριστοῦ ('faith in/of Christ'),[13] it is clear that the death and resurrection of Jesus has brought about a new way of reckoning the people of God, and faith is integral to this identification. Wright is in concert with the so-called 'New Perspective' on Paul in that it is on the basis of faith rather than such Jewish ethnic identity markers as circumcision, Law, Sabbath, etc., that one is identified as a person of the covenant. Because God was in Christ reconciling the world to himself, and this Christ, the kingly representative of Israel, fulfilled the promise of Abraham as a blessing to all the families of the earth, the people of God now consists of both Jews and Gentiles who have faith in Christ.

It might seem odd to bring in consideration of Paul's understanding of justification by faith at this point rather than in the previous section of our discussion. But in Wright's understanding of the doctrine, which has brought him into heated conflict with many

---

[12] Wright, *WSPRS*, chs. 7 and 8; Wright, *Romans*, pp. 508-619, 700-59; Wright, *RSG*, pp. 248-59, 263-67, ch. 6; Wright, *Paul*, pp. 120-22, 145-50, ch. 8; Wright, *SH*, chs. 12-15; Wright, *Justification*, ch. 4.

[13] For a discussion of the issues, see Richard B. Hays, *The Faith of Jesus Christ: The Narrative Substructure of Galatians 3:1–4:11* (Grand Rapids: Eerdmans, 2001).

from Lutheran and Reformed camps,[14] the focus is not on how one becomes a Christian, but rather on who is declared by God to be the people of the covenant, vindicated in the divine law court, anticipating in the present the future eschatological vindication in the resurrection of the dead when God puts the world to rights. Faith in the redemptive work of Christ is that which presently marks out the covenantal people of the Messiah whose reality this is.

There is, as a result of Christ's work, a new humanity (cf. 2 Cor. 5.17), identified by faith, whose task is to spread throughout the world and proclaim the gospel of Christ. This people also receives the promise of the Holy Spirit, who both marks out believers as people of the covenant as well as empowers them to live as citizens of the new order breaking forth in the world. It is by empowerment of the Spirit that this people engages in mission in the world, testifying to the presence of God's Kingdom in the face of demonic resistance personified in the structures of human existence. Much of Wright's recent work focuses on Paul's critique of and engagement with the powers of the Roman Empire. It is by the power of the Spirit that the people of God are emboldened to announce that Jesus is Lord in the face of all pretentious claims to power.

This new people of God is also, by the power of the Spirit, endued with power over sin. In this respect, the new humanity in Christ, through the Spirit, anticipates the ultimate eschatological deliverance from sin in the present. Much of Romans 6 and 8 attests to the reality of genuine holiness as characteristic of Spirit-led living in the present age. It is on the basis of Spirit-empowered living that believers, those justified by faith, anticipate in the present the future verdict of justification to be pronounced in the final judgment.

For Wright, it comes down to this. The new humanity in Christ, brought into being through the work of God in setting the world to rights, is the agency through which God continues this work in anticipation of the eschatological consummation of this work. The nature and mission of this people embodies a foretaste of what is to

---

[14] E.g. the two-volume response to the New Perspective in general edited by D.A. Carson, Peter T. O'Brien, and Mark Seifrid (eds.), *Justification and Variegated Nomism* (Grand Rapids: Baker, 2001, 2004). More recently, John Piper has challenged Wright's position in *The Future of Justification: A Response to N.T. Wright* (Wheaton, IL: Crossway, 2007). Wright's response to Piper is found in *Justification*.

be in the new heavens and earth. It is a new humanity patterned on the last Adam, transformed from the pattern of the first Adam (1 Cor. 15.45).

God's Creation Set to Rights[15]

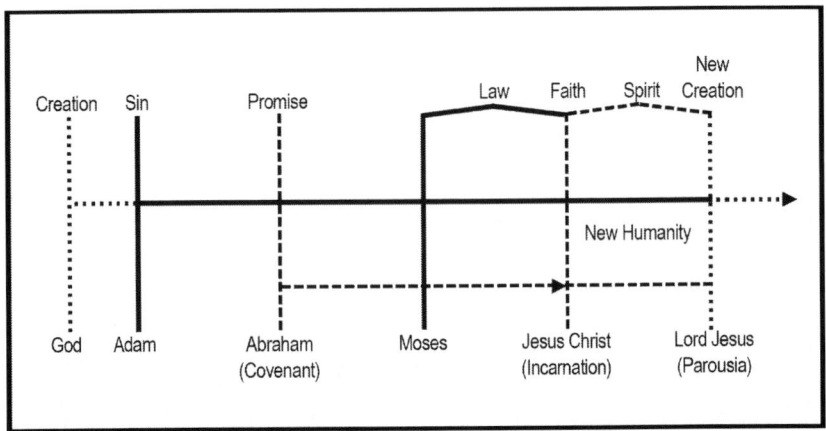

The final stage of the redemptive drama occurs with the *parousia*, in which the ascended Christ, who is declared to be cosmic Lord of all creation in the mission and message of the new humanity, is established as the reigning Lord of the new creation. At this point, the absent but reigning Lord Jesus becomes the present reigning Lord in the joined new heaven and new earth, setting the world to rights through his judgment. Here Wright diverges with some popular conceptions of final judgment. In many constructions, Jesus is depicted as a warrior coming from heaven to execute horrific wrath on the wicked, culminating in the destruction of the cosmos. Wright argues that in the Old Testament, God's judgment is viewed as that by which the groaning creation is vindicated by making right that which has been wrong. In other words, God's judgment is the establishment of God's justice throughout creation, the establishment of new creation. At the *parousia*, Jesus establishes God's justice throughout the cosmos, transforming it such that God will be all in all.

---

[15]Wright, *RSG*, ch. 7; Wright, *Paul*, pp. 140-44; Wright, *SH*, pp. 94-108, 118-43.

One of Wright's more provocative views regards the nature of the new creation, particularly as it compares to some popular conceptions of eschatology. As Wright reads Paul and the rest of the New Testament, popular notions such as the world will end and redeemed believers will all go dwell with God in some sort of spiritual state of existence in heaven up in the sky are gross distortions of biblical teaching that have dramatic ramifications for the present mission of the Church in the world. The hope of Christians is precisely that God will set the world to rights, radically transforming the created order, renewing it from the effects of sin and decay, and that the people of God will be raised bodily and transformed to inhabit this new creation. This is the net effect of Paul's teaching in Rom. 8.18-25, which Wright sees as cut from the same cloth as the vision of Revelation 21–22, the coming together of heaven and earth in the new creation in which God and his people dwell together eternally. The notion that God will destroy the cosmos in the end and that Jesus will lead his people in the great escape into heaven is one that Wright believes owes more to Gnosticism than to biblical Christianity. So the new creation, both in its human and other-than-human components, is characterized by a transformed physicality rid of its bondage to sin, corruption, decay, and death.

Wright is often taken to task for his denial of the doctrine of the rapture. One strand of popular teaching on 1 Thess. 4.13–5.11 holds that at some point prior to the consummation of the Kingdom, Christ descends and removes his people from the earth, setting in motion the sequence of events that leads to the eschatological climax of the consummation of the Kingdom. With many others,[16] Wright sees Paul's language here as reflecting the cultural custom of welcoming a visiting dignitary, in which a welcome party goes out of the city to receive the dignitary, and then leads him back into the city. So rather than removing believers from the earth, the image indicates quite the opposite: believers at the end of the age receive their Lord and dwell with him on the earth.

For Wright, this view of the new creation must inform and motivate the mission of God's people in the present time. Since God is not going to destroy physicality, but rather transform it, the Church

---

[16] E.g. John Dominic Crossan and Jonathan L. Reed, *In Search of Paul* (New York: HarperCollins, 1994), pp. 167-74.

must focus its energies on fulfilling the words of Jesus in the Lord's Prayer, 'on earth as it is in heaven'. That is, the Church, in its essence and its mission, must embody and establish in some anticipatory sense the new creation toward which God is taking history. In a series of dialogues with Wright, J.D. Crossan called this 'collaborative eschatology'.[17] Believers must work to bring something of the eschatological new creation back into the present. It is in this sense that Paul can presently say of believers, 'if anyone is in Christ, behold, new creation' (2 Cor. 5.17).

Wright and the Pentecostals

Though the preceding discussion painted Wright's thought in broad, brief strokes, at detail level there are certainly areas where Pentecostals might either agree or disagree with Wright. We will leave detailed analyses for the essays to come in this volume, and focus instead on three areas in which Pentecostals and Wright have great affinity in order to provide a framework for more detailed interaction.

The first of these is the importance that each places upon the role of *narrative* in theological orientation. As our discussion has demonstrated, Wright sees God's redemption in Christ not primarily in theological categories, but rather as a drama, the drama of God's dealings with his world and human beings. As the diagram indicates, theological vocabulary emerges from the drama but is never detached from the drama. The story of God's dealings in the world is not simply the medium of the message, but is the message itself. Abstraction, however helpful and necessary, diminishes the power present in the story. If the story is discarded once propositional truth is gleaned, then the story form becomes unnecessary. But Wright is clear that story is more than simply the window dressing for propositions. Rather, what story reveals is an active, interested God, one who is immanently and intimately present with his people in the outworking of the drama.

---

[17] Robert B. Stewart, John Dominic Crossan, and N.T. Wright, *The Resurrection of Jesus: John Dominic Crossan and N.T. Wright in Dialogue* (Minneapolis: Fortress, 2006).

An analogy Wright frequently employs is one of a recently discovered long lost play, one that is five acts long. It is apparent that only the first four acts and the final page of the play are extant. A troupe of actors decides to create the fifth act. They have a choice – they can write the fifth act by quoting lines directly from the first four acts, or they can become saturated with the story of the first four acts and create the fifth act. For Wright, this is what the Bible is, a drama of four acts – creation, sin, Israel, Jesus – that is to inform the Church so that it might continue in the present the commission given her by Jesus as she works in the world toward the day of the consummation of the Kingdom of God. So the people of God in the world today is essentially a people of a story, shaped by the story up to this point and creatively contributing to the ongoing development of that story.[18]

Pentecostals, too, are a people shaped by narrative.[19] Much of the early and ongoing self-identity of the movement is derived from a narrative, the book of Acts.[20] Their creative contribution to the story is a new experience of the Spirit that equips believers for their distinctive role in the Church and the world. At the levels of individual experience and corporate liturgy, testimony to the ongoing work of God through the Spirit is a mainstay of Pentecostal spiritu-

---

[18] A brief synopsis of this scheme is found in Wright, *NTPG*, pp. 141-43. This scheme has been adopted and enhanced by Craig G. Bartholomew and Michael W. Goheen, *The Drama of Scripture: Finding Our Place in the Biblical Story* (Grand Rapids: Baker, 2004).

[19] Walter J. Hollenweger goes so far as to argue that narrativity is that which functions as the distinctive uniting Pentecostals over against any doctrinal formulation. See *The Pentecostals* (Peabody, MA: Hendrickson, 2nd edn, 1988); 'Priorities in Pentecostal Research: Historiography, Missiology, Hermeneutics, and Pneumatology', in J.A.B. Jongeneel (ed.), *Experiences in the Spirit* (Bern: Peter Lang, 1989), pp. 9-10; and 'From Azusa Street to the Toronto Phenomenon', in Jürgen Moltmann and Karl-Josef Kuschel (eds.), *Pentecostal Movements as Ecumenical Challenge* (Concilium 3; London: SCM Press, 1996), p. 7. Frank D. Macchia, *Baptized in the Spirit: A Global Pentecostal Theology* (Grand Rapids: Zondervan, 2006), pp. 49-57, while acknowledging the importance of narrativity in Pentecostal identity, criticizes Hollenweger's argument as insufficient to describe the totality of Pentecostal distinctiveness and himself opts for Spirit baptism as a doctrinal unifier.

[20] E.g. Robert Menzies, *Empowered for Witness: The Spirit in Luke-Acts* (JPTSup 6; Sheffield: Sheffield Academic Press, 1994); J.M. Penney, *The Missionary Emphasis of Lukan Pneumatology* (JPTSup 12; Sheffield: Sheffield Academic Press, 1997); Macchia, *Baptized in the Spirit*; and Amos Yong, *The Spirit Poured out on All Flesh: Pentecostalism and the Possibility of Global Theology* (Grand Rapids: Baker Academic, 2005).

ality. Familiarity with Wright's overall program of describing the narrative of God's dealings with the world might provide Pentecostals with a depth reading of the first four acts of the drama as they navigate their way through the drama not only as a people with a distinctive identity, but also as a people in continuity and communion with the universal Church across the ages.

The second area of affinity between Wright and Pentecostals is in the area of *mission*. As the diagram indicates, the drama of redemption is cast largely in terms of the creation of a people to carry out God's redemptive mission in the world. This began with Adam, the image bearer who would reflect God's benevolence throughout creation. With Abraham came the promise of a people that would be a blessing in the world. The culmination of the Abrahamic promise is Jesus, the Last Adam, who, through his death, resurrection, and ascension, brings about the formation of a people that is to make incursions in the world, establishing beachheads for the Kingdom of God. This people participates with God in setting the world to rights. This theme is evident in *Surprised by Hope*, where Wright passionately urges the Church to live out the implications of her story, not just in evangelism, but also in all areas of life in the world. Here Wright brings together his roles as scholar and pastor, advocating a life of mission that springs forth from a well-informed reading of the Church's story.

This, too, is a significant aspect of Pentecostal identity. Initially, Pentecostals understood Spirit baptism as equipment for mission in the world. Though this has often manifested exclusively in terms of evangelism, Pentecostals have also engaged in so-called 'social gospel' efforts throughout the history of the movement.[21] In our day this is evident in groups such as Pentecostals and Charismatics for Peace and Justice as well as in concern for environmental stewardship.[22] Wright's focus on Spirit empowerment for this mission is certainly one with which Pentecostals can resonate.

---

[21] E.g. Veli-Matti Kärkkäinen, 'Are Pentecostals Oblivious to Social Justice? Theological and Ecumenical Perspectives', *Missionalia* 29 (2001), pp. 387-404; Kärkkäinen, 'Spirituality as a Resource for Social Justice: Reflections from the Roman Catholic-Pentecostal Dialogue', *Asian Journal of Pentecostal Theology* 6 (2003), pp. 75-88.

[22] Amos Yong (ed.), *The Spirit Renews the Face of the Earth: Pentecostal Forays in Science and Theology of Creation* (Eugene, OR: Pickwick, 2009).

One final area of affinity merits brief mention here, that of *glossolalia*. Wright addressed the matter of glossolalia and other charismata in a lecture given at the inaugural Fulcrum Conference, a gathering of evangelical Anglicans in London in 2005. Wright affirms both the existence and importance of such manifestations of the Spirit. However, Wright frames his understanding firmly within the structure of thought we have developed in this discussion, and at this point, what these charismatic giftings actually represent differs between Wright and some Pentecostal formulations. Wright notes that in some traditional understandings, the Pentecostal view of spiritual gifts assumes a worldview in which there is a radical disconnect between heaven and earth. So the gifts represent a sort of invasion of a foreign supernatural power into the earth. For Wright, the manifestations of the Spirit are among the many instances in which heaven and earth overlap and interlock in the present in anticipation of the ultimate coming together of heaven and earth in the eschaton. So the gifts, in Wright's estimation, represent the presence of the Spirit among the people of God who are at work bringing about God's Kingdom on earth as it is in heaven. Wright states, 'those in whom the Spirit comes to live are God's renewed Temple. They are, individually and corporately, locations where heaven and earth meet.'[23]

Conclusion

With a scholar as prolific as Wright, there is opportunity to engage his thought on many heads. Pentecostals certainly have a stake in many of these issues. Our discussion here has established that the broad contours of his historical and theological program certainly strike chords of affinity with the interests of Pentecostals, and has suggested a context within which more detailed engagements with his thought in this volume might take place. Pentecostals are joining the throngs of those who have recognized in N.T. Wright a thinker

---

[23] See Wright, *Simply Christian: Why Christianity Makes Sense* (San Francisco: Harper Collins, 2006), p. 110. See also his more pastoral presentation of spiritual gifts in *Paul for Everyone: 1 Corinthians* (Louisville: Westminster John Knox, 2004), pp. 166-70, 179-201. Of glossolalia he writes, 'Tongues, then and now, remain a gift of great value which God gives to some people (not all; see [1 Cor] 12:30)' (p. 183).

of extraordinary creativity and productivity whose ideas have and will continue to have significant impact upon both the academy and the Church as these institutions struggle to work out their missions in the world.[24]

---

[24] I would like to thank my research assistant, Donna Divine, for assisting me with tracking down the references in Wright's works. The task would have been much more time consuming and difficult without her invaluable assistance.

2

'WHO DO I SAY I AM?' A CONSTRUCTIVE CRITIQUE OF N.T. WRIGHT'S VIEW OF JESUS' SELF-UNDERSTANDING

CHRIS GREEN*

Introduction

N.T. Wright has made clear his disappointment that more theologians have not thoughtfully engaged his account of Jesus' self-interpretation.[1] Admitting that his proposals are unconventional, he insists they nonetheless remain true to orthodox Christology.[2] In my judgment, Wright's account of Jesus' self-understanding deserves careful consideration and in spite of its weaknesses promises to prove rewarding for Pentecostal preaching and catechesis, the reading of Scripture, and theological reflection – primarily because it emphasizes Jesus' exemplary faith. What follows is an attempt to critique Wright sympathetically and constructively, seeking to make Pentecostal, theological sense both of the content of his proposals

---

* Chris Green (PhD, Bangor University) is Associate Professor of Theology at Pentecostal Theological Seminary, Cleveland, Tennessee. He formerly was a pastor of a church related to the Pentecostal Holiness tradition in Oklahoma City, Oklahoma.

[1] N.T. Wright, 'Jesus' Self-Understanding', in Stephen T. Davis, Daniel Kendall, and Gerald O'Collins (eds.), *Incarnation: An Interdisciplinary Symposium* (Oxford: Oxford University Press, 2002), p. 54.

[2] 'Wrightsaid Q&A for June 2007', http://www.ntwrightpage.com/Wrightsaid_June2007.html, 2007.

on Jesus' self-interpretation and of the methodology Wright uses to formulate those proposals.

Who Does N.T. Wright's Jesus Say He Is?

Jesus as Israel and YHWH-in-Person

The basics of Wright's proposal are easily summarized. In short, he holds that the mature Jesus believed he had to live, suffer, and die as the agent through whom God's purposes for Israel and the nations would be brought about, exactly as Israel's Scriptures predicted. In other words, Jesus understood himself as one called to act as Israel's *messiah*. Everything he said and did, from his scandalous baptism in the waters of Jordan to his even more scandalous death outside the city walls of Jerusalem, arose from and was carried along by this messianic self-understanding.[3]

Over the years, Wright's opinion on these issues has changed slightly, if at all, although he has experimented with different forms of expression. In his magisterial *Jesus and the Victory of God*, Wright explained at length what in his view Jesus must have thought of himself:

> [W]ho did Jesus think he was? The first answer must be: Israel-in-person, Israel's representative, the one in whom Israel's destiny was reaching its climax. He thought he was the Messiah. Jesus' actions, his message, his warning, and his welcome, make sense only within this framework ... He believed himself called, by Israel's god, to *evoke* the traditions which promised YHWH's return to Zion, and the somewhat more nebulous but still important traditions which spoke of a human figure sharing the divine throne; to *enact* those traditions in his own journey to Jerusalem, his messianic act in the Temple, and his death at the hands of the pagans (in the hope of subsequent vindication); and thereby to *embody* YHWH's return.[4]

---

[3] See Robert B. Stewart, *The Quest of the Hermeneutical Jesus: the Impact of Hermeneutics on the Jesus Research of John Dominic Crossan and N.T. Wright* (Lanham: University Press of America, 2008), pp. 90-96.

[4] N.T. Wright, *Jesus and the Victory of God* (Minneapolis: Fortress Press, 1996), pp. 538, 651. Cited hereafter as *JVG*. See also, N.T. Wright, 'Jesus', in David F.

In the following years, Wright has continued to explain this in much the same way: 'Jesus believed that Israel's history had arrived at its focal point [and] he believed that he was himself the bearer of Israel's destiny at this critical time. He was the Messiah who would take that destiny on himself and draw it to its focal point.'[5] Recently, in his best-selling introduction to the Christian life[6] and his work on the Christian virtues, Wright has reasserted these claims in more popular terms.[7]

Vocation, Risk, and Faithful Obedience

Jesus, Wright contends, understood himself *vocationally*. That is, he knew himself as someone with a particular task to perform, a work to do on God's behalf: 'He believed himself called to do and be what in the Scriptures only Israel's God did and was'.[8] Rather than thinking of himself in abstract terms, Jesus knew himself as the bearer of a calling, burdened to perform the messianic task on God's behalf. By Wright's accounting, Jesus did *not* know himself as God the Son, at least not 'in the same way that one knows one is male or female, hungry or thirsty'. Instead, his self-knowing was 'of a more risky, but perhaps more significant, sort: like knowing one is loved'.[9]

This riskiness is essential to Wright's view of Jesus and Jesus' self-understanding. Even if Christ lived with a vivid awareness of his uniqueness and the extraordinariness of his mission, Wright stands convinced that his sense of calling was just that – a *sense*, a 'faith awareness'.[10] Christ's vocation was 'grasped in faith, sustained in prayer, tested in confrontation, agonized over in further prayer

---

Wright *et al.* (eds.), *New Dictionary of Theology* (Downers Grove: IVP, 1988), pp. 348-51.

[5] N.T. Wright, *The Challenge of Jesus: Rediscovering Who Jesus Was and Is* (Downers Grove: IVP, 1999), p. 89. See also, N.T. Wright, 'Jesus and the Identity of God', *Ex Auditu* 14 (1998), pp. 42-56; N.T. Wright, 'Jesus' Self-Understanding', pp. 47-61.

[6] N.T. Wright, *Simply Christian: Why Christianity Makes Sense* (San Francisco: Harper Collins, 2006), pp. 108-20.

[7] N.T. Wright, *After You Believe: Why Christian Character Matters* (San Francisco: Harper Collins, 2010), p. 109.

[8] Wright, 'Jesus and the Identity of God', p. 53.

[9] Wright, *JVG*, pp. 652-53.

[10] Wright, *JVG*, pp. 651.

and doubt, and implemented in action'.[11] Again and again, Wright directs attention to what he takes to be the outlandishness of Jesus' self-understanding, to what he calls Jesus' 'great wager of faith'.[12] By acting and speaking as Israel's messiah, Jesus was taking an 'enormous risk',[13] giving himself up in faith to a 'crazy and utterly risky vocation'.[14] While he remained unwaveringly faithful to his call, Christ did so with the knowledge that he could be making a 'terrible, lunatic mistake'.[15]

Wright's Jesus is a man who lived humanly, from faith. He did not soar above the fray, beyond jeopardy, but instead willingly, trustingly put himself at hazard for God's sake, and in remaining true to his vocation accomplished the 'ultimate fulfillment of the purpose of creation itself'.[16] God wins God's victory over sin and death through Jesus' messianic faithfulness, his always precarious and severely-tested but finally unerring fidelity to his *Abba*.

As Wright sees it, Jesus matured into the awareness of his vocation through his 'own fresh and prayerful reading of Israel's Scriptures'.[17] To live faithfully, Jesus had to learn the faithfulness and obedience that would make possible the completion of his task as God's messiah. As Christ matured, he became 'the fully developed human being',[18] and as he gave himself up to do (and have done to him) what God had promised to do for Israel and for the world. In his reading of the Psalms,[19] particularly, as well as Daniel, Zechariah, and Isaiah,[20] Jesus came to believe he was 'bringing the story of Scripture to its climax'.[21] Over time, he recognized that he had to do

---

[11] Wright, *JVG*, pp. 653.

[12] N.T. Wright, *The Lord and His Prayer* (Grand Rapids: Eerdmans, 1997), p. 17.

[13] Wright, *The Lord and His Prayer*, p. 17.

[14] Wright, *The Lord and His Prayer*, p. 29.

[15] Wright, 'Jesus' Self-Understanding', p. 59.

[16] Wright, *Simply Christian*, p. 118.

[17] Wright, *After You Believe*, pp. 109-10. See also N.T. Wright, *The Crown and the Fire: Meditations on the Cross and the Life of the Spirit* (Grand Rapids: Eerdmans, 1995), pp. 122-23; N.T. Wright, *The Last Word: Scripture and the Authority of God – Getting Beyond the Bible Wars* (San Francisco: Harper Collins, 2005), p. 43.

[18] Wright, *After You Believe*, p. 131.

[19] Wright, *JVG*, p. 600.

[20] See Wright, *JVG*, pp. 597-604.

[21] Wright, *The Last Word*, p. 42.

Scripture-like work in his own speaking and acting.[22] This conviction carried him along, sustaining and energizing him, especially during the climactic events of his final days in and around Jerusalem, events that led to his death.

Jesus and Christology, History, and Doctrine

Because so much depends on the trusting *faithfulness* of Jesus, on the fully human dimension of his obedience, Wright finds it impossible to accept that Jesus knew himself as God, at least in any direct sense, rejecting in no uncertain terms the 'attempts to make Jesus of Nazareth conscious of being the second person of the Trinity' as 'unthinking' and 'pseudo-orthodox'.[23] Wright does so, he says, 'not to diminish the full incarnation of Jesus but to explore its deepest dimensions'.[24] In his judgment, if Jesus had known himself as God, then he could not have experienced the events of his life in any recognizably human way,[25] and this would subvert the purpose of the incarnation, rendering it finally inexplicable and inapplicable to us, here and now.

That Jesus believed himself in some sense the 'embodiment of Israel's God' bound to 'die for the sins of the world', Wright does not doubt. Jesus 'knew' he was doing what Scripture says only YHWH can do and be. Wright only wants to rethink what 'knowing' means in such a context. He wants to call into question the notion that Jesus *thought* of himself as 'the second person of the Trinity' or 'God incarnate' in the way most Christian theologians have assumed.[26] As he puts it, he wants to know Jesus from Jesus' own 'point of view', rather than seeking to understand him primarily through the lens of the Church's dogmatic witness. Wright is confident that biblical theology of this kind casts new light on the liturgical-dogmatic tradition – even corrects it at points.[27]

Wright believes the Church has from the second century made the mistake of trying to fit Jesus into an already-formulated philo-

---

[22] Wright, *The Last Word*, p. 43.
[23] Wright, *JVG*, p. 653.
[24] Wright, *Simply Christian*, p. 118.
[25] Wright, *Simply Christian*, p. 118.
[26] See Wright, 'Jesus and the Identity of God', p. 51.
[27] See N.T. Wright, 'Reading Paul, Thinking Scripture', in Markus Bockmuehl and Alan J. Torrance (eds.), *Scripture's Doctrine and Theology's Bible: How the New Testament Shapes Christian Dogmatics* (Grand Rapids: Eerdmans, 2008), p. 71.

sophical notion of God.²⁸ This is a result, he argues, of the Church losing contact with its Jewishness, taking on the language and conceptual framework of ancient Hellenistic philosophy. Reading Scripture through this alien grammar, Christian thought bit by bit set loose to 'the actuality of Jesus, to his Jewishness, to his own aims and objectives'. The traditional reading of the messianic title 'Son of God' as 'straightforwardly Nicene Christology' serves Wright as an example of this loss of contact with Jesus' Jewishness.²⁹

> The Great Tradition has seriously and demonstrably distorted the Gospels. Eager to explain who 'God' really was, the church highlighted Christology; wanting to show that Jesus was divine, it read the Gospels with that as the question; looking for Jesus' divinity, it ignored other central themes such as the kingdom of God.³⁰

Contrary to this tradition, Wright calls for an approach that pushes through to the thought-world of ancient Judaism, to what Jesus must have believed about himself and his ministry in such a context.³¹ If one wants to know here and now what it means to say Jesus saves, then Wright contends one must discover what Jesus was up to then and there, what he and his contemporaries understood him to be doing: 'that is where we must look for it and not somewhere else'. Christology must remain grounded in the first-century significance of such notions as 'Kingdom of God' and 'Son of man'.³² In other words, Wright the Jesus scholar does not want to trade in the language and concepts of the Nicene tradition,³³ but in the currency of ancient Palestinian Judaism.³⁴

---

²⁸ Wright, 'Jesus and the Identity of God', p. 54.

²⁹ Wright, 'Jesus and the Identity of God', p. 48.

³⁰ N.T. Wright, 'Response to Richard Hays', in Nicholas Perrin and Richard B. Hays (eds.), *Jesus, Paul, and the People of God: a Theological Dialogue with N.T. Wright* (Downers Grove: IVP, 2011), p. 63.

³¹ Wright, 'Jesus' Self-Understanding', p. 53.

³² Wright, 'Jesus and the Identity of God', p. 50.

³³ See Richard B. Hays, 'Knowing Jesus: Story, History, and the Question of Truth', in *Jesus, Paul, and the People of God*, pp. 42-43.

³⁴ Wright, 'Jesus and the Identity of God', p. 55.

Wright is critical of the creeds mostly because they do not afford *sufficient* attention to Jesus' and Israel's story.³⁵ He feels that by leaping from 'born of a virgin' to 'suffered under Pontius Pilate', they fail 'to do justice to the place of Jesus' public career, and especially to his proclamation of God's Kingdom'.³⁶ He also faults the creeds for taking up a language and conceptual framework different from that used by the biblical authors:

> [I]f it is in the human life of Jesus of Nazareth that the living, saving God is revealed, [then] that means that John and Paul themselves would urge us to consider Jesus himself – not merely by asking about the hypostatic union and the like (we can be sure that Jesus of Nazareth would have found that puzzling!), or by cleaning up the categories of Aquinas, Calvin, or anyone else, but by enquiring once more about the worldview and mindset of a first-century Jew possessed of a particular vocation.³⁷

Recently, Wright summed up his position pithily and forcefully: 'I believe in the creeds. But I believe in the Jesus of the Gospels a good deal more.'³⁸

To be fair, Wright does not suggest the Church's dogmas should be rejected out of hand. He does celebrate the use of the creeds in Christian worship,³⁹ and understands this confession as basic to his own way of life. He sometimes appeals to and celebrates the creeds' narrative structure, going so far as to describe creeds as 'portable stories' that in fact bear the imprint of 'deep fidelity to the Gospel tradition'.⁴⁰ He sees the creeds, specifically, and Christian doctrine, generally, as enabling the Church to make manageable the 'big picture' of Scripture. What is more, some take Wright's description of Jesus as not only consonant with the creedal tradition, but as in fact

---

³⁵ See Matthew Levering, *Scripture and Metaphysics: Aquinas and the Renewal of Trinitarian Theology* (Malden, MA: Blackwell, 2004), p. 112.

³⁶ Wright, *For All the Saints? Remembering the Christian Departed* (Harrisburg, PA: Morehouse, 2003), p. 57.

³⁷ Wright, 'Jesus' Self-Understanding', p. 52.

³⁸ Wright, 'Response to Richard Hays', p. 64.

³⁹ See, for example, Wright, *For All God's Worth: True Worship and the Calling of the Church* (Grand Rapids: Eerdmans, 1997), p. 31; see also Wright, *Simply Christian*, p. 209.

⁴⁰ Wright, 'Reading Paul, Thinking Scripture', pp. 59-71.

providing support for the creeds' truthfulness and contemporary legitimacy.[41]

Wright finds in the New Testament an 'incipient trinitarian theology' that works apart from 'any of the technical terms that later centuries would adopt for the same purpose'. In fact, once historical-critical research has shown how this incipient trinitarianism works, 'we discover that it actually does the job considerably better than the later formulations'.[42] By contrast, Chalcedon smells 'a bit like a confidence trick'. Patristic Christology had to work so hard to express the truth because the fathers worked with 'one hand, the biblical one, tied behind their backs'. From that time, Christian theology has been 'playing away from home', attempting to express Christian truth in 'non-biblical patristic ... formulations'.[43] Wright hopes to reverse that trend, to free up the Scriptures from these alien philosophical formulations.

The Shape of Wright's Methodology

Wright comes to his conclusions by means of a particular methodology, which he defends at considerable length.[44] On the strength of his knowledge of Second Temple Judaism and the Hebrew Scriptures coupled with a synthetic reading of the Synoptic Gospels,[45] he constructs a hypothetical model of Jesus' ministry, teasing out in detail how first-century Jews would have made sense of Jesus' words and symbolic actions. From that, he works back to discover in the Gospel texts clues to Jesus' mindset or worldview, i.e. the underlying and motivating beliefs, aims, and intentions that energized and directed Jesus' ministry. Having discovered these, he works even further back to Jesus' own self-understanding.[46] In his view, this remains a rather straightforward project – even if it requires meticulous research, keen discernment, and innovative thinking all along the way – and the reconstruction of a true-to-life repre-

---

[41] See Carey C. Newman, *Jesus and the Restoration of Israel: A Critical Assessment of N.T. Wright's Jesus and the Victory of God* (Downers Grove: IVP, 1999), p. 59.

[42] Wright, 'Jesus and the Identity of God', p. 46.

[43] Wright, 'Jesus and the Identity of God', p. 46.

[44] N.T. Wright, *The New Testament and the People of God* (Minneapolis: Fortress Press, 1992), pp. 29-144. Also, Wright, *JVG*, pp. 137-44.

[45] Wright, *Reflecting the Glory: Meditations for Living Christ's Life in the World* (Minneapolis: Augsburg Fortress, 1998), p. 138.

[46] See Stewart, *The Quest of the Hermeneutical Jesus*, pp. 88-89.

sentation of the historical Jesus, the drawing of a critically verifiable, and therefore credible 'picture'[47] is far from impossible. Wright intends to make this picture central to the reading of the Gospels and the preaching of the good news. 'All readers of the Gospels have a mental picture of who Jesus was, what he was thinking, what he was like'.[48] His own agenda is to make this mental picture correspond as closely as possible to the historical truth:

> The point of having Jesus at the centre is that one has *Jesus:* not a cypher, a strange silhouetted Christ-figure, nor yet an icon, but the one Jesus the New Testament writers knew, the one born in Palestine in the reign of Augustus Caesar, and crucified outside Jerusalem.[49]

Wright harbors no uncertainties about the 'value of the history of Jesus' life in relation to the theological and hermeneutical task',[50] insisting that 'historical research is part of our God-given cultural mandate'.[51] Good historical investigation in fact is the only way to 'clear away the overgrown thickets of misunderstanding, misreading, sheer bad history, and sometimes willful obfuscation', that have distorted readings of the Gospels and kept the truly important questions obscured.[52] Therefore, historical study is not merely a 'possibly helpful source for theology' but nothing less than a 'vital and non-negotiable resource'. It is 'not just part of the possible *bene esse*, but of the *esse* itself'. This is so, he maintains, because without that kind of work, 'we condemn ourselves to talking about abstractions, even perhaps to making Jesus himself an abstraction'.[53]

Conclusions

Summing up, we can say Wright stands convinced that Jesus of Nazareth lived and worked from a *messianic consciousness*, a sense of vocation. Wright's own Christology stresses the riskiness of Jesus'

---

[47] Wright, *JVG*, p. 653.
[48] Wright, 'Response to Richard Hays', p. 63.
[49] Wright, *JVG*, pp. 10-11.
[50] Wright, *JVG*, pp. 15-16.
[51] Wright, 'Jesus and the Identity of God', p. 50.
[52] Wright, 'Jesus' Resurrection and Christian Origins', http://www.ntwrightpage.com/Wright_Jesus_Resurrection.html, 2002.
[53] Wright, 'Jesus' Self-Understanding', p. 59.

life, his radical faith and almost-unimaginable readiness to venture everything for the sake of the one he called 'Father'. Although he in fact *was* the co-equal, co-eternal Son, he did not think of himself or his mission in such abstracted terms – and *could not* have. Instead, Jesus made sense of his calling and his personal identity in the language of the temple theology of his day, which, if rightly understood, remains consonant with the high Christology of the Christian theological tradition, even if it does not adhere to it precisely. Christ is known most truly when the Gospels are read and understood in the language and concepts of Palestinian Judaism, rather than the Hellenistic categories taken up by the Nicene tradition.

What to Do with Wright's Jesus? A Pentecostal Theological Response

Grappling with Jesus' Self-Understanding

What are we, as Pentecostals, to make of Wright's proposals about Jesus' self-understanding? We should not dismiss them, even if we cannot agree to them without qualification. Instead, we should grapple with them, allowing them to wound us, if necessary, so we can receive the promised blessing. They are worth the trouble because they forcefully express what it meant for Jesus to live from faith into faith, how it is that he opened the way of perfect obedience, and they afford immense significance to the *story* of Jesus. This should appeal to us as Pentecostals, not only because we know our lives as *storied*, but also because our way of being-in-the-world is a form of *imitatio Christi* – a way of life that simply makes no sense if Jesus is not the *exemplar* as well as the *executor* of salvation. We have to agree with Wright that the narrative integrity of the Gospels' (and the gospel's) story must be maintained. It cannot be ruined by thinking or talking about Jesus as if he lived on a kind of auto-pilot, as if he were not really *tempted*, as if he were not in fact *agonizing* in the olive grove, as if he did not in fact feel himself abandoned on Golgotha. Unlike Wright, however, we should attempt to say this in ways that are self-consciously faithful to the Christian theological tradition. We have to attempt to make sense of Jesus' self-understanding and his faith with Pentecostal spirituality, on the one hand, and the Nicene and Chalcedonian descriptions of Jesus' identity, on the other hand.

Jesus, Self-Understanding, and Divine Risk

We have no need to believe that Jesus thought of himself in philosophical terms. We have only to keep clear the difference between divine and human ways of knowing. Herbert McCabe puts it saucily: God does not assent 'to *any* proposition at all'!⁵⁴ The truth is that God's freedom does not limit human freedom, but makes it *possible*. In the same way, Jesus' knowledge of himself as the divine Son – whatever that knowledge must have been – would not have in any way limited the fullness of his humanity. In this light, we can affirm Wright's suggestion that Jesus' self-understanding belongs to a radically different order than one's knowledge of, say, mathematical theorems, as exactly on key.

What of his claims about Jesus' *faith* and the terrible *riskiness* of Jesus' mission? Is it possible to find a credible way to agree with Wright that Jesus *was* indeed at risk? As already mentioned, such a view intensifies the drama of Jesus' story, and Pentecostals are sure to welcome a teaching that does that. How we are to square such a view with the Christian theological tradition remains unclear, however. Someone may yet find a way to do it, but it will only 'count' if it manages to do justice to the creedal tradition – a feat Wright clearly has not even attempted.

Re-imagining Jesus' Obedience & Faith(fulness)

While the Christian tradition affirms that Jesus lived a life of *obedience*, no dogma has been set down about whether or not Jesus lived from *faith*. Scripture says comparatively little about Jesus' faith, although Heb. 12.2, 'Jesus the pioneer and perfecter of our faith', seems clear enough⁵⁵ and the general tenor of Hebrews and the Synoptic Gospels resonate to it. In the history of doctrine, some have insisted Jesus could *not* have lived from faith because he enjoyed unbroken and unbreakable communion with the Father.⁵⁶ Aquinas, for example, held that Jesus enjoyed the beatific vision throughout his human life,⁵⁷ and much of the Roman Catholic tra-

---

⁵⁴ Herbert McCabe, *God Matters* (London: Continuum, 1987), p. 59 (emphasis original).

⁵⁵ See Gerald O'Collins, *Christology: A Biblical, Historical, and Systematic Study of Jesus* (Oxford: University Press, 2009), p. 263.

⁵⁶ See Ian G. Wallis, *The Faith of Jesus Christ in Early Christian Traditions* (New York: Cambridge University Press, 1995), pp. 208-10.

⁵⁷ See O'Collins, *Christology*, pp. 266-68.

dition followed him in this, at least until recently.[58] Such a claim means, as Gerald O' Collins recognizes, that Jesus lived by *sight*, not faith,[59] making it absurd to speak of Jesus experiencing anything like risk. Others, conversely, have held and do hold that Jesus did in fact live from faith, even if he never really ran the risk of failing in his vocation.[60]

Early Pentecostal theology, shaped by the Christologies of Hebrews and John, emphasized Jesus' faith and faithful obedience. Mary Boddy, wife of the Anglican vicar and prominent early Pentecostal, Alexander A. Boddy, provides an example. In an early *Confidence* article, she puzzles over Heb. 5.8, seeking to explain how Christ, who was 'always absolutely abandoned to His Father's will', could nonetheless 'learn obedience'. She explains that obedience is not only obeying commands, but in its higher forms is a carrying out of ever more difficult tasks with an increasing *delight* in pleasing God. Jesus, she concludes, moved from faith to faith, graduating from one realm of perfect obedience to another, submitting himself again and again to the Father's will, until his faith climaxed in 'the supreme act of obedience' of death on the cross.[61] Through it all, the source of Jesus' obedience was his 'implicit and perfect faith in His Father, which never once wavered'.[62] His faith radiated out from the 'infinite love and understanding' that existed between him and his Father.[63]

Like Wright, Boddy manages to emphasize the integrity of Jesus' story, never talking as if his faith were supra-human, mechanical. Nonetheless, her description of Jesus' faith differs from Wright's in at least two respects. First, she assumes that Jesus *did* know himself as God the Son. Second, she believes Jesus was never genuinely in danger of failing in his mission; although he did suffer and was truly tempted, he never could have sinned. In her construal, the Son's

---

[58] For a defense of these positions, see F. Ocariz, L.F. Mateo Seco, and J.A. Riestra, *The Mystery of Jesus Christ* (Portland, OR: Four Courts Press, 1994).

[59] Gerald O'Collins and Daniel Kendall, *Focus on Jesus: Essays in Christology and Soteriology* (Herefordshire: Fowler Wright Books, 1996), p. 13; Jean Galot, *Who Is Christ?* (Chicago: Franciscan Herald Press, 1989), p. 354.

[60] See Wallis, *The Faith of Jesus Christ in Early Christian Traditions*, p. 215.

[61] Mary Boddy, 'Obedience', *Confidence* 7.9 (June 1915), p. 110.

[62] Boddy, 'Obedience', p. 111.

[63] Boddy, 'Obedience', p. 111.

faith is his human response to the divine knowledge of his oneness with the Father, his intimacy with the Father the source and content of his faith. For her, faith is sight, although not the kind of sight that comes only in the end.[64] In my judgment, her description of Jesus' faith, whatever its shortcomings, makes better sense of the Fourth Gospel's 'high Christology' than Wright's can hope to do, and she does this without rejecting the Church's theological tradition or history of interpretation.

Evaluating Wright's Methodology

Gospel-Truth and Gospel-Method

Wright is a *biblical* theologian. What R.R. Reno says of Irenaeus applies in basic ways to Wright, as well: 'Arranging the details' of Scripture is not regarded as a mere prerequisite to theology, a necessary first step, but simply *is* theology; theology is the name of the work of 'draw[ing] the diffuse elements of Scripture into ever closer and more intimate interconnections', and gives definition to the task of 'expounding "the whole picture"'.[65] Wright departs from Irenaeus in that he does not read Scripture in harmony with the *regula fidei*. Instead, he reads Scripture in harmony with (a version of) the findings of historical-critical research. It seems to me, however, that Hans Frei was right: if we hope to remain true to the gospel, we must not look for Jesus' identity 'in back of the story', still less make it up by means of 'extraneous analytical schemes',[66] God does not *intend* us to find him in that way. Frei overstates his case against the reliability of historical Jesus research, but he correctly insists that the Gospels serve as the God-given access to the risen Jesus. The Christian tradition has maintained at every point that Christ can be known only as God the Spirit makes him known in the 'foolishness of preaching' and in the 'breaking of bread'. Precisely by the faithful reading and preaching of the Scriptures and celebration of the sacraments we 'see' and 'hear' Jesus as he is (and was) – and we simply

---

[64] See O'Collins, *Christology*, pp. 275-80.

[65] R.R. Reno, 'Biblical Theology and Theological Exegesis', in Craig Bartholomew *et al.* (eds.), *Out of Egypt: Biblical Theology and Biblical Interpretation* (Grand Rapids: Zondervan, 2004), pp. 403-404.

[66] Hans W. Frei, *The Identity of Jesus Christ: The Hermeneutical Bases of Dogmatic Theology* (Philadelphia: Fortress Press, 1975), p. 138.

cannot now see and hear him in any other reliable way.[67] Christ's 'identity' is revealed not to the one who masters the historical record but to the one disciplined in the Church's lively witness to the gospel. We can no more separate Jesus from the witness to him than we can separate the head from the body: 'the apostolic witness, interpretative though it may be, is of a piece with the event itself'.[68] We are called to trust that as we read the fourfold Gospel, attuned to the literary and theological glory of each Gospel, we position ourselves to encounter the risen Lord.[69] As Hauerwas explains, each evangelist 'has told us what we need to know to be transformed into a follower of Jesus'. Historical-critical research can help to make sense of what the Gospels say, but it must *not* set itself up as 'a more determinative historical explanation for what must have "really been going on"'. To make such a move is to play false to the gospel.[70]

What Has Nazareth to Do with Nicea? The Normativity of the Creedal Tradition

Wright correctly insists that Scripture can and should inform Christian dogmatics at every point. He is also correct to hold that 'without historical investigation of the factuality of the Gospels, the story is vacuous'.[71] The creeds cannot be confessed faithfully without the witness of Scripture, and historical investigation belongs to this process.[72] That said, as Pentecostals we also can and must allow the dogmatic, creedal tradition to inform and direct our readings of the canonical texts. Just as it is impossible to identify rightly the 'Lord' of the creeds apart from the Scriptures, it is *impossible* to identify the Jesus of the Gospels without the creeds. Historical-critical exegesis helps to detail what the promise of the Kingdom was taken to mean

---

[67] See Brevard S. Childs, 'The Nature of the Christian Bible: One Book, Two Testaments', in Ephraim Radner and George Sumner (eds.), *The Rule of Faith: Scripture, Canon, and Creed in a Critical Age* (Harrisburg, PA: Morehouse Publishing, 1998), p. 121.

[68] Christopher A. Brown, 'More than Affirmation: The Incarnation as Judgment', in *The Rule of Faith*, p. 85.

[69] Hays, 'Knowing Jesus', p. 55.

[70] Stanley Hauerwas, *Matthew* (Grand Rapids: Brazos, 2006), pp. 20-21.

[71] Hays, 'Knowing Jesus', p. 61.

[72] Robert Jenson, *Canon and Creed* (Louisville: Westminster John Knox, 2010), p. 50.

in Jesus' day, but only the Church's confession of Jesus Christ as the Father's Spirit-baptized Son can reveal the *identity* of the king whose rule means salvation and peace for all creation. Therefore, in spite of what Wright sometimes suggests, the Church's confessional tradition is not superfluous, not an alien and obscure imposition. On this score, many, if not all, Pentecostals would agree with Robert Jenson's rule: 'when we ask about the identity of Jesus, historical and systematic questions cannot be separated'. Any reconstruction of a historical Jesus that does not make Nicene sense must be rejected.

This is not by any means to act as if questions of history are finally beside the point.[73] Instead, it is a confession that the only way to get at the historical truth is to work *with* the Christological and Trinitarian teaching of the Church.[74] As Hays puts it, 'the historical figure of Jesus cannot be rightly known or understood apart from the epistemological insight articulated precisely in the confession that Jesus is Lord – Jesus is the *kyrios*'.[75] The Church's confessions are nothing less than a 'necessary hermeneutical principle of historical reading' because without the confessional tradition, whatever its limitations, we cannot get at the 'the true ontology of historical being'.[76] If the Church is right in identifying Christ as the eternal Word, then even the historical truth of Jesus belongs in its own category.[77] Jesus' earthly career, his life 'in the flesh', simply *exceeds* historiography, although it does not evade it altogether.[78] As a result, history, even at its most faithful and productive, can only do so much, and only with the help of the Church's dogmas can we begin to understand rightly who Jesus was and is.

A Pentecostal Counter-Example

What would an acceptably Pentecostal and Nicene methodology look like? Consider the reflections of Elisabeth Sisson, an early Pentecostal evangelist and lay theologian. On the strength of her read-

---

[73] Wolfhart Pannenberg, *Systematic Theology* (Grand Rapids: Eerdmans, 1991), I, p. 232.
[74] Jenson, 'Identity, Jesus, and Exegesis', p. 48.
[75] Hays, 'Knowing Jesus', p. 60.
[76] Jenson, 'Identity, Jesus, and Exegesis', p. 50.
[77] See Hays, 'Knowing Jesus', p. 61.
[78] Jenson, 'Identity, Jesus, and Exegesis', p. 49.

ing of Jn 5.30, 'I can of mine own self do nothing', she argues that in his incarnational *kenosis* Jesus 'renounced the power of His own [divine] being', submitting himself entirely to the Father's will. Drawing on Isa. 18.19-21 and Heb. 1.3, Sisson portrays Jesus as 'the emptiness which let in the fullness of the seal or stamp' of God's nature.[79]

> So Christ in His mortal life perpetually gave place in His emptiness to the fullness of the Father. He renounced all independent thought or action, and just let, so to speak, God the Key, turn in Christ the Lock; God the Ball, play in Christ the Socket. Thus does God say of Him delightedly, seeing His utter self-abnegation, 'Who is blind but My Servant? or deaf as My Messenger that I sent?'[80]

Sisson believes Christ's 'flesh' was *sinful* flesh, that he participated in *fallen* human nature. She contends Jesus had to live life as 'very man of very man' as well as 'very God of very God', for only in this way could he 'stand in the sinner's stead, feeling the pressure of a sin-broken nature, and getting the sinner's victory, that is through grace, and not because of inherent strength, over that nature'. How could Christ live sinlessly if he was subject to the 'sinner's nature'? By living as an emptiness, doing nothing of or from his own will. He lived a fully human life, but he 'never live[d] in His humanity, never move[d] from it for one single instant'.[81] He was the 'full overcomer' because he, 'Himself the omnipotent God',[82] lived 'in the flesh, against the flesh, above the flesh'. Because he was willing to 'do nothing' – not even God's work of redeeming creation – of his own will, Jesus 'lived the divine life in the human nature'.[83] In a striking move, she reads his agony in the garden as a request to be delivered not from the cross but from a 'premature death, before He had come to the place and hour of His sacrificial offering'.[84] He had to become willing, Sisson believes, to give up the 'holy call …

---

[79] Elisabeth Sisson, 'Resurrection Paper No. 7', *Latter Rain Evangel* 10.3 (July 1911), p. 21.
[80] Sisson, 'Resurrection Paper No. 7', p. 21.
[81] Sisson, 'Resurrection Paper No. 7', p. 18.
[82] Sisson, 'Resurrection Paper No. 7', p. 18.
[83] Sisson, 'Resurrection Paper No. 7', p. 20.
[84] Sisson, 'Resurrection Paper No. 7', p. 19.

to die for a wrecked world', and not allow even his loving compassion to determine his course of action. 'With a certain knowledge that His sacrificial death was a lost world's only life, [Christ had to be willing] to give that sacrifice all up ... if such be the will of God'.[85] To achieve truly the nothingness he was called to, the Lord had to be willing to 'drop out of human life' with 'nothing accomplished'. Only in that way would he be prepared in fact to do the work of dying for the world.[86]

Whatever the faults of her theological formulations, Sisson provides an example of thinking theologically about the problem of Jesus' faith and self-understanding and her methodology is exemplary. First, she reads the Scripture *canonically*, allowing Scripture to interpret Scripture, even allowing Isaiah to speak *directly* of Jesus' self-understanding. Second, she insists on the narrative authenticity of Jesus' decisions to follow the Father's will, working (creatively!) within the framework of Nicene and Chalcedonian Christology. Third, she keeps the application of her reflections always in mind. This, in my judgment, is exactly as it should be.

---

[85] Sisson, 'Resurrection Paper No. 7', p. 19.
[86] Sisson, 'Resurrection Paper No. 7', p. 21.

3

A Pneumatological Addition to N.T. Wright's Hermeneutic Done in the Pentecostal Tradition

Timothy Senapatiratne[*]

Introduction

This essay suggests that Wright's hermeneutic, which is most clearly explained in the first five chapters of his *The New Testament and the People of God*, could be improved with the addition of a pneumatological component. This pneumatological component would help to solve the historical problem that he addresses in the section entitled 'Critical Realism and the Threat of the Disappearing Object'. Wright says this problem arises when attempting to read the Bible in a way that is in some 'sense normatively Christian' and at the same time attempts 'to be faithful to history'.[1] This essay argues that biblical studies done within the Pentecostal theological tradition can help solve this problem of history and offer a more robust and ultimately better Trinitarian biblical hermeneutic.

---

[*] Timothy Senapatiratne (PhD, Marquette University) is Reference Librarian at Bethel Seminary, St. Paul, Minnesota. Growing up Assemblies of God in Sri Lanka has motivated him to wonder about what hermeneutical structures look like when doing biblical studies in a non-Western context.

[1] N.T. Wright, *The New Testament and the People of God* (Minneapolis: Fortress, 1992), p. 9. Cited hereafter as *NTPG*.

Statement of the Problem

As Wright describes it, the problem is that there is a fear that '"actual events" [of history] will disappear beneath a welter of particular people's perceptions'.[2] Wright rejects this concern as 'groundless'.[3] The tension that Wright struggles to overcome, however, is that without some historical grounding, the biblical text (and the Christian faith for that matter) might become as subjective as 'mere observation' and lead to the 'conclusion that there are therefore, no such things as "facts"'.[4] By facts, it seems that he is referring to epistemologically verifiable data.[5] Wright argues that those Christian communities who have chosen to ignore the historical components of the Christian faith are wrong because the Gospel writers themselves 'think they're talking about things that actually happened'.[6] Wright suggests that the way to reconcile these different readings (historical and theological) is by finding a *via media* among a 'pre-modern emphasis on the text as in some sense authoritative, the modern emphasis on the text (and Christianity itself) as irreducibly integrated into history, and irreducibly involved with theology, and the post-modern emphasis on reading the text'.[7] Wright's solution is to use the philosophical method of Critical Realism (CR). CR, he believes, allows for the diversity of perspective (both historically and theologically) without completely giving up on the objective claim of history that 'something happened'.[8]

---

[2] Wright, *NTPG*, p. 89.

[3] Wright, *NTPG*, p. 89.

[4] Wright, *NTPG*, p. 88.

[5] See his definition of 'truth' and 'fact' in Wright, *The Last Word: Beyond the Bible Wars to a New Understanding of the Authority of Scripture* (San Francisco: HarperSanFrancisco, 2005), p. 8.

[6] Wright, 'N.T. Wright Talks About History and Belief: Resurrection Faith', *Christian Century* 119.26 (December 18, 2002), p. 28.

[7] Wright, *NTPG*, 27. Thorsten Moritz, 'Reflecting on N.T. Wright's Tools for the Task', in Craig Bartholomew *et al.* (eds.), *Renewing Biblical Interpretation* (Grand Rapids: Zondervan, 2000), p. 179. Wright states that he is not arguing for some form of modernism, nor 'a return to pre-modernism', nor even a 'capitulation to post-modernism' but rather his hope is to find a 'way through the entire mess and muddle' (Wright, *Last Word*, p. 10).

[8] Wright, *NTPG*, p. 90.

Critical Realism

Wright details what he means by CR in chapters three and four of *The New Testament and the People of God*. For him CR is a middle way between the positivists, who believe that there are at least some things 'about which we can have definite knowledge', and those who reject positivism and conclude that 'all that is left is subjectivity and relativity'.[9] CR offers an epistemology, says Wright, that 'acknowledges the *reality of the thing known, as something other than the knower*', which defines the *realism* of CR.[10] Wright describes the *critical* in these terms: 'the only access we have to this reality lies along the spiraling path of *appropriate dialogue or conversation between the knower and thing known*'.[11] Thus, knowledge is never independent of the knower (the subjective), but this does not negate that there is something real to be observed and understood.[12]

Wright argues that a worldview (which is comprised of stories) is what 'forms the basis of the observer's way of being in relation to the world'.[13] By this he means that the epistemological foundation for most people is formed by those stories which help them '*find things that fit* with the particular story or (more likely) stories to which they are accustomed to give allegiance'.[14] Wright says that stories are 'one of the most basic modes of human life', and thus, the universality of the use of stories provides some antidote to the relativism about which the modernists are concerned.[15] Wright distinguishes between stories that illustrate some point of life (which are not part of one's worldview) and stories that are epistemologically more fundamental 'than explicitly formulated beliefs, including theological beliefs'.[16] It is these stories that create 'a vital framework

---

[9] Wright, NTPG, pp. 32-33.
[10] Wright, NTPG, p. 35.
[11] Wright, NTPG, p. 35.
[12] Wright, NTPG, p. 35.
[13] Wright, NTPG, p. 37.
[14] Wright, NTPG, p. 37.
[15] Wright, NTPG, p. 38.
[16] Wright, NTPG, p. 38.

for experiencing the world'.[17] They also provide a 'means by which views may be challenged'.[18]

What is significant for Pentecostal hermeneutics is how Wright understands the way that stories inform one's epistemology and ultimately shape his or her worldview. Wright says that a worldview does four things. First, a worldview provides the stories 'through which humans view reality'.[19] This means that stories become the lens by which people understand the world. Second, it is through these stories that people are able to answer the basic questions of life.[20] These questions include, 'Who are we? Where are we? What is wrong? And What is the solution?'[21] Third, these stories are expressed in cultural symbols, and fourth, these symbols imply a certain praxis, 'a way of being in the world'.[22] Later it will be shown how this definition of worldview actually is quite similar to the hermeneutical model of many Pentecostals.

The implication of this model is that the stories of theology and the Bible offer readers of the Bible answers to the basic questions of life and also offer advice and insight into ways of creating a system of praxis by which to live. Furthermore, says Wright, these theological stories are not 'reducible to materialist analysis', and thus, can form the basis of a worldview.[23] Moritz describes this approach as a 'recalibration' that attempts to 'account for the textually embodied intentionality of the author' rather than the typical Evangelical (and, although Moritz does not state this, it would seem Pentecostal) method of starting 'from the bottom up (by privileging dictionaries and grammars)'.[24] Wright acknowledges, however, that this has not solved the historical problem since theology could simply be 'a fanciful way of attempting to invest reality with a significance

---

[17] Wright, *NTPG*, p. 39.
[18] Wright, *NTPG*, p. 39.
[19] Wright, *NTPG*, p. 123.
[20] Wright, *NTPG*, p. 123.
[21] Wright, *NTPG*, p. 123.
[22] Wright, *NTPG*, pp. 123-24.
[23] Wright, *NTPG*, p. 127.
[24] Thorsten Moritz, 'Critical Realism', in Kevin J. Vanhoozer *et al.* (eds.), *Dictionary for Theological Interpretation of the Bible* (Grand Rapids: Baker Academic, 2005), p. 149.

not always perceived' rather than describing 'real entities beyond space-time reality'.[25]

For Wright the reason one is justified in believing that theological language actually refers to real entities is that the nature of the language of theology even though 'fundamentally metaphorical does not mean that it does not have a referent'.[26] Rather than being problematic, Wright believes that these metaphors can be considered stories in their own right and as a result help solve the problem rather than complicate it.[27] He does emphasize that the possibility of theological language having a referent (in this case God) does not make all language about God true, but rather this allows theological language to be 'in principle, on the same footing as language about anything else'.[28]

So from Wright's point of view the way in which to fly between the horns of the dilemma between positivism (and the post-modern critique of positivism) and relativity (which brings into question and historical claims of Christianity) is to understand that it is stories (and their subjective nature) which comprise worldviews that allow us to interpret the world, theology, and the Bible as real 'things' while not getting gored on either side of the dilemma. The question, of course, is whether or not Wright has succeeded. Even those sympathetic to Wright's solution can wonder if perhaps Wright is simply a 'historical positivist'.[29] Moritz wonders if 'Wright the historian' is still operating in these positivistic ways since he 'is still very much interested in what happened, why it happened and what was intended to happen'.[30]

Wright's Historical Problem

Wright's historical problem becomes clear when he looks at the actual text of the Bible. He writes:

---

[25] Wright, *NTPG*, p. 128.
[26] Wright, *NTPG*, p. 129.
[27] Wright, *NTPG*, p. 130.
[28] Wright, *NTPG*, p. 130.
[29] Moritz, 'Tools', p. 179.
[30] Moritz, 'Tools', p. 180.

The discovery, therefore, that someone has a 'point of view', or has selected or arranged material, or has a characteristic style or turn of phrase, does nothing whatever to tell us whether what the writer is talking about (if he or she purports to be describing events) actually happened or not.[31]

It is here that a challenge to Wright must be raised. Has he really solved anything? While Wright's understanding of worldview and the role that stories play in those perceptions seems to be correct, has he really solved the historical problem, or has Wright only pushed the question back one or two steps? Yes, embedding stories in a worldview (which is correct) alleviates the epistemological problem of certainty for the biblical text, that is, the worldview has accepted the stories as true (irrespective of their correspondence to actual historical events), but this still questions the actual historicity of the stories as they are told. In other words, simply because I confess that Jesus was raised from the dead (a claim the Gospels make) does not mean that this resurrection actually happened, even if a whole group of people agree with me (that is, through the stories symbolized by Eucharist, Easter celebrations, or whatever). My confession of the resurrection has potentially become a confession about the story rather than in the event itself.

Wright's answer to this problem is to use a 'visual metaphor' of a telescope. He describes someone who has never seen or used a telescope and the need for this person to learn how to use it through trial and error. This process, which leads to many distorted pictures of reality, does not change the fact, says Wright, that 'there are objects out there in the real world, and I am really looking at them, albeit of course (a) from my own point of view and (b) through a particular set of lenses'.[32] For Wright the solution to this perspective problem is CR and not an 'abandonment of knowledge of the extra-linguistic world', because being aware of the Gospels' biases does not take away from the fact that they were describing something that happened in history.[33] Thus, Wright tries to combine the concern for bias vis-à-vis historical objectivity by saying the Gospels'

---

[31] Wright, *NTPG*, p. 90.
[32] Wright, *NTPG*, p. 90.
[33] Wright, *NTPG*, pp. 90-91.

bias, for example, is, in fact, part of the historical record and as such is not to be rejected on this basis alone.

Furthermore, Wright insists that this does not mean that all interpretations of history are 'equally valid or proper'.[34] He argues that a new set of historical criteria are needed because, 'the epistemological tools of our age seem inadequate for the data before us'.[35] Wright suggests that biblical studies, rather than being problematic, might actually be the solution for creating 'a reappraisal of the theory of knowledge itself'.[36] What is this reappraisal? Wright answers that people should listen to 'stories other than those by which they habitually order their lives, and to ask themselves whether those other stories ought not to be allowed to subvert their usual ones'.[37]

Wright's Problematic Solution

At this point the problem becomes very clear. What one person will accept as 'fact' varies based on the stories that he or she has already accepted as reflecting the 'truth' of an event. To use an historical example, determining whether the United States won the Vietnam war (or if it actually was a war) rests largely on one's worldview (and accompanying stories) and has little to do with their epistemic theory as it relates to history. Even if one could speak philosophically about history (and few outside academia could) how could there be adjudication between the stories of different people? Another example of this is manifest in the current Evangelical debate surrounding women in ministry. Good people, good scholars, and people sincere in their faith line up on both sides of the debate and argue using the same verses. Certainly Paul meant something when he wrote, but in our current situation what counts for truth (even at the level of hermeneutical methodology) cannot be adjudicated by simple (or complex) exegesis of a text.

Where does Wright place subjectivity? He places it in the process of interpretation which is, of course, where it lies, but in doing so

---

[34] Wright, *NTPG*, pp. 90-91. He notes that the *Gospel of Thomas* is an example of an inaccurate recounting of history since it is less accurate than the Gospel of Mark.
[35] Wright, *NTPG*, p. 96.
[36] Wright, *NTPG*, p. 96.
[37] Wright, *NTPG*, p. 97.

Wright has not really solved any problems. This is because for Wright the text, along with the bias of its authors, is static. By static it is not meant that the text is not the Word of God, but rather that the text as we have it does not change. As a result the interpreter's job is to uncover the stories of the text and let them interact with (or become) the stories of our lives (our worldview). The problem with this approach is that subjectivity has simply been moved from the text (which is a good thing), and placed on interpretation (which is true, but does not solve the problem). This problem, however, may be solved using a Trinitarian hermeneutic that is informed by the Pentecostal theological tradition.

A Pentecostal Approach to Hermeneutics

Since currently there is no agreement within the Pentecostal movement on what exactly constitutes a Pentecostal hermeneutic, it is hoped that this essay will serve not only as a suggestion for improvement of Wright's hermeneutic, but also as a suggestion for further exploration of what a Pentecostal biblical hermeneutic might look like.[38]

An important distinction needs to be made before starting this discussion. Traditionally Pentecostals, although not children of the Evangelical theological tradition, have generally used hermeneutical methods formulated in this tradition even though these approaches are not generally part of the Pentecostal historical heritage.[39] It is also from the Evangelical tradition that Pentecostals have inherited, sometimes uncritically, much of their systematic theology, including much of their doctrine of the Bible. One of these legacies is the doctrine of biblical inerrancy.[40] While few Pentecostal denominations have a stated theological doctrine of inerrancy, most Pentecostals assume biblical inerrancy in their hermeneutics. This may seem like a detour from the question of Wright's historical problem, but it is, in fact, very germane.

---

[38] For a summary of Pentecostal Hermeneutics (more theological than biblical) see the first four chapters of Kenneth J. Archer, *A Pentecostal Hermeneutic for the Twenty-First Century* (JPTSup 28; New York: T&T Clark, 2004).

[39] Archer, *Hermeneutic*, p. 2.

[40] This is not to suggest that all Evangelicals affirm inerrancy.

Most Evangelical traditions start their statements of faith with an affirmation about the Bible and then secondarily move to the doctrines of God and Church.[41] This, of course, is necessary in foundational philosophical systems since in order for each doctrinal statement to be true the prior one must also be true.[42] Thus, many Evangelical traditions for good or bad affirm a priori that the Bible is inerrant. Paul Merritt Bassett notes that 'Such confessions seem usually to affirm that one must accept the authority of the Bible in order to come to a living relationship with God'.[43] This affirmation solves one problem by giving these doctrinal statements the philosophical grounding and foundation that they need, but they do so at the expense of making their adherents adopt a historical positivist approach to the Bible. They thus fall prey to the very problem that Wright seeks to avoid. This type of biblical scholarship is what has characterized much Evangelical scholarship, especially in the last couple of decades.

On the other hand, the Anglican (of which Wright is a part), Wesleyan, and classical Pentecostal traditions usually start with the Trinitarian God and only secondarily move to the Bible.[44] The significance of this is that the Bible can be considered the accurate self-revelation of God and does not need to be affirmed as a priori inerrant. Among other things, this places the Bible in its correct place subservient to God. If the Bible is a self-revelation of God, then the goal of biblical studies (in Christian perspective) is to understand what the Bible reveals about God. This removes the need to be a biblical apologist. Instead the Bible becomes a human (and divine) explanation of who God is.[45]

---

[41] The following paragraphs are largely based on an article by Paul Merritt Bassett, 'The Theological Identity of the North American Holiness Movement: Its Understanding of the Nature and Role of the Bible', in Donald W. Dayton and Robert K. Johnston (eds.), *The Variety of American Evangelicalism* (Knoxville: University of Tennessee Press, 1991), pp. 72-108.

[42] See Bassett, 'Theological Identity', p. 81. Of course, he is not interacting with Wright.

[43] Bassett, 'Theological Identity', p. 77.

[44] Bassett, 'Theological Identity', pp. 77-79. Bassett does not mention Pentecostals in his article, but rather writes about holiness churches. Because of the similarities on this issue between Holiness and Pentecostal churches, I have taken the liberty of inserting Pentecostals into Bassett's analysis.

[45] Bassett, 'Theological Identity', pp. 77-79.

This may seem like the splitting of very thin theological hairs, but the significance cannot be overstated. Rather than placing one's faith in the Bible's accurate transmission of history, one is freed to read the Bible for what it is: a subjective relating of God's interaction with the world. Bassett, describing John Wesley's understanding of the Bible, writes, 'Authority belongs to Scripture as the means attested by the Spirit, and the Spirit's attestation is that Scripture is sufficient for salvation'.[46] This pneumatological subjectivity does not threaten faith, but rather strengthens one's faith in the Spirit that initiates that faith. This allows for an epistemology that can start with the self-revelation of Jesus who claims to be 'the way, the truth, and the life'. Jesus' claim is an epistemological 'clue' to our own postmodern understanding of hermeneutics. If Jesus is the 'ground' by which all truth is measured then a relationship with him is what 'provides' truth.

Building on this idea of a relational epistemology, if we consider a relational model of the Trinity, we can then conceive of the Spirit continually drawing us into relationship with the Triune God for the purpose of self-revelation.[47] Wesleyans and Pentecostals call this Spirit-facilitated relationality between human and divine 'prevenient grace'. (Catholics understand this process as the giving of grace through the sacraments.)[48] Thus, it is through the mitigation or drawing of the Spirit that one comes to Christ.

For hermeneutics, the Spirit is where the objective text (the Bible as it is prior to interpretation) intersects with the subjective (the Word of God). 'Word of God' does not refer to the words on the page of the Bible, but rather the Bible as it becomes alive through

---

[46] Bassett, 'Theological Identity', p. 79.

[47] It is not necessary to defend this assertion here; however, two examples of this formulation are Karl Barth and Wolfhart Pannenberg. See Pannenberg's *Systematic Theology* (Grand Rapids: Eerdmans, 1991), I, ch. 5; and Barth's *Church Dogmatics* (eds. G.W. Bromiley and T.F. Torrance; trans. A.T. Mackay and T.H.L. Parker; repr., Peabody, MA: Hendrickson, 2010), I:1, ch. 2. For a Pentecostal articulation of the relationality of the Trinity see Amos Yong, *Spirit-Word-Community: Theological Hermeneutics in Trinitarian Perspective* (Eugene, OR: Wipf & Stock, 2002), ch. 2. For the argument that the Spirit draws all people see Amos Yong's carefully defended articulation of this in *The Spirit Poured Out on All Flesh: Pentecostalism and the Possibility of Global Theology* (Grand Rapids: Baker Academic, 2005), ch. 2.

[48] David M. Coffey, *Grace: The Gift of the Holy Spirit* (Milwaukee: Marquette University Press, 2011), see especially ch. 9.

the Spirit.[49] Then the biblical text can transform people into the persons that God wants them to be. This happens through the inspiration of the Holy Spirit, which operates in the life of the hearer or reader. The Spirit who inspired the biblical authors to write is the same Spirit who inspires the reader today. It is only when the text becomes alive to the reader (interpreter) through the inspiration of the Spirit that the words actually become the Word of God.

What guards this process from wrong interpretation? Both the Spirit and the Church do. The Spirit keeps interpreters honest in their own readings of the text by keeping the pious interpreter faithful to the text (this does not presume that the interpreter will not be educated, but rather presumes that all interpreters will be called to study the text carefully). The (universal) Church keeps the interpreter from spreading false notions for selfish gain through both its God-given authority and through its traditions. This protects the Word of God from misinterpretation while at the same time elevating subjective human readings of the text to become the Word of God. To be clear, this is not a theological reading that downplays historical-critical methods as advocated by Daniel Trier and others.[50] Trier fails, not because of his concern for the text, but because he privileges tradition at the expense of biblical interpretation.

This is why Wright's work is not without great value. Wright's arguments about worldview and historical reconstruction are accurate, but they must be used in combination with the history of scholarship, Church tradition, and personal faith so that there can be an adjudication between varying interpretations and ultimately varying applications. The final section of this essay suggests that infusing a pneumatological theology into Wright's biblical hermeneutic offers a solution to the historical problem that troubles him and many other interpreters. The reason that Wright's work is more helpful than many other formulations is that the hermeneutical

---

[49] The first volume of Barth's *Church Dogmatics*, of course, is famous for this claim, but one need not agree with all of Barth's understanding of revelation (especially his rejection of natural revelation) to make the claim that it is only through the work of the Spirit that the words of the Bible become the Word of God.

[50] Daniel J. Treier, *Introducing Theological Interpretation of Scripture: Recovering a Christian Practice* (Grand Rapids: Baker Academic, 2008).

method which he has developed easily lends itself to the insertion of pneumatological language.

Pneumatological Solution

It is surprising that Wright does not address pneumatology more in his hermeneutic. For example, in his well-known essay on the authority of Scripture he answers the rhetorical question of how God exercises authority with the Bible by saying that in 'the biblical story itself we see that he does so through human agents anointed and equipped by the Holy Spirit'.[51] Wright reiterates this when he says, 'New Testament authors believed themselves called to exercise their calling as "authorized" teachers, by the guidance and the power of the Spirit'.[52] Unfortunately, Wright does not explain what he means by this comment.

One way to illustrate a rudimentary Pentecostal hermeneutic is with the use of the Wesleyan quadrilateral.[53] The quadrilateral with its four vertices of Scripture, tradition, reason, and experience (with Scripture given primacy on the top of the quadrilateral), illustrates the way in which knowledge for Christian living is developed. The reason why the quadrilateral serves as a helpful Pentecostal hermeneutical model is that it includes, along with the traditional triad of Scripture, tradition, and reason, the affirmation that experience also plays a role in informing the Christian life. It is through the experience of the Spirit that Scripture (mitigated through the guides of tradition and reason) once again breathes. It is not going too far to suggest that the same Spirit that inspired the original authors of the Bible continues to inspire, not the composition of the text, but the reading of the text, making the reading of the text not just intellectual practice, but an intellectual practice. Furthermore, reading the

---

[51] Wright, 'How Can the Bible Be Authoritative?', *Vox Evangelica* 21 (1991), p. 16.

[52] Wright, *Last Word*, p. 51.

[53] Ever since Albert Outler coined the phrase 'Wesleyan Quadrilateral' to help illustrate Wesley's theology it has been used in many different ways, some which Outler himself found troubling. For this particular discussion, however, the term is completely germane since this discussion relates to the role in which Scripture informs the rest of Christian life. See Outler's essay 'The Wesleyan Quadrilateral – in John Wesley', in Thomas C. Oden and Leicester R. Longden (eds.), *The Wesleyan Theological Heritage* (Grand Rapids: Zondervan, 1991), pp. 21-38.

text is not just affirming Christian tradition, but it is an affirming Christian tradition. Reading, affirming, and practicing are all existential aspects of biblical interpretation that cannot be removed from the process. While rarely carefully articulated, this is the way in which Pentecostals have historically done biblical studies (sometimes with good results and sometimes with disastrous ones).

To be clear, for Pentecostals the justification for the hermeneutical integration between human experiences and the Spirit is simply the belief that the Spirit both inspires the text and indwells the believer who reads the text. The Spirit continues the Spirit's work in the world. The Pentecostal acknowledges this Spirit activity in the world and looks for (even expects) the witness of the Spirit in daily life. Infusing the Spirit into one's hermeneutic makes the interpretive process not just an exercise in history (recovering the triad of Scripture, reason, and tradition), but also a spiritual exercise in the experience of the Spirit. Finally, this move also alleviates the subjectivity problem of history. The subjectivity of the historical interpretation can be avoided, not by ignoring or denying Lessing's Ditch, but rather by placing the subjectivity of the enterprise in the correct location. The correct location is with the Spirit itself. For it would be accurate to say that the Spirit is, by definition, pure subjectivity. The Spirit does what the Spirit wills. Experience of the Spirit is also subjective, but this need not be a worry, since, while the experience of the Spirit is subjective, the experience itself is not. So, when one reads Scripture the subjective experience of the Spirit integrates with the objective Word.

No one but the most strident fundamentalist would deny the influence of tradition and reason in the interpretation of the Bible. It is the existential claim, however, that is often denied and it is this very element that, it would seem, solves Wright's historical problem. How does this solve Wright's problem? Wright's hermeneutic will fall apart if there is no way of recapturing history. While he does not demand that history be proven, the need for an objective history that is in some way able to be proven is necessary. A strong pneumatology, however, mitigates this problem by bridging the gap of history with a contemporary experience of the same Spirit that inspired the text. Although Wright does not use Spirit language in his definition of revelation, he is very close when he writes, 'there is a much older notion of "revelation", according to which God is continually revealing himself to and within the world he has made'.[54]

What is fascinating is that the way Wright has developed his hermeneutic lends itself to this kind of a suggestion. In his discussion on worldviews he offers a quadrilateral of his own that, in a way similar to the Wesleyan model, connects each vertex of the quadrilateral to the others with arrows indicating the interdependency of each element on the other.[55] His four points are story, question, symbol, and praxis. For Wright these four elements constitute a worldview. Similarly the Wesleyan quadrilateral's points constitute what informs and defines the Christian life, thus developing a worldview of sorts. Wright's four points actually match up with those on the Wesleyan quadrilateral, although he does not identify them as such. Wright's story vertex, of course, is analogous to Scripture, since Scripture is where all Christians get at least some of their stories. The questions vertex that Wright describes ultimately reflects the same idea as reason in the Wesleyan quadrilateral. Questions about the stories in Wright's model are generated through reason. The symbols vertex is complementary to Wesley's tradition since both are ways of describing the past in representative form. Finally, Wright's praxis vertex is without question the same as the Wesleyan quadrilateral's experience.

In *The Last Word* Wright does mention the Wesleyan quadrilateral and the addition of experience to the 'three legged stool' of biblical authority.[56] Wright is clearly not in favor of adding experience to the 'stool'. He argues correctly that for Wesley 'scripture remained the primary authority' and that experience only referred to 'the living experience of God's love and power of the Holy Spirit, through which what the Bible said was proved true in the life of the believer'.[57] Wright is incorrect, however, when he says:

> It is quite an illegitimate use of all this to see 'experience' as a separate source of authority to be played off against scripture it-

---

[54] Wright, *Last Word*, p. 31.
[55] See Wright, *NTPG*, p. 124.
[56] Wright, *Last Word*, pp. 100-101.
[57] Wright, *Last Word*, pp. 100-101.

self, though this move is now frequent, almost routine, in many theological circles.[58]

If Wright's point is that experience should not trump Scripture, most Pentecostals, at least in theory, would agree. If, however, Wright's point is that experience has no place in interpretation, it seems he has failed in his attempt to offer a hermeneutic that is not thoroughly modernist in its approach to history. Experience can (and does) play an important role in interpretation and ultimately a hermeneutic that incorporates a pneumatological experience can solve the historical problem that seems to trouble Wright's exegetical method.

It is worth anticipating three possible critiques to the inclusion of a pneumatologically-led experiential component into one's hermeneutic. The first might be that reliance on experiential interpretations could result in particular readings of the Bible that are propped up on the basis of an individual's own questionable exegesis defended by the claim of special spirituality. One does not need to look far to see the destructive nature that certain biblical interpretations can have. This is where a robust pneumatology once again solves the problem. The Spirit is not the exclusive domain of a particular church denomination or leader; instead the Spirit is available to all and will witness consistently to the community of believers. Similarly, the historical tradition of the Church also serves as a corrective means. While many in the Pentecostal movement have justifiably been cautious of incorporating tradition into their hermeneutic, the notion that the Church of today is Acts 29 (a common folk-Pentecostal statement) and has no need of knowing Church history is misguided. Hermeneutics is never done in a vacuum and while experience does illuminate the text it will constantly be checked by the tradition of the Church and the guidance of the Spirit within the community of believers.

A second critique that might be argued is that this Spirit-infused hermeneutic may imply that historical-critical work is not necessary or at least less helpful when interpreting the Bible. This also is not true. The academic methods of biblical interpretation continue to offer insight into the ways in which the Bible can be understood. Often these methods tell us less about what the Bible says and more

---

[58] Wright, *Last Word*, p. 101.

about what the Bible does not say. They highlight what Paul could not have meant or illustrate ways in which Genesis 1 should not be read. Thus, formal biblical studies of the kind that Wright and others do serve as a guardrail to biblical interpretive options and keep the Church on course. Furthermore, these critical methods of study affirm the need mentioned in the Wesleyan quadrilateral for a rational approach to Scripture.

Finally, some may argue that this type of Spirit-led hermeneutic could exclude the non-believer, that is, those that at least theologically speaking were not regenerated by the Spirit and therefore have no access to the Spirit's help in the interpretive process. This, however, is a faulty understanding of regeneration. As has already been shown, the Spirit is accessible to all regardless of their spiritual state. Thus, the Spirit may, in fact, use the study of Scripture as a means of drawing a person into grace.

Conclusion

What impact does the inclusion of a pneumatologically driven experiential element make on Wright's hermeneutic? It may be a small contribution, but it 'tweaks' his understanding of the subjective. The subjective is no longer found within the process of the interpreter's attempt to understand history, but rather it is found in the experience of the Spirit who is the inspirer of the writer and reader of the text. This alleviates the angst of history, while admittedly not relieving the hard work of the historian, whose job now becomes even more important. It is the subjectivity of the Spirit that bears the brunt of the postmodern critique. This is, however, a better place to attribute subjectivity, since Christian faith must always be subjective. An objective faith is by definition no faith at all.

A larger impact is that now the Spirit is 'back in our hermeneutic'. This gives an opportunity to read afresh the breath of God in the text. The text is no longer a static document available for stodgy study of grammar and words, but it is the confessional document of believers of old that continues to inspire believers of today with the Word of God. Wright's work, far from being dry, offers new insights into the Bible and when infused with the Spirit offers not only an intellectual advancement, but a true transformation of the soul.

4

N.T. Wright's 'Justification' and the Cry of the Spirit

Rick Wadholm Jr.[*]

Introduction

The Spirit has at times played second fiddle to the Father and Son in much of Christian theology, particularly with regard to the doctrine of justification – perhaps particularly among Protestants.[1] While the Spirit is attributed with leading believers to justification and with the work of sanctification that is typically conceived as flowing from justification, there simply has been too little thought given to the role of the Spirit in the actual work of justification. One almost wonders what to make of Paul's question to the Galatians: 'Having begun by the Spirit, are you now being perfected by the flesh?' (Gal. 3.3). This is not to say that Christian theology has not considered the Spirit to be in some way working out the justification of the believer, but that justification has been considered by and large to be primarily the work of the Father and the Son. In Protestantism, most of the focus on the Spirit has been given to works considered antecedent and posterior to justification. The warning of N.T. Wright seems fitting: 'Any attempt to give an ac-

---

[*] Rick Wadholm, Jr. (PhD Candidate, Bangor University, Wales) is Assistant Professor of Biblical and Theological Studies at Trinity Bible College in Ellendale, North Dakota.

[1] Frank D. Macchia, *Justified in the Spirit: Creation, Redemption, and the Triune God* (Grand Rapids: Eerdmans, 2010).

count of a doctrine which screens out the call of Israel, the gift of the spirit, and/or the redemption of all creation is doomed to be less than fully biblical'.[2]

One might wonder just how a richer doctrine of the Trinity might be fleshed out in relation to the doctrine of justification. Is there room for a reprioritization of the discussion in order to facilitate better a more thoroughly pneumatological approach to the doctrine of justification? There have been those who are turning their focus upon the pneumatological elements of theology that have been for too long neglected, but the doctrine of justification is still somewhat in its nascent stage in this regard.[3] What might the current debate over justification have to offer towards this more robust pneumatology leading to an enriched Trinitarian doctrine of justification? It will be the contention of this paper that the person and work of the Spirit indwelling the believer works out the life of the Son as son in the midst of the believing community and thereby assures of that justification before the Father.[4]

N.T. Wright has, I will contend, rightly reminded us that the 'Spirit is the path by which Paul traces the route from justification by faith in the present to justification, by the complete life lived, in the future'.[5] What follows is a brief discussion of N.T. Wright's view of justification with specific attention to his pneumatological direction. This will be followed by a brief analysis and biblical exposition of the 'cry of the Spirit' in relation to justification in Rom. 8.15 and Gal. 4.6 using some of Wright's pneumatological insights. The concluding remarks will suggest a more pragmatic and robustly pneumatological theology of justification that will (it is hoped) also be more thoroughly Trinitarian than other models that have been postulated.

---

[2] N.T. Wright, *Justification: God's Plan & Paul's Vision* (Downers Grove: IVP Academic, 2009), p. 222. There is no distinction intended by Wright's use of lower-case 'spirit' versus upper-case 'Spirit'. It is simply characteristic of his mode of expression in certain volumes compared to others. Throughout this article all references which are not quotations of Wright use the upper-case form.

[3] For a fine summary of several theologians working in the field of pneumatology in its relation to justification see Macchia, *Justified*, p. 85, n. 38.

[4] John Piper, *The Future of Justification: A Response to N.T. Wright* (Wheaton: Crossway Books, 2007), pp. 181-88.

[5] Wright, *Paul: In Fresh Perspective* (Minneapolis: Fortress, 2005), p. 148. Cited hereafter as *Paul*.

Wright's Justification and Its Pneumatological Orientation

N.T. Wright's view of justification is firmly rooted in *'God's single plan, through Abraham and his family, to bless the whole world'*.[6] He further defines justification as that righteousness which one receives as the decision of the judge, rather than as an imputed righteousness.[7] 'It isn't that God basically wants to condemn and then finds a way to rescue some from that disaster. It is that God longs to bless, to bless lavishly, and so to rescue and bless those in danger of tragedy – and therefore *must* curse everything that thwarts and destroys the blessing of his world and his people'.

Wright's primary contention is against the wrong direction he feels the doctrine of justification has been taken and his desire to see it brought back to a more Pauline (and therefore a more biblical) perspective. Wright quotes Alister McGrath as saying,

> The *doctrine* of justification has come to develop a meaning quite independent of its biblical origins, and concerns *the means by which man's relationship to God is established*. The Church has chosen to subsume its discussion of the reconciliation of man to God under the aegis of justification, thereby giving the concept an emphasis quite absent in the New Testament. The 'doctrine of justification' has come to bear a meaning within dogmatic theology which is quite independent of its Pauline origins.[8]

According to Wright, '[T]he verb *dikaioō*, "to justify" ... does not denote *an action which transforms someone* so much as *a declaration which grants them a status*'.[9] Wright goes on to state:

> the church has indeed taken off at an oblique angle from what Paul had said, so that, yes, ever since the time of Augustine, the discussions about *what has been called* 'justification' have borne a tangled, but ultimately only tangential, relation to what Paul was talking about.

---

[6] Wright, *Justification*, p. 48.
[7] Wright, *Justification*, p. 50.
[8] Wright, *Justification*, p. 60.
[9] Wright, *Justification*, p. 70.

For Wright the early Christians were asking the question of 'how we can tell, in the present who is implicitly included in the death and resurrection of Jesus?'[10] This set the Jewishness of the original question of justification in the Old Testament into a new context.

Justification as Covenant

Wright reads justification in covenantal terms and in the context of Old Testament and Second Temple usage, but with a decidedly Christological reorientation. Citing Richard Hays, he writes,

> Paul's understanding of justification must be interpreted resolutely in terms of OT affirmations of God's faithfulness to the covenant, a faithfulness surprisingly but definitively confirmed through Christ's death and resurrection.

'The *tsedeqah elohim*, the *dikaiosynē theou*, is an outward-looking characteristic of God, linked of course to the concern for God's own glory but essentially going, as it were, in the opposite direction, that of God's creative, healing, restorative love'. Wright argues,

> Paul believed, in short, that what Israel had longed for God to do for it and for the world, God had done for Jesus, bringing him through death and into the life of the age to come. Eschatology: the new world was inaugurated! Covenant: God's promises to Abraham had been fulfilled! Lawcourt: Jesus had been vindicated – and so all those who belonged to Jesus were vindicated as well! And these, for Paul, were not three, but one. Welcome to Paul's doctrine of justification, rooted in the single scriptural narrative as he read it, reaching out to the waiting world.[11]

The covenant was for 'dealing-with-sin-and-rescuing-people-from-it, on the one hand and bringing-Jews-and-Gentiles-together-into-a-single-family, on the other, always were bound up together, as they always were in Paul'. God has at last brought His judgment into the world and history

---

[10] Wright, *The New Testament and the People of God* (Christian Origins and the Questions of God 1; Minneapolis: Fortress, 1992), p. 458. Cited hereafter as *NTPG*.

[11] Wright, *Justification*, p. 80.

precisely in the covenant-fulfilling work of Jesus Christ, dealing with sin through his death, launching the new world in his resurrection, and sending his spirit to enable human beings, through repentance and faith, to become little walking and breathing advance parts of that eventual new creation.[12]

This covenant has created 'the single multi-ethnic family, constituted in the Messiah and indwelt by the spirit ... designed as God's powerful sign to the pagan world that Israel's God, Abraham's God, is its creator, lord and judge'.[13] Thus, justification for Wright is intimately related to sonship within the family rather than being myopically focused upon the traditional Protestant legal paradigm. The traditional legal paradigm of Protestantism is not absent from Wright's interpretation, but it is only one part of his view of justification.

Justification in Relation to Sonship

As Wright understands it 'for Paul, "justification", whatever else it included, always had in mind God's declaration of membership, and that this always referred specifically to the coming together of Jews and Gentiles in faithful membership of the Christian family'.[14] This is explicitly covenantal language rather than moralistic, which is why he can state that justification 'denotes a *status*, not a moral quality. It means "membership in God's true family".'[15] For Wright it is the 'faith of the individual' which 'marks out those who now belong to him, to the Messiah-redefined family'.[16]

The family paradigm as indicative of covenantal relationship is crucial.

> *There is a single family*, because this is the whole point: the one God, the creator, always intended to call into being a single family for Abraham. The single plan through Israel for the world has turned out to be the single plan through *Israel's representative, the*

---

[12] Wright, *Justification*, p. 106.
[13] Wright, *Justification*, p. 106.
[14] Wright, *Justification*, p. 96.
[15] Wright, *Justification*, p. 100.
[16] Wright, *Justification*, p. 97.

Messiah, for the world *including Israel*, and all those who belong to the Messiah now form the one promised family.[17]

The one family wherein Gentile and Jew are all one in the Messiah has come about through the single plan of God. This is the work of justification.

> God is now creating a worldwide family where ethnic origin, social class and gender are irrelevant, and where each member receives the affirmation 'you are my beloved children', because that is what God says to his son, the Messiah, and because 'as many as were baptized into the Messiah have clothed themselves with the Messiah'.[18]

Wright conceives the future verdict to have been given concerning faith: '"righteous", "my child"'.[19] These declarations – 'righteous' and 'my child' – are understood to be the very terms of justification and they are best related through the indwelling evidence of the Spirit.

Thus Wright considers that 'we are now and forever part of the family to whose every member God says what he said to Jesus at his baptism: you are my beloved child, with you I am well pleased'.[20] As Christ received evidence of the Spirit at his baptism testifying to his being the well pleasing Son of the Father, so the Spirit-endowed believers give spiritual testimony to being well pleasing sons in the cry of the Spirit to the Father.

Justification in Relation to the Spirit

The 'Spirit of the Son' that we have received necessitates a doctrine of justification that is pneumatological according to Wright. 'The Spirit is the path by which Paul traces the route from justification by faith in the present to justification, by the complete life lived, in the future'.[21]

---

[17] Wright, *Justification*, p. 109.
[18] Wright, *Justification*, p. 112.
[19] Wright, *Justification*, p. 117.
[20] Wright, 'New Perspectives on Paul', in Bruce L. McCormack (ed.), *Justification in Perspective: Historical Developments and Contemporary Challenges* (Grand Rapids: Baker Academic, 2006), p. 261.
[21] Wright, *Paul*, p. 148.

> [T]he 'spirit of the son' (Galatians 4.6), the 'spirit of the Messiah' (Romans 8.9), is poured out upon the Messiah's people, so that they become in reality what they already are by God's declaration: God's people indeed, his 'children' (Romans 8.12-17; Galatians 4.4-7) within a context replete with overtones of Israel as 'God's son' at the exodus. The extremely close interconnection of Romans 8 and Galatians 4 with the discourse of justification in the earlier chapters of both letters warns us against attempting to construct a complete 'doctrine of justification' without reference to the spirit. Indeed, I and others have long insisted that the doctrine is Trinitarian in shape. This is the point at which it is idle to complain that I, or others who take a similar position, are encouraging people to 'trust in anyone or anything other than the crucified and resurrected Savior'. Is it wrong, or heretical, to declare that *as well as* and also *because of* our absolute faith in the crucified and resurrected Savior, we *also* trust in the life-giving spirit who enables us to say 'Abba, father' (Romans 8.12-16) and 'Jesus is Lord' (1 Corinthians 12.3)? Of course not. For Paul, faith in Jesus Christ *includes* a trust in the spirit; not least, a sure trust that 'he who began a good work in you will bring it to completion at the day of the Messiah' (Philippians 1.6).[22]

The relation of the Spirit to the work of present and final justification is left for his exegesis, although he says far less than one might like him to say on this subject.

Wright proposes that Paul would have understood the reason Christ was made a curse for us (*negative* justification) was 'that the blessing of Abraham might come upon the Gentiles, and so that we (presumably Jews who believe in Jesus) might receive the promise of the Spirit through faith' (*positive* justification). Thus, the promised anointed one of God became a curse, in accord with Deuteronomy, successfully passing through that curse 'into the time of renewal when the Gentiles would at last come into Abraham's family, while Jews could have the possibility of covenant renewal, of receiving the promised spirit through faith'.[23]

When one's trust is in the Holy Spirit

---

[22] Wright, *Justification*, pp. 85-86.
[23] Wright, *Justification*, pp. 103-104.

within Trinitarian theology one is quick to say that this is not something other than trust in Jesus the Messiah, since it is his own spirit; the Father who sent Jesus is now sending 'the Spirit of the Son' (Gal. 4.4-7). But the point about the Holy Spirit, at least within Paul's theology, is that when the spirit comes the result is human freedom rather than human slavery.

The 'Spirit of the Son' is the spirit of freedom and liberation from sin and all of its consequences. The reception of the Spirit thus means the justification of the believer into the freedom of new life or real life.

True freedom is the gift of the spirit, the result of grace; but, precisely because it is freedom *for* as well as freedom *from*, it isn't simply a matter of being forced now to be good, against our wills and without our co-operation … but a matter of being released from slavery precisely into responsibility, into being able at last to choose, to exercise moral muscle, knowing both that one is doing it oneself and that the spirit is at work within, that God himself is doing that which I too am doing. If we don't believe that, we don't believe in the spirit, and we don't believe Paul's teaching.

It is not as if this cry of the Spirit, and this new life lived in the Spirit, is somehow other than that very life of the vindicated believer. '[T]he spirit is the one through whose agency God's people are renewed and reconstituted *as* God's people. And it is by the energy of the spirit, working in those who belong to the Messiah, that the new paradox comes about in which the Christian really does exercise free moral will and effort but at the same time ascribes this free activity to the spirit'.

How might this be accomplished in Wright's system? It appears primarily to be accomplished through the preaching of the Word (which is noticeably central to all Reformed theology).

Paul's conception of how people are drawn into salvation starts with the preaching of the gospel, continues with the work of the Spirit in and through that preaching, and the effect of the Spirit's work on the hearts of the hearers, and concludes with the coming to birth of faith, and entry into the family through baptism.[24]

While Wright has structured a certain continuum of the work of salvation, it is centered on the proclamation of the good news in Christ preached in the power of the Spirit.

> [T]he preaching of the gospel, in the power of the spirit, is the means by which, as an act of sheer grace, God evokes this faith in people from Abraham to the present day and beyond. It is a mystery, but it is held within the larger mystery of that same overarching divine grace. 'Nobody can say "Jesus is Lord" (the basic Christian confession of faith) except by the Holy Spirit.' When the word of the gospel is proclaimed, the spirit goes to work in ways that the preacher cannot predict or control which often take the hearers, and the responders, by surprise as well.[25]

How could this be conceived as anything different than the 'Abba, Father' cry of the Spirit of the Son? Is this not the preaching of the gospel by the Spirit in the mouth of the believing and vindicated community of faith? Or at the very least a cry of affirmation to that Word and by that very Word?

In what sense should this be understood to be present (or future) vindication by the Spirit? Is it merely a hopeful cry or the certain cry of assurance? According to Wright, 'You cannot ... have a Pauline doctrine of assurance (and the glory of the Reformation doctrine of justification is precisely assurance) without the Pauline doctrine of the spirit'. '"Justification by faith" is about the *present*, about how you can already tell who the people are who will be vindicated on the last day'. Wright, however, makes a clear comment as to his understanding of future justification. It will 'truly reflect what people have actually done'. He immediately explains that this in no way means they will have earned the final verdict or that their works will be perfect and complete, but that they are 'seeking it through that patient, spirit-driven Christian living' wherein from one perspective it is entirely the work of the Spirit and from another it is the renewed and recreated humanity freely offering itself in obedi-

---

[24] Wright, *What Saint Paul Really Said: Was Paul of Tarsus the Real Founder of Christianity?* (Grand Rapids: Eerdmans, 1997), p. 125. Cited hereafter as *WSPRS*.
[25] Wright, *WSPRS*, p. 184.

ence to the Lord.[26] Wright's conclusion concerning Spirit reception and justification needs bearing in mind: 'What Paul says about Christians could be said about the doctrine of justification itself: if you don't have the spirit, you're not on the map'.[27]

The Cry of the Spirit in Romans 8.15 and Galatians 4.6

> For you did not receive the spirit of slavery to fall back into fear, but you have received the Spirit of adoption as sons, by whom we cry, 'Abba! Father!' (Rom. 8.15)

> And because you are sons, God has sent the Spirit of his Son into our hearts, crying, 'Abba! Father!' (Gal. 4.6).

As we turn to examine the 'cry of the Spirit' in Rom. 8.15 and Gal. 4.6, we will be able to deepen our understanding of Wright's discussion of the covenantal and familial declaration of justification in accord with the Spirit. 'The Spirit enables Christians to share in the unique relation of the Son but it is not the good works of the Christian that make him a son of God nor is it his physical descent'.[28] This becomes clearer when we recognize justification as related to the 'cry of the Spirit'. 'The Abba cry is confirmation of sonship, not merely in the reception of the "Spirit producing sonship" but in the actual status as sons and daughters of God'.[29] Indeed, it can and should be argued that 'Paul believes it is the Spirit that puts life into believers and gives them a basis for spiritual kinship with God' and thus any doctrine of justification lacking pneumatological emphasis is a doctrine of justification lacking altogether.[30]

The wedge which has been too often driven between the gift of sonship and the reception of the Spirit in Gal. 4.6 has been ruled

---

[26] Wright, *Justification*, p. 167.

[27] Wright, *Justification*, p. 165.

[28] E.A. Obeng, 'Abba Father: The Prayer of the Sons of God', *The Expository Times* 99 (1987–1988), p. 364.

[29] Robert Jewett, *Romans: A Commentary* (Hermeneia; Minneapolis: Fortress, 2007), p. 500.

[30] Ben Witherington III and Darlene Hyatt, *Paul's Letter to the Romans: A Socio-Rhetorical Commentary* (Grand Rapids: Eerdmans, 2004), p. 217.

too long by 'dogmatic and philosophical categories'.[31] 'For Paul, it seems, sonship and receiving the Spirit are so intimately related that one can speak of them in either order ... with only the circumstances of a particular audience, to be used at any given time or place'.[32] 'Paul is not here setting out stages in the Christian life, whether logical or chronological. Rather, his emphasis is on the reciprocal relation or correlational nature of sonship and the reception of the Spirit'. In fact, for Longenecker, the Spirit can justly be called 'the Spirit of the Son'[33] because of the 'two mutually dependent and intertwined features in the subjective experience of salvation'.[34] This is because there are not two experiences of salvation, but only one. The reception of the Spirit and sonship are spoken of separately, but identified together as two aspects emphasizing the relation to the Son and to the Spirit. However, even here, one has to do with the 'Spirit of the Son' and not simply 'the Spirit'. It is impossible to conceive of the Spirit as separate from the Son in Paul's writings; he lays special emphasis upon the relation of the Son and Spirit. Gordon Fee argues that while the Spirit is not ultimately responsible for *procuring* this sonship, the Spirit *actualizes* the adoption as sons.[35] The Son has been sent by the Father making us to be sons of God and the Spirit of the Son has been sent also by the Father (even 'into our hearts') who Himself cries out 'Abba, Father!'. 'Paul then has here spoken of the objective and subjective dimensions of conversion, and in each case it has to do with being conformed to the image and status of the Son.'[36]

This adoption has been both enacted and declared by the reception of the Spirit and Paul may at times (as in Gal. 4.6) emphasize one aspect over another. But at another time he puts the other aspect forward (as in Rom 8.15). These two aspects are not to be con-

---

[31] Hans Dieter Betz, *Galatians: A Commentary* (Hermeneia; Philadelphia: Fortress, 1979), p. 209.

[32] Richard N. Longenecker, *Galatians* (Word Biblical Commentary 41; Dallas: Word, 1990), p. 173.

[33] Though τοῦ υἱοῦ is omitted by P[46], Marcion, and Augustine.

[34] Longenecker, *Galatians*, p. 174.

[35] Gordon Fee, *God's Empowering Presence: The Holy Spirit in the Letters of Paul* (Peabody, MA: Hendrickson, 1994), p. 408.

[36] Witherington, *Grace in Galatia: A Commentary on Paul's Letter to the Galatians* (Grand Rapids: Eerdmans, 1998), p. 291.

sidered in absolute terms, but need to be seen pragmatically as a way of emphasizing the complex relation of the Spirit and Son in the justification of the believer. Whereas there is some sense of grammatical ambiguity in the text of Gal. 4.6 (due to the conjunctive ὅτι) as to whether there is something other than the Spirit that might constitute sonship, yet Paul has cleared that up in Romans 8. 'Spirit-led Christians are children of God. The gift of the Spirit *constitutes* the sonship, and it is thus the basis of the *huiothesia*'.[37] However, Fee correctly points out that whereas in Gal. 4.6 Paul clarifies that 'adoption was secured for us by Christ … here [in Rom. 8.15] it has been made effective in the life of the believer through the work of the Spirit'.[38] Thus, for Paul, sonship is a thoroughly Trinitarian work attributable at one moment primarily to the Son and at another to the Spirit, but in both cases the Son and Spirit are intimately involved.

Gordon Fee argues that the 'presence of the Son by means of the Spirit of the Son actualizes our own "sonship"' which was 'secured for us' by Jesus' death, resurrection, and ascension.[39] The adoption as sons is something that *has* happened and yet has 'its eschatological consequences'.[40] This eschatological dimension of justification and the cry of the Spirit recognizes the ongoing work which is both firmly established and yet sought after by the very being of God indwelling redeemed creation. 'The Christian cry is likewise the cry of the Spirit. The inspired *Abba* cry reveals that Christians are children of God and destined for glory.'[41] 'The divine sonship is and remains an eschatological reality'.[42] For Paul, 'the confident articulation that God is one's Father stems from a certainty in the heart that transcends human comprehension'.[43] This

---

[37] Joseph A. Fitzmyer, *Romans: A New Translation with Introduction and Commentary* (Anchor Bible 33; New York: Doubleday, 1993), p. 498.
[38] Fee, *God's Empowering Presence*, p. 566.
[39] Fee, *Pauline Christology: An Exegetical-Theological Study* (Peabody, MA: Hendrickson, 2007), p. 590.
[40] Fitzmyer, *Romans*, p. 497.
[41] Fitzmyer, *Romans*, p. 501.
[42] Ernst Käsemann, *Commentary on Romans* (trans. G.W. Bromiley; Grand Rapids: Eerdmans, 1980), p. 227.
[43] Thomas R. Schreiner, *Romans* (Baker Exegetical Commentary on the New Testament 6; Grand Rapids: Baker, 1998), p. 427.

cry of the Spirit is offered in the deeds of the body as well. Cranfield writes:

> This is what it means to live after the Spirit, to mortify by the Spirit the deeds of the body, and to be led by the Spirit of God – simply to be enabled by that same Spirit to cry, 'Abba, Father.' And it is here expressed not as an imperative but as an indicative: Christians do as a matter of fact do this. The implicit imperative is that they should continue to do just this, and do it more and more consistently more and more sincerely, soberly and responsibly. This is all that is required of them … Nothing more is required of us than that we should cry to the one true God 'Abba, Father' with full sincerity and with full seriousness.[44]

Cranfield goes on to say, 'In the accomplishment of this work of obedience the δικαίωμα τοῦ νόμου is fulfilled (Rom. 8.4)' and in this: sonship, justification, and the Spirit cry are bound up in the finished work of the Son.[45]

Toward a Spirit – Trinitarian – Theology of Justification

This pneumatological – and because pneumatological, ultimately Trinitarian – orientation for understanding justification is the direction toward which Paul has pointed us. N.T. Wright clearly thinks this a path toward which the Church needs to be re-oriented. Where to from here? Is the 'cry of the Spirit' nothing more than a subjective ground by which one recognizes the community of those who are being declared as justified? Is there a sense in which the 'cry of the Spirit' is also the objective declaration of the Father that indeed we are sons? Has there been any positive move towards a more pneumatological doctrine of justification whereby the Spirit might be recognized as working our justification?

The familial/covenantal motif of N.T. Wright offers far more towards a Spirit theology of justification than the more traditional motif of the legal setting for justification. Where, however, might the Spirit be found in such a legal motif if it is not to be discarded

---

[44] C.E.B. Cranfield, *A Critical and Exegetical Commentary on the Epistle to the Romans* (International Critical Commentary; Edinburgh: T&T Clark, 1975), I, p. 401.
[45] Cranfield, *Romans*, pp. 401-402.

(as it most certainly should not be)? In what sense might the indwelling and imparted person of God as the Spirit of God be related through such a motif?[46] How should justice be done to the doctrine of justification as understood and articulated according to Scripture without doing an injustice to the person and work of the Spirit?

Two theologians in particular may offer some helpful direction for us in conjunction with the forgoing exegesis of Romans and Galatians and the theological work of N.T. Wright – Karl Barth and Dietrich Bonhoeffer. Their reflections on Scripture and theology offer much in the way of careful exegesis and Trinitarian fullness and so we shall turn to them for some closing suggestions toward a fuller Trinitarian theology of justification. Barth suggests the necessity and privilege of our justified praying in the 'Spirit of the Son' to the Father. Bonhoeffer writes regarding the Christological and communal (Spirit-inspired?) word spoken aloud as our justification before the Father. I believe they both offer, in their own way, a further affirming word to the Church concerning the necessity of the justified and justifying cry of the Spirit.

Karl Barth writes in his *Church Dogmatics* concerning prayer and the relation of the Spirit and Christ:

> It is not a twofold but a single fact that both Jesus Christ with His prayer and also the Holy Spirit with 'unutterable groanings' is our Mediator and Intercessor. This can and must be said both of Jesus Christ and of the Holy Spirit, and in both cases it concerns the one event of laying a foundation for prayer, i.e. for the cry, Abba, Father. It is He – Jesus Christ through the Spirit, the Spirit as the Spirit of Jesus Christ – who makes good that which we of ourselves cannot make good, who brings our prayer before God and therefore makes it possible as prayer, and who in so doing makes it necessary for us. For Jesus Christ is in us through His Spirit, so that for His sake, praying after Him as the one who leads us in prayer, we for our part may and must pray, calling upon God as our Father. And the Spirit who frees us for this and incites us to the power in which we are with Him the children of God and are addressed as such, so that irrespective

---

[46] Macchia, *Justified*, pp. 121-27, 131-85.

of what we ourselves can offer and perform we can call God our Father and go to Him with our requests.[47]

In other words, Barth proposes that our prayer, even our 'Abba, Father' cry, is permitted, enabled, and necessitated by the 'Spirit of the Son' within us. There is a divine imperative wherein we are compelled by our justification to cry to our Father, but wherein we are also freed to cry and enabled to do so. This is the glory of our sonship whereby the Spirit within makes and declares us to be sons of the Father. This is why Paul could say that the 'cry of the Spirit' is both our cry and the Spirit's cry. Neither contradicts the other, because there is a divine indwelling, enabling, and compulsion of transformation towards the ultimate redemption of the sons and of all creation in the Son. These words also serve to remind the Church that Paul calls the inward witness of the Spirit that we are indeed sons a 'cry'. Barth recognizes this 'cry' as outward prayer and confession.[48] The Spirit will always give evidence of sonship. By the indwelling 'Spirit of the Son', our prayers are necessary, though freely given. We cry 'Father!' because we can and must.

Dietrich Bonhoeffer in his little work entitled *Life Together* wrote about the perspective of 'alien righteousness' which in Luther's doctrine of justification was "outside of us".[49] He explained the need, based upon this doctrine of 'alien righteousness', for community and the spoken Word of Christ:

> If they are asked 'Where is your salvation, your blessedness, your righteousness?', they can never point to themselves. Instead, they point to the Word of God in Jesus Christ that grants salvation, blessedness, and righteousness. They watch for this Word wherever they can. Because they daily hunger and thirst for righteousness, they long for the redeeming Word again and again. It can only come from the outside. In themselves they are only destitute and dead. Help must come from the outside; and it has

---

[47] Karl Barth, *Church Dogmatics* (G.W. Bromiley and T.F. Torrance [eds.]; trans. A.T. Mackay and T.H.L. Parker; repr.; Peabody, MA: Hendrickson, 2010), III:4, p. 94.

[48] Fee, *God's Empowering Presence*, p. 569.

[49] Dietrich Bonhoeffer, *Life Together, Prayerbook of the Bible* (Geoffrey B. Kelly [ed.]; trans. Daniel W. Bloesch and James H. Burtness; Minneapolis: Fortress, 1996), p. 31, n. 10.

come and comes daily and anew in the Word of Jesus Christ, bringing us redemption, righteousness, innocence, and blessedness. But God put this Word into the mouth of human beings so that it may be passed on to others. When people are deeply affected by the Word, they tell it to other people. God has willed that we should seek and find God's living Word in the testimony of other Christians ... They need them again and again when they become uncertain and disheartened ... They need other Christians as bearers and proclaimers of the divine word of salvation.[50]

The 'alien righteousness' of Luther, which Bonhoeffer has taken up, seems to fail to do justice to the justification of the believer in the Spirit in the very midst of the believing and confessing community. I believe Bonhoeffer has in some respects redeemed Luther in this by reminding the Church that we speak the Word of God as righteousness ... one to another. We confess the forgiveness of sins as fully granted. We are a community that is redeemed and redeeming, justified by the Spirit which cries aloud 'Abba, Father!' that others may hear, believe, and take heart. Let this be the cry of the gathered worshipping community full of the Spirit of the Son confessing the Father as our father.[51] Let us confess, hear, believe and take heart ... together having been justified that we may also be glorified with our Lord Jesus Christ.

---

[50] Bonhoeffer, *Life Together*, p. 32.
[51] Fee, *God's Empowering Presence*, pp. 409-10.

5

JUSTIFICATION AND THE SPIRIT: AN APPRECIATIVE INTERACTION WITH N.T. WRIGHT

FRANK D. MACCHIA[*]

Justification by faith has been termed 'one doctrine with many debates'.[1] Among these many debates are those grouped loosely under the so-called 'new perspectives on Paul'. Starting with Krister Stendahl's historic piece entitled, 'Paul and the Introspective Conscience of the West'[2] the new perspectives have attempted in part to free Paul from the medieval debates over one's personal salvation in order to locate justification within a refreshingly larger theological framework more in touch with ancient Jewish covenantal concerns. Stendahl put forward the insightful thesis that Paul's message of justification by faith tended to decrease in significance after the first century due partly to the waning of the theological vision that originally couched the doctrine, namely, the vision of the new *ekklesia*

---

[*] Frank D. Macchia (DTheol, University of Basel; DD, Pentecostal Theological Seminary) is Professor of Theology at Vanguard University, Costa Mesa, California and Associate Director of the Centre for Pentecostal and Charismatic Studies at Bangor University, Bangor, Wales. He has served as president of the Society for Pentecostal Studies and for more than a decade was senior editor of its journal, *Pneuma*. He has also served on the Faith and Order Commission of the National Council of Churches.

[1] Peter Segwick, 'Justification by Faith: One Doctrine, Many Debates?', *Theology* 93.751 (1990), pp. 5-13.

[2] Krister Stendahl, 'Paul and the Introspective Conscience of the West', *Harvard Theological Review* 56 (1963), pp. 199-215.

that consisted of the joining together of Jew and Gentile in Christ. When the doctrine is revived by Augustine in the fifth century, it is wielded in the service of his anti-Pelagian polemic that focused on one's personal salvation.[3]

The so-called new perspective on Paul has taken on other accents after Stendahl and has fragmented into several different approaches to a variety of issues (though with some continuity of accents). N.T. Wright has undoubtedly taken his place as one of the most innovative and challenging voices from within this larger trend. The most compelling feature of Wright's approach to justification was his insistence that Paul, true to his Jewish influence, viewed justification within a larger narrative that centered on God's covenant promise to Abraham to bless the nations. Briefly put, Israel was the linchpin of this plan. The covenant, however, not only involved promises but also curses, as indicated in Deuteronomy 28–30. Under the curse of disobeying the law, Israel found itself unable to fulfill the Torah and to play its role as a means by which the covenant promises given to Abraham would reach the nations. Faced with Roman occupation, Israel was being cursed by the nations rather than blessing the nations as God had intended. Within this crisis, Paul proposes that the Messiah Jesus had borne the curse on the cross, the curse that belongs not only to Israel but to everyone by virtue of Adam's disobedience. By bearing the curse on the cross, Jesus in his resurrection provided a way beyond it so that the blessing promised to the nations through Israel might be fulfilled. The end result of this blessing is the formation of the one body consisting of both Jew and Gentile taken up into Christ as the reason for this shared covenant status. The astounding fact highlighted by Paul is that God had intended all along that the plan to bless the world through Abraham and Israel would be fulfilled through and in the Messiah in precisely the way that it was.

Wright's conclusion is that justification is precisely God's act of making the world right through the formation of the covenant community in Christ. As the gift of covenant membership, justification is social, historical, and eschatological in nature. Though justifi-

---

[3] Augustine's doctrine of justification was actually broader than that, since it also involved the resurrection of the dead. Yet, Stendahl rightly maintained that the ecclesial and social nature of the doctrine was not developed at this point in the tradition.

cation is social for Wright, it is also forensic and declarative. Justification makes people right by declaring them members of the covenant community. Justification is covenant status bestowed by God and received by faith in Christ. Justification is not the reception of divine righteousness, since divine righteousness as God's covenant faithfulness lies *behind* the gift of justification but is not that gift. Similarly, justification is not receiving Christ's righteousness, since Christ's righteousness is the Son's faithfulness to bear the curse and to open the door to the fulfillment of the promise to bless the nations. No, the blessing of justification itself is none other than the gift of covenant membership, covenant status granted by God through Christ.

Wright thus wishes both to *expand* and *constrict* the doctrine of justification. More expansively, Wright grants the doctrine vast historical and global boundaries beyond one's quest for personal salvation by locating the doctrine within a covenantal and social framework. But, more constrictively, Wright wishes to keep justification focused on the declaration of covenant membership rather than on the entire span of personal salvation. If one likens one's salvation to a car, justification might be compared to its steering wheel, vitally important to the rest of the car's function but still only one component of a larger reality. As covenant membership, justification is not detached from personal salvation, since it functions to distinguish those who will one day be vindicated as 'just' through resurrection. Wright expands justification through a larger story of covenant promise, curse, and fulfillment, but he also constricts the doctrine to covenant membership or status declared as a reality to those who embrace Christ by faith.

Allow me to make a few general remarks about these two moves of expansion and constriction. First, I find Wright's expansive move to be very convincing. I believe that Wright has persuasively made his case concerning the larger covenantal framework of Paul's remarks concerning justification. Though the term 'covenant' is not always present in texts dealing with the 'righteousing' of humanity in the Old Testament or the justification of humanity in the New, the theological contexts of such texts are at least implicitly covenantal in nature. Clearly, Paul does not just 'mention' Abraham in Romans 4 or Galatians 3 as an 'example' of justification by faith but rather in order to indicate the larger narrative framework within which the reality of justification by faith is to be understood.[4] As further support for this insight, Romans 9–11 is obviously the place where Paul rehearses the entire story of how Jesus fulfilled Israel's calling to bless the nations by being essential to the 'olive tree' into which the Gentiles have been incorporated. How can one help but to connect the conclusion of these chapters to the larger theme of justification dealt with earlier in the book? Romans 11.32's conclusion of chs. 9–11 is key: 'For God has bound everyone over to disobedience so that he may have mercy on them all'. This verse simply restates the key text about justification in Rom. 3.23-24: 'for all have sinned and fall short of the glory of God, and all are justified freely by his grace through the redemption that came by Christ Jesus'. Clearly, justification is not only to be understood within one's personal quest for forgiveness but within the larger narrative of God's plan to open up the covenant blessings enjoyed by Israel to the nations. To be made right is to be brought together in covenant community in Christ to enjoy the fulfillment of the promises made to Abraham. Second, it thus seems legitimate to me to see justification as a profoundly covenantal and ecclesial gift and not just a personal one. In other words, justification does not just signal the divine embrace of an individual who is now in Christ by faith but also the covenantal embrace of all peoples, both Jew and Gentile, taken up together into Christ by faith. This social or ecclesial context for understanding justification holds potential for developing the larger pneumatological, eschatological, and Trinitarian framework for the doctrine. There is breathing room here for overcoming the rift between forensic and participationist understandings of justification and for revealing the implications of justification for ethical concerns that relate to our corporate life together as human beings. Partly under the influence of Wright's work, I have attempted to develop these implications in my recent work entitled, *Justified in the Spirit: Creation, Redemption, and the Triune God*.[5] More recently, Michael Gorman's new covenant interpretation of the atonement holds promise for developing Wright's basic insights. Following Jesus' own interpretation of his coming death (Mt. 26.28; Mk 14.24;

---

[4] N.T. Wright, *Justification: God's Plan & Paul's Vision* (Downers Grove: IVP Academic, 2009), pp. 55-57.

[5] Frank D. Macchia, *Justified in the Spirit: Creation, Redemption, and the Triune God* (Grand Rapids: Eerdmans, 2010).

Lk. 22.20), Gorman argues that the atonement was meant to establish the new covenant with God's people, a covenant that reconciles, forgives, and opens up the new community to the life of the Spirit.[6] Support for Gorman's understanding of the atonement may be found in the way in which John implicitly ties atonement to the bestowal of the Spirit and the opening up of the covenant community to diverse peoples by noting that the seed cannot spread until it first dies (Jn 12.24).

Gorman's pneumatological doctrine of atonement, however, implies that justification within a new covenant context might be more than mere 'right status', a concept I suspect would have been foreign to Paul. Interestingly, Paul writes about justification as the fulfillment of the covenant promise given to Abraham precisely in the context of the gift of the Spirit. Justification is by faith; so is receiving the Spirit (Gal. 2.17; 3.1-5). The blessing of Abraham is justification (Gal. 3.8), but so is receiving the Spirit (Gal. 3.14). One gets the impression here, as James Dunn notes, that Paul is somehow equating justification with the gift of the Spirit.[7] Acceptance in the reconciled and reconciling community implies more than 'status' as an abstract term but is more deeply a being taken up into the life of the community through the embrace of the Spirit.[8] My research in this area has thus caused me to find Wright's constrictive move to be too constrictive. I am not entirely certain why he insists so adamantly that justification is limited to the reception by faith of membership 'status' within the covenant community when he has nowhere convincingly shown that Paul always has something so narrow or abstract in mind when writing about incorporation through justification into the new covenant community.[9] I find much more convincing here E.P. Sanders' conclusion that Paul's language concerning justification mixes indiscriminately with participationist language, making it impossible to restrict this language systematically to a single forensic metaphor.[10]

---

[6] Michael Gorman, 'Effecting the Covenant: A (Not So) New New Testament Model for the Atonement', *Ex Auditu* 26 (2010), pp. 60-74.

[7] James Dunn, *Baptism in the Holy Spirit* (London: SCM Press, 1970), p. 108.

[8] See my development of this idea in *Justified in the Spirit*.

[9] Wright, *Justification*, p. 102.

[10] E.P. Sanders, *Paul and Palestinian Judaism: A Comparison of Patterns of Religion* (Philadelphia: Fortress, 1977), pp. 506-507.

It seems to me that texts concerning justification are more robustly pneumatological and participatory than the bestowal of a mere status. For example, Paul describes justification by faith in Gal. 2.17-20 as nothing short of a spiritual rebirth. In the very next chapter, as noted above, he seems to equate justified existence with pneumatic existence, or with life in the Spirit (Gal. 3.8, 14). I suppose one could argue that justification is the bestowal of a new status that then *leads to* participation through death and rebirth in the blessings of being in Christ and in the Spirit, but I don't think Paul consistently preserves such a fine distinction. Merely noting as Wright does that Paul has the law court in mind when talking about justification is not enough to limit justification to a legal status. The law court metaphor that Paul assumes when writing about justification has in view the Hebraic world court of Yahweh, which is not forensic in any way that we in the West would recognize. The divine verdict imparts more than a mere change in legal 'status'. In such a court, Yahweh's declared will is richly accomplished in concrete victory over the resistance of the opposition. The righteousness imparted flows like a mighty stream or pours down like a torrent rain (Hos. 10.12; Isa. 32.14-16). It imparts not only a new status but also a new mode of life. Such fulfillment in my view cannot consistently and persuasively be limited to something as narrow as a new 'status'.

In fact, Wright implies as much when stating on occasion that justification leads to making the entire creation right.[11] He seems to imply here that justification involves more than a change in status. In Romans and Galatians, God makes things right for creation not only by bestowing a new status upon it (whatever that might mean) but by embracing it within a new mode of existence, one that has the Spirit and the reality of divine *koinonia* at its essence. A more holistic understanding of justification is also implied in Wright's understanding of justifying faith as involving an *embodiment* of the gospel. Though he says that justification is a status and not a change in character,[12] the future verdict is said to be brought into the pre-

---

[11] For Wright, justification involves God's 'faithfulness to, and his powerful commitment to rescue, creation itself' (Wright, *Justification*, pp. 65, 164).

[12] Wright, *Justification*, p. 91.

sent 'visibly and community-formingly'.[13] What is this status but a new mode of existence in the embrace of Christ, of the Spirit, of the covenant community? How can we conceive of it apart from a fundamental change in the very conditions and direction of our existence? Certainly, the verdict of justification does not merely have at its essence a new status but also a new mode of existence involving the Spirit and genuine *koinonia*. Wright's occasional reference to the Spirit or the Trinity as the new frontiers of justification by faith[14] remain undeveloped by him so long as justification relates directly to legal status only. In other words, justification in the New Testament proves to be more essentially relational, participatory, and transformational than Wright seems willing to admit within his narrower definition, though he implies here and there a richer concept. To use Wright's car metaphor, justification is not only the steering wheel of the car but is rather a way of looking at the function of the entire car from a certain angle. It is a way of looking at the entire Christian life from the angle of an understanding of divine justice that overturns conventional wisdom, a notion that involves the bestowal of new life, new covenant existence, from Christ and by the Spirit, upon those who are estranged and condemned.

One can detect part of the problem involved in Wright's constrictive understanding of justification by examining how he deals with the issue of Israel's failure to fulfill the law. The issue of the law is not just right standing (guilty or innocent) but the quality of existence (death or life). On the positive side, Wright helpfully shows that obedience to the law in ancient Judaism was to demonstrate who belonged to the covenant and would be vindicated eschatologically. He shows how a living faith in the Messiah now fulfills this function. But Wright follows the traditional line of argument that Israel did not claim the fulfillment of the promises because Israel simply could not adequately demonstrate obedience to the law in a way that would bring about this fulfillment. Though accurate as far as it goes, more is needed. More promising is Wright's suggestion that the law does not justify because God has reconstituted the people of God around the Messiah and his ful-

---

[13] Wright, *Justification*, p. 147.
[14] Wright, *Justification*, pp. 107, 189.

fillment.[15] Yet this suggestion requires pneumatological development. Paul does not just point to the failure of sinful flesh in explaining why justification is fulfilled by the Messiah and not the law. *The law has limits too because the law needs the Spirit.* Paul also notes that the Spirit and *not* the letter gives life (2 Cor. 3.6), 'for if a law had been given that could impart life, then righteousness would certainly have come by the law' (Gal. 3.21). *The problem is thus not only Israel's failure but the law's limitation.* Thus the law itself bore witness to the fulfillment of righteousness that would come *apart* from the law (Rom. 3.21)! The law witnesses to its own limitations.

The key issue when it comes to the law is thus the *promise of life*. The law that promises life cannot impart it because it is a letter and not the Spirit. Only the Spirit imparts life and the Messiah fulfills the law not only through atonement but also by bearing and imparting the Spirit (the very goal of atonement and resurrection). I thus see Rom. 1.4 as programmatic: the Christ was declared to be the Son by the resurrection 'according to the Spirit of holiness'. We are declared righteous as we partake of the new life unleashed in the resurrection of the Messiah and the establishment of his covenant community. The verse quoted in Rom. 1.17 from Habakkuk that the 'just shall live by faith' would in the light of this programmatic verse be better translated: 'the just by faith shall *live*'. The new justice received by faith occurs in the receiving of new life. Indeed, Jesus was offered up for our transgressions and *raised for our justification* (Rom. 4.25). By faith the justified are reckoned not only as having a right status but as having through the Spirit of the resurrection a foretaste of the life to come right in the midst of condemnation and death, for Abraham himself believed in 'the God who gives life to the dead' (Rom. 4.17) and God 'will credit righteousness – for us who believe in him who raised Jesus our Lord from the dead' (Rom. 4.23). Sin leads to death but righteousness to life; the righteous act of Jesus brings us 'justification and life' (Rom. 5.18, 21). What gets credited to us who believe is life in the midst of death. This is the promise of the law. As Deut. 30.16 notes, 'keep his commands, decrees and laws; then you will *live and increase*'.

Actually, I have found significant help developing the pneumatological dimension of justification from Wright in parts of his discus-

---

[15] Wright, *Justification*, p. 118.

sion not directly related to the topic of justification. I refer especially to his insights into how Jesus the Messiah replaced the Jewish Temple as the new locus of God's presence and favor.[16] I had already been deeply influenced by Irenaeus' striking comment that the Holy Spirit had rested on Jesus in order to 'get accustomed to dwell in the human race, to repose on men, to reside within the work God has modeled, working the Father's will in them and renewing them from oldness to newness in Christ'.[17] The Spirit gave the Son an anointed body at the incarnation in order through him to anoint all bodies! I then came to see Jesus as the temple of the Spirit who descended at the cross into God-forsakenness in order through resurrection to bring the God-forsaken into the realm of the Spirit, the realm of participation in sonship and in the covenant community. The essence of justification is thus not just a new status but a new pneumatic, christoformistic mode of existence caught up in the justice of Trinitarian *koinonia*. This is what it means to be 'righteoused' or justified. This is justification at its essence, justification in the Spirit.

I am deeply appreciative of the various insights that I have gained from Wright. Even where I find him too narrowly constrictive, I discover hints and resources for expanding the boundaries of those limits. He is a brilliant and innovative mind who has helped me to think about justification within a compellingly expansive narrative context. I am deeply grateful for his contribution to my work.

---

[16] Wright, *Jesus and the Victory of God* (Christian Origins and the Question of God 2; Minneapolis: Fortress, 1996), pp. 333-428.

[17] Irenaeus, 'Against Heresies', in *The Apostolic Fathers: Justin Martyr and Irenaeus* (Ante-Nicene Fathers I; Alexander Roberts and James Donaldson (eds.); trans. A. Cleveland Coxe; Peabody, MA: Hendrickson, 1994), p. 3.17.1.

6

ASSESSING N.T. WRIGHT'S READING OF PAUL THROUGH THE LENS OF DISPENSATIONALISM

GLEN W. MENZIES[*]

Introduction

I grew up attending church three times a week – Sunday morning, Sunday night, and Wednesday night – unless our church was holding a revival. In that case, I attended church every night of the week. When I was a boy, sermons in Pentecostal churches were longer than they are today and they were organized differently. Most of them were actually one larger sermon joined to at least a couple of sermonettes. I believe that in two-thirds to three-quarters of the sermons I heard some significant portion of the sermon was devoted to the second coming of Christ or the rapture of the Church (or both), virtually all ringing with heavy Dispensationalist overtones. We were constantly reminded, 'Jesus is coming soon!' I

---

[*] Glen W. Menzies (PhD, University of Minnesota) is Dean of the Institute for Biblical and Theological Studies and Professor of New Testament and Early Christian Literature at North Central University, Minneapolis, Minnesota. His office is located only a few blocks from Bethlehem Baptist Church, where John Piper serves the Preaching Pastor. As many will recognize, Piper is not fond of Wright's biblical theology and holds himself up as a champion of Reformed orthodoxy in his book, *The Future of Justification: A Response to N.T. Wright* (Wheaton: Crossway Books, 2007). This paper originally took shape as a response to this controversy and the publication of Wright's book, *Justification: God's Plan & Paul's Vision* (Downers Grove: IVP Academic, 2009).

have never read any of the 'Left Behind' books or watched any of the 'Left Behind' movies because 'I've been there, done that'. I could have written the books myself.

There seems little doubt that N.T. Wright is the preeminent New Testament specialist in the world today. There is also little chance that he would have liked the many sermons and sermonettes on the rapture and second coming I heard in the Pentecostal churches of my youth, to judge from his snide comments about notions of 'Christians flying around in mid-air on clouds'.[1]

This essay will focus on Wright's reading of Paul in relation to the issues of Dispensationalism. I teach at a Pentecostal university and there I find that many of my students are captivated by Wright's scholarship. No doubt this illustrates the changing character of Pentecostalism and the diminished impact of Dispensationalism on its present-day theology, but it also raises questions about what the Bible in fact teaches and what Pentecostals ought to proclaim. In the interest of full disclosure I should point out that I do not consider myself a Dispensationalist. Nevertheless, I will attempt to be fair to that hermeneutical tradition.

Why This Analysis Is Significant for Pentecostals

From its beginning Pentecostalism has been caught up in the fervor of premillennial expectancy. Not only was the Church believed to be in 'the last days' with the second coming of Christ expected soon, the restoration of tongues to the Church was understood as a sign of 'the latter rain' which would shortly usher in a final worldwide revival and the end of the age. Since the remaining time was short, evangelism and missionary work were of the highest priority. Many understood tongues as a supernatural gift intended to erase the barriers of language that had hindered global evangelization. Others understood tongues simply as a sign of charismatic empowering that would equip the individual to proclaim the gospel with power.

While Dispensationalists are uniformly Premillennialists, it is possible to be a Premillennialist and not be a Dispensationalist. In

---

[1] N.T. Wright, *The Resurrection of the Son of God* (Christian Origins and the Question of God 3; Minneapolis: Fortress, 2003), p. 215. Cited hereafter as *RSG*.

fact, most of the earliest Pentecostals seem not to have shared Dispensationalism's rigid distinction between God's two peoples, Israel and the Church. Nevertheless, the impact of the *Scofield Reference Bible*, first published in 1909 just as the Azusa Street Revival began to wane, and the eschatological expectancy that was characteristic of Dispensationalism, soon led to its widespread embrace within American Pentecostal circles. Some have claimed that Dispensationalism is incompatible with Pentecostalism, since Dispensationalists have often relegated tongues, prophecy, and other oral and power gifts of the Spirit to 'the Apostolic Age'. However, many manifestly did not find Dispensationalism incompatible with their Pentecostalism, and soon Dispensationalism was being widely taught in Pentecostal schools. As progressive Dispensationalist scholar Craig Blaising once emphasized to me in a private conversation, Dispensationalists have never regarded the Apostolic Age as a unique dispensation. Rather both the Apostolic Age and the post-Apostolic Age are part of the Church Age. Moreover, those who embrace Calvin's covenant theology, which maintains that the Church has replaced Israel as the people of God, are just as likely to be Cessationists as are Dispensationalists.

Dissecting Dispensationalism

One of the difficulties with exploring similarities and differences between Wright's perspective and Dispensationalism is crafting an adequate description of Dispensationalism. Part of the problem is that the general outline of Dispensationalism has changed over time. Beginning in the 1950s the revised Dispensationalism of Charles Ryrie, John Walvoord, and Dwight Pentecost significantly modified the classical Dispensationalism of J. Nelson Darby, C.I. Scofield, and Lewis Sperry Chafer. Over the past twenty-five years the progressive Dispensationalism of Craig Blaising, Darrell Bock, Robert Saucy, and Gerry Breshears has led to further modifications.

This picture is complicated further by the emergence within mainline Protestant circles of a similar schema known as 'dual covenant' theology. A leading voice championing this approach was the late Krister Stendahl. Locating Stendahl and Walvoord in similar camps feels somewhat audacious; they are certainly strange bedfellows.

While the name 'Dispensationalism' has led many to conclude that a division of salvation-history into distinct eras is the most basic characteristic of Dispensationalism, this is somewhat misleading. Some measure of division into epochs is probably inevitable in any sketch of salvation-history. Certainly the covenant theology of John Calvin would presuppose a few dispensations, even if Calvin did not call them dispensations.

Instead of dispensations, the *sine qua non* of Dispensationalism is its separation of two distinct peoples of God, Israel and the Church, and its corollary rejection of the notion that the Church in any way replaces Israel as the people of God. Traditionally, the language of 2 Tim. 2.15 in the King James, 'rightly dividing the word of truth', served as a slogan summarizing the Dispensationalist program of slicing up Scripture into one set of passages that discusses God's plan and purposes for Israel and another set that discusses God's plan and purposes for the Church.

The area in which most development has occurred in Dispensationalist thought concerns the terms under which Israel will be saved. While Darby and Scofield believed the Mosaic Covenant obligated Israel to keep the Law, and that as a result the people of Israel would be judged by their success in this regard independently of the atoning work of Christ, later Dispensationalist thinkers have concluded that at least since the first advent of Christ the people of Israel could only be saved through faith in him. Thus, while there remain two peoples of God, the manner in which both peoples are saved is not fundamentally different.

The following is a partial list of characteristics typically associated with Dispensationalism today:

1) Identification of two separate peoples of God, Israel, and the Church;

2) Insistence that the Old Testament prophecies about an eternal Kingdom promised to David and his posterity (e.g. in 2 Samuel 7) have not been fulfilled through the inauguration of the Church and in fact have nothing to do with the Church;

3) Belief that the Old Testament prophecies of this 'eternal Kingdom' will be fulfilled literally during the Millennium (Rev. 20.1-6), with Jesus sitting on a physical throne in Jerusalem and ruling over all the nations of the earth;

4) The idea that because Israel as a whole refused to recognize Jesus as the promised Messiah and instead rejected him, in order to make his people Israel 'jealous' (Rom. 11.11) and lead them to repentance, God constituted another people (the Church) from among the gentiles, who are offered salvation through faith in Jesus Christ, 'until the full number of the gentiles should come in' (Rom. 11.25);

5) An eschatological expectation that links the end of Jerusalem's being 'trodden down by the gentiles' and the end of 'the times of the gentiles' (Lk. 21.24) with an imminent secret rapture of the Church and the Great Tribulation, followed by the second coming of Christ and the conversion of national Israel at the appearance of its triumphant king;

6) Expectation of a Millennium of peace during which the Kingdom of God will be established (or reestablished) and King Jesus will reign from a physical throne in Jerusalem over all the nations of the earth;

7) Belief in a final judgment of every individual, which is often called 'the great white throne judgment' (Rev. 20.11).

Some of these characteristics are shared by other non-Dispensationalist systems.

While the central thrust of 'dual covenant' theology is similar to that of Dispensationalism – that God has two distinct peoples – the fundamental impetus propelling each is quite different. The primary motivation driving Dispensationalism is to safeguard the authority of Scripture by refusing to 'spiritualize' biblical prophecy. In contrast, there are two main drivers behind dual covenant theology. The first came in the wake of the Holocaust. There was great embarrassment in certain quarters of mainline Protestantism over the Church's moral irresponsibility in the face of German National Socialism. There was also a fear that 'replacement theology', which claimed that the Church had replaced Israel as God's chosen people, had contributed to the Church's moral paralysis. The second driver was the growing belief that tolerance was a Christian virtue. This led to a growing interest in interfaith dialogue and acceptance of theological pluralism.

Of particular note is the role Krister Stendahl had in promoting this dual covenant theory. Stendahl argued that in the New Testament the name 'Israel' is never applied to the Church. He translated the καί of Gal. 6.16 adjunctively ('also') rather than epexegetically ('even'). Thus, he rendered the verse, 'Peace and mercy be upon all who walk by this rule, and also upon the Israel of God', rather than the more traditional, 'Peace and mercy be upon all who walk by this rule, that is, upon the Israel of God'.

I remember attending a presentation given a number of years ago on the exegesis of the famous crux Rom. 11.25-26. It was at the annual meeting of the Society of Biblical Literature. I found myself sitting right in front of Stendahl and Peter Schäfer, the noted expert on Judaism. The presenter echoed Calvin's exegesis of the passage: when Paul stated, 'All Israel will be saved', he meant that an amalgam of Jews and gentiles had been joined together in the Church to become the people of God: it is this group that 'will be saved'. Stendahl would have none of this. Luther believed that 'all Israel' in this passage referred to the Jewish people, and so did Stendahl. In the preceding verse Paul speaks of 'a hardening that has come in part (ἀπὸ μέρους) upon Israel'. Stendahl understood ἀπὸ μέρους to form a contrast with the πᾶς ('all') of v. 26. Thus, according to Stendahl, the contrast in this passage was not between the partial hardening of ethnic Israel (along with the complete exclusion of the gentiles) and the unified 'all Israel' that would ultimately include both believing Jews and believing gentiles. Rather the contrast was between the partially hardened ethnic Israel in the present and the ultimate salvation of all ethnic Israel in the future. The bottom line was that Stendahl considered it arrogant for Christians to suggest that Jews without Christ were separated from God and consequently they would not be saved. We will see that Wright agrees with Calvin and the mocked presenter rather than with Stendahl on this point.

Reprising Wright

It is difficult to summarize Wright's work because he has proposed so many excellent insights one is left in a quandary about what to exclude. Nevertheless, I will try to summarize Wright's contributions – at least as they relate to Paul and Dispensationalism – under seven headings.

1) The Continuing Exile of Israel

A foundation of Wright's work is the premise that most Jews at the time of Jesus and Paul believed they were in exile.[2] Yes, the geographic exile to Babylon had ended, and Jeremiah's prophecy of a seventy-year exile – perhaps understood as a hiatus in the temple service – had technically been fulfilled. But there were other voices expressing a more negative evaluation. Ezra describes 'many of the priests and Levites and heads of fathers' households, the old men who had seen the first temple' weeping when they see the newly laid foundation of the second temple (Ezra 3.13). Haggai asks, 'Who is left among you who saw this temple in its former glory? And how do you see it now? Does it not seem to you like nothing in comparison?' (Hag. 2.3). And then Daniel reinterpreted Jeremiah's seventy years as seventy sevens of years, or a total of 490 years – a clear judgment that the rebuilding of the temple did not imply the end of exile.

The fact was that the people remained in bondage. As Ezra flatly states, 'For we are enslaved; yet in our bondage God has not forsaken us' (Ezra 9.9). Wright further explains:

> Similar statements can be found in a variety of literature of the time, from Qumran to Tobit, from the book of Baruch to Second Maccabees, and on into rabbinic literature ... The exile (the real exile, as opposed to the merely geographical exile in Babylon) is still continuing. And this exile is, in turn, to be understood, relatively straightforwardly, as the result of the 'covenantal curse' articulated so strikingly in Deuteronomy 27–29. Scripture said that YHWH would bring the curse on his people if they disobeyed, and that the curse would end in exile under foreign overlords; that is a good description (thought many first-century Jews) of where we still are; therefore we are still under the curse, still in exile.[3]

---

[2] This is discussed in numerous places in numerous ways in Wright's various books. A particularly pithy discussion is found in Wright, *Justification*, pp. 57-63.

[3] Wright, *Justification*, p. 60.

The hard reality was that Israel had failed in her vocation. The prophetic vision Isaiah expressed that 'Zion will be filled with justice and righteousness' (Isa. 33.5) seemed an empty hope. The expectation that Israel would serve as a 'light to the nations' (Isa. 42.6; 49.6) had resulted instead in God's name being profaned (Rom. 2.24; Isa. 52.5; Ezek. 36.22). The Torah, which was believed to mark Israel as God's chosen people, instead indicted her and sentenced her to the curse described in Deuteronomy 27–29.

2) The Messiah as the Incorporative Representative of Israel
Another foundation of Wright's work is his belief that the Messiah encapsulated the entire people of Israel, so that what the Messiah accomplished could be understood as Israel's accomplishment. Ultimately it is in this way, through the personal exaltation and rule of Jesus the Messiah of Israel, that Paul understood the 'eternal Kingdom' Israel had long hoped for to have been actualized.

As Wright understands this, there is a two-step linkage. First, Israel is pictured as God's true humanity, the heir to Adam's glory. Second, the Messiah is understood as a second Adam or – to use Paul's words from 1 Cor. 15.45 – the 'last Adam'. Adam Christology is possibly evident in several other passages: Rom. 1.18-23; 5.12-21; 7.7-12; Phil. 2.5-11; and Col. 1.15.

Space limitations preclude an exhaustive presentation of the evidence adduced by Wright. After quoting Gen. 1.28, 'And God blessed them, and God said to them, "Be fruitful and multiply, and fill the earth and subdue it; and have dominion"', Wright quotes several patriarchal blessings that speak of blessing, fruitfulness, and dominion over the land. As he explains,

> Thus at key moments – Abraham's call, his circumcision, the offering of Isaac, the transitions from Abraham to Isaac and from Isaac to Jacob, and in the sojourn in Egypt – the narrative quietly makes the point that Abraham and his family inherit, in a measure, the role of Adam and Eve.[4]

Wright is aware that to present Paul's view of Messiahship in this way is to swim against the tide of conventional scholarship. As he says,

---

[4] Wright, *The Climax of the Covenant: Christ and the Law in Pauline Theology* (Minneapolis: Fortress, 1992), p. 22.

[T]he majority of Pauline scholars do not read 'Christos' in Paul as a title, retaining its Jewish significance of 'Messiah', but simply as a proper name. I want now to suggest that this consensus is wrong; that Χριστός in Paul should regularly be read as 'Messiah'; and that one of the chief significances which his word then carries is *incorporative*, that is, that it refers to the Messiah as the one in whom the people of God are summed up, so that they can be referred to as being 'in' him, as coming or growing 'into' him, and so forth.[5]

3) Wright's 'Inaugurated Eschatology'

Although the impact of C.H. Dodd is evident throughout Wright's work, it would be inaccurate to say he shares Dodd's 'realized eschatology'. 'Inaugurated eschatology' is a more apt descriptor, and one he seems willing to embrace.[6] Jesus' ministry, particularly his cleansing of the temple and his death that resulted from challenging the religious establishment, marked the beginning of YHWH's return to rule as king. The results of this change are immediate and concrete. As Paul states, Christian believers at the present time must walk worthy of the God who calls them 'into his own Kingdom and glory'.[7]

Still Wright insists on a future dimension of the Kingdom as well. In 1 Cor. 4.8 Paul mocks the over-realized eschatology of some in the church at Corinth: 'Already you are filled! Already you have become rich! Without us you have become kings!'[8] The sin lists found in 1 Cor. 6.9-11 and Gal. 5.19-21 both conclude with declarations that those who practice such 'will not inherit the Kingdom of God'. And 1 Cor. 15.24 describes the ultimate goal, when Christ 'delivers the Kingdom to God the Father after destroying every rule and every authority and power'.

4) Wright's Rejection of Heaven as a Place of Final Reward

Wright makes abundantly clear that Paul's conception of the afterlife has nothing whatsoever to do with Platonic immortality, 'in which a preexistent immortal soul comes to live for a while in a

---

[5] Wright, *Climax*, p. 41.
[6] See, for example, Wright, *RSG*, p. 217.
[7] 1 Thessalonians 2.12. See also Wright, *RSG*, p. 214.
[8] Wright, *RSG*, 279.

mortal body, from which it is happily released at death'.⁹ Instead, Paul retains the concept of bodily resurrection that he had learned as a Pharisee, so that one's final reward takes place in the body and on the earth. As he puts it, 'Resurrection ... meant life *after* "life after death": a two-stage future hope, as opposed to the single-stage expectation of those who believed in a non-bodily future life'.¹⁰

Concomitant with this is belief in an intermediate state. As Wright explains,

> [A]ny Jew who believed in resurrection, from Daniel to the Pharisees and beyond, naturally believed also in an intermediate state in which some kind of personal identity was guaranteed between physical death and the physical re-embodiment of resurrection.¹¹

Upon death believers depart and go to be with the Messiah, as Phil. 1.23 says, and this intermediate state is conscious.¹² This, however, is not the fullness of what is promised to those who are 'in the Messiah'. Like the Messiah, those who place their hope in him will one day live again in a body, but in a body that cannot die.

Wright repeatedly notes his opposition to a view of the *eschaton* that involves 'the end of the space-time universe'.¹³ He explains:

> [Such a] 'cosmic meltdown' (the phrase is Borg's) has regularly been supposed to be the event predicted or expected by second-Temple Jews and by Jesus himself. This assumption has been made by scholars from Schweitzer to the present day, and equally by literalists and/or fundamentalists.¹⁴

Although Wright never uses this term and would not accept it for himself, I consider myself a 'historic Premillennialist' as opposed to an Amillennialist, precisely because I believe some of these same things as Wright. The *eschaton* the New Testament depicts is not the end of the space-time continuum, and the Christian's ultimate reward is life in a resurrected body on a renewed earth, not

---

⁹ Wright, *RSG*, p. 164.

¹⁰ Wright, *RSG*, p. 130.

¹¹ Wright, *RSG*, p. 164.

¹² Wright, *RSG*, pp. 216, n. 14; 226.

¹³ Wright, *Jesus and the Victory of God* (Christian Origins and the Question of God 2; Minneapolis: Fortress, 1996), p. 207 Cited hereafter as *JVG*.

¹⁴ Wright, *JVG*, p. 207.

disembodied bliss in heaven. Premillennialism is not predicated solely on a literal interpretation of Revelation 20; it is also a statement about the nature of the eschatological reward Christians are promised.

5) Wright's 'Partial Preterism'

One of the most controversial aspects of Wright's program is his 'partial preterism'. 'Full preterism' would imply that all the eschatological predictions made by Jesus and the apostles took place in the first century, specifically by the end of the First Jewish War. Wright's partial preterism allows for a future second coming of Christ and for a future general resurrection of the dead, but it allows for no Millennium and no future earthly Kingdom for Israel. It regards the entirety of Jesus' Olivet Discourse to have been fulfilled in the first century.

In addition, Wright rejects the notion that the belief of Paul and other early Christians in a second coming of Christ was based on the teaching of Jesus. In particular, he insists that the expression 'the Son of Man coming in clouds with great power and glory', found in the synoptic tradition,[15] depicts the vindication of Jesus, who comes *to* heaven to take his seat beside the Ancient of Days, as is described in Daniel 7, rather than the traditional portrait of Christ coming *from* heaven to earth as a righteous warrior who will judge the wicked and collect the saints.

Wright maintains that the reason many commentators see the situation differently is because they misunderstand the way apocalyptic language works:

> In the post-Bultmannian New Quest it was assumed that talk of the 'kingdom of god', or of the 'son of man coming on the clouds of heaven', was to be taken as a literal prediction of events, shortly to take place, which would close the space-time order. But not only is it unnecessary to read apocalyptic language in this way: it is actually necessary, as historians, that we refuse to do so. Apocalyptic language was (among other things, to be sure) an elaborate metaphor-system for investing historical events with theological significance. This understanding of the literature has at any rate a good *prima facie* claim to be historically

---

[15] Mk 13.26//Mt. 24.30//Lk. 21.27.

on target, in contrast with the contrived literalism in which the Bultmann school find themselves as uncomfortable bedfellows of mainstream fundamentalism.[16]

Some Pentecostals will no doubt find this non-literal explanation unsatisfying, particularly for a passage such as Lk. 21.23-24. The Dispensationalist will point to 1948 and the founding of the modern state of Israel or perhaps even to 1967's Six-Day War, when Old Jerusalem including the Temple Mount came under the control of Israel, as the end of 'the times of the gentiles', which is to say, when Jerusalem first ceased to be 'trodden down' by non-Jewish nations. To remain consistent, Wright must claim that the events of AD 66–74 alone are described here. To state things differently, Wright takes 'trodden down by the gentiles' in its maximal sense, that is, to mean 'occupied by large-scale invading armies', and he concludes that the 'times of the gentiles' ended when the Roman legions left Palestine in AD 74.

Wright considers it improbable that Jesus taught his followers that he would come again:

> [A]lthough the idea of Jesus' return (the so-called 'second coming') has a place in Luke's writings, it is neither central nor major, and in any case occurs, within the Lukan corpus only in Acts [Acts 1:11]. It looks much more like a post-Easter innovation than a feature of Jesus' own teaching. Even granted that Jesus' hearers did not always grasp what he said, it strains probability a long way to think of him attempting to explain, to people who had not grasped the fact of his imminent death, that there would follow an indeterminate period after which he would 'return' in some spectacular fashion, for which nothing in their tradition had prepared them.[17]

Similarly, many Pentecostals will find Wright's interpretation of Mt. 24.36-44 to be problematic. This passage is widely cited by Pentecostals as evidence for the doctrine of the rapture, with its vivid imagery of the suddenness of the hour and the results of the coming of the Son of Man. Wright, of course, has a different understanding. The key to Wright's interpretation of this passage is the

---

[16] Wright, *JVG*, p. 96.
[17] Wright, *JVG*, p. 635.

reference to Noah and the suddenness with which the flood overtook his contemporaries. When in vv. 40 and 41 this pericope twice says, 'One is taken and one is left', it is the one who is *taken* that experiences judgment, not the one left. Jesus' point is that the prudent will flee; they should not try to wait the calamity out. Nor should they expect a miraculous rescue. As he explains,

> There is no hint, here, of a 'rapture', a sudden 'supernatural' event which would remove individuals from *terra firma*. Such an idea would look as odd, in these synoptic passages, as a Cadillac in a camel train. It is a matter, rather, of secret police coming in the night, or of enemies sweeping through a village or city and seizing all they can. If the disciples were to escape, if they were to be 'left', it would be by the skin of their teeth.[18]

While this is not an impossible reading, it also does not seem the most obvious way to understand this passage. Matthew 24.31 describes the Son of Man sending out his angels to gather the elect from the four winds. It seems plausible to assume that these 'elect' are the ones 'taken' in vv. 40 and 41, and that they are taken to safety.

If Paul's belief in the *parousia* was not based on the teaching of Jesus because Jesus never taught that he would return, from where did this expectation come? I do not think Wright has yet made this clear. Even if Wright's thesis is correct and Paul did not learn of the *parousia* from careful transmission of what Jesus had taught, as a first-century Jew steeped in the religious environment of a people living 'in exile', he expressed his eschatology using apocalyptic language similar to the apocalyptic language of Jesus. According to Wright, Paul's language about the *parousia* should not be interpreted literally any more than Jesus' comments about the coming of the Son of Man should. When the apostle says in 1 Thess. 4.16-17, 'And the dead in Christ will rise first; and then we who are alive, who are left, shall be caught up together with them in the clouds to meet the Lord in the air', this too is an echo of Daniel 7, and speaks of the vindication of those who are 'in the Messiah'. Just as the Messiah himself was first vindicated, those who are 'in him' will also

---

[18] Wright, *JVG*, p. 366.

be vindicated at the general resurrection, and this will not involve 'Christians flying around in mid-air on clouds'.[19]

One advantage to Wright's partial preterism is that it resolves the problem associated with the 'this generation' sayings of Jesus by asserting that all were fulfilled prior to AD 74. Solutions such as 'the eternal wandering Jew' or translating ἡ γενεὰ αὕτη as 'this race' (i.e. the Jews) are no solution at all. And understanding 'this generation' as necessarily 'the final generation preceding the *parousia*' appears to be an solution manufactured from the problem itself.

6) Wright's View of Justification

Recently Wright has become best known – 'notorious' might be the better word – for his rejection of the classic Protestant understanding of justification as the imputation of Christ's alien righteousness to believers. Perhaps even more fundamentally he does not place justification at the center of Paul's theology as Luther and his followers did. Instead, incorporation into Jesus, the triumphant Messiah of Israel who has fulfilled Israel's vocation, is Paul's central focus.

Wright's argument against the classic doctrine of imputation may be summarized as follows:

1) The phrase δικαιοσύνη θεοῦ ('righteousness of God') does not mean, as Luther understood it, 'God's own righteousness that is imputed to the believer'. Instead it means 'the acquittal that God declares as judge'.

2) The phrase δικαιοσύνη θεοῦ always relates to the divine verdict about humanity. According to Wright, Paul never envisions God being put on trial or that God's own righteousness is at issue in Paul's writings.

3) While Paul does say that Abraham's faith was 'reckoned to him as righteousness' (Rom. 4.3, 9), nowhere does he say that it is *the righteousness of Christ* that is reckoned or imputed to the believer. That the imputed righteousness must come from Christ is a construct Protestants project almost reflexively and uncon-

---

[19] Wright, *RSG*, p. 215. If Wright does not want to take being 'caught up . . . in the clouds to meet the Lord in the air' at face value, will he not at least admit that graves must be opened for resurrection to serve as anything more than a metaphor?

sciously onto the words of Paul because of the overwhelming influence of Luther's exegesis and his narrative of Christian conversion.

4) While Paul argues that no one will ever be justified by 'works of the law' (Rom. 3.20),[20] he has good things to say about works themselves. Romans 2.6 says that God 'will render to every person according to his works'.[21] His 'sin lists' (e.g. 1 Cor. 6.9-10; Gal. 5.19-21) also suggest much the same, that those whose lives are characterized by such sin 'will not inherit the Kingdom of God'. Wright suggests that present-day justification by faith, in some mysterious way, reliably predicts the eschatological judgment of God when he will 'render to every person according to his works'.

5) The true value to the believer of faith in Christ is that it incorporates that person into the Messiah/people of God. Because the Messiah has accomplished God's will in a way that neither Adam nor Israel was able to do, the blessings and dominion promised to both Adam and Israel become the believer's heritage.

7) Wright's 'Replacement' Theology

For Paul, faith in the Messiah of Israel rather than observance of the Torah marks one's continuing inclusion in God's people, and this applies to both Jew and gentile. Thus, one's Jewishness or gentileness, as marked by the Torah, may remain a cultural artifact, but it ceases to be important theologically.

Paul does not abandon the word 'Israel' – even though the new way he uses it risks confusing his audience – because it is important to him for God to be shown having remained faithful to his promises to Israel. Nevertheless, as Wright sees it, the word 'Israel' in-

---

[20] On the only extant use of the phrase 'works of the Law' outside of Paul, see Wright, '4QMMT and Paul: Justification, "Works", and Eschatology', in Aang-Won [Aaron] Son (ed.), *History and Exegesis: New Testament Essays in Honor of Dr E. Earle Ellis for His 80th Birthday* (New York and London: T&T Clark, 2006), pp. 104-32. In the letter, probably written by the Teacher of Righteousness, that comprises Section C of 4QMMT, 'works of the Law' seems to represent some specific program of *halakhah*.

[21] For those who are inclined to accept Ephesians as an authentic epistle of Paul, Eph. 2.10 says, 'we [presumably all Christians] were created in Christ Jesus for good works'.

cludes believing gentiles along with believing Jews when in Rom. 11.26 he says, 'And thus all Israel will be saved'. The word 'Israel' also includes believing gentiles when in Gal. 6.16 he refers to 'the Israel of God'. Moreover, this is not much different from Paul's claim in Phil. 3.2 that 'we are the circumcision', where he clearly has in mind both Jewish and gentile believers.[22] Paul sometimes uses the word 'gentile' to refer to those who are not 'in Christ' (1 Cor. 12.2; Eph. 4.17; 1 Thess. 4.5). In this sense the word comes to mean something like 'outsiders' or 'non-Christians', spoken from a perspective in which the 'insiders' are the Christian community that includes both Jews and gentiles, the 'Israel' that will be saved.

To return to Rom. 11.25-26, Wright dismisses the prospect of an end-time conversion of national Israel:

> It is usually held that, in Romans 11, Paul predicts a large-scale entry of Jews into the kingdom in fulfillment of the ancestral promise, after the Gentiles have been saved. There are, of course, numerous variations on this theme. Some see this sudden event as happening immediately before the Parousia, while others see it as concurrent. Some see it as involving actual conversion to Christ, while for others it is a salvation which takes place apart from Christ. Some see it as involving all Jews living at the time, others as including a large number but not all. Whatever the variation, this basic view always seems to fit very badly with Romans 9–10, where, following Galatians and Romans 1–8, Paul makes it abundantly clear that there is no covenant membership, and consequently no salvation, for those who simply rest on their ancestral privilege. This tension is then explained either as a reassertion of an illogical patriotism, or as mere apocalyptic speculation about the sequence of events in the end-time, or as a 'new mystery' (cf. v. 25) suddenly revealed to Paul during the writing of the letter, or as a textual corruption whereby

---

[22] In addition, Paul sometimes uses the word 'circumcision' (περιτομή) as a metonym for 'righteousness'. He contends that disobedience to the Torah can effectively undo circumcision (Rom. 2.25) and keeping the precepts of the Torah will be reckoned as circumcision (Rom. 2.26). For this line of analysis, see especially ch. 13 ('Christ, the Law and the People of God: the Problem of Romans 9–11') in Wright, *Climax*, pp. 231-57.

11.25-7 has been inserted into a chapter about something else, so colouring the whole.[23]

Wright regards the key to the interpretation of Rom. 11.25-26 to be Rom. 11.13-14:[24] 'Now I am speaking to you gentiles. Inasmuch then as I am an apostle to the gentiles, I magnify my ministry in order to make my flesh (i.e. fellow Jews) jealous, and thus save some of them'. His point is that for Paul the jealousy to which Israel will be provoked is not some future event, but rather is a central dynamic of Paul's present ministry, and is part of why God's olive tree contains both Jewish and gentile grafts.

Since the tenor of Wright's argument largely mirrors the covenant theology of Calvinism, and today theologians often rail against Calvin as the paradigmatic 'replacement theologian', an important question presents itself: Is Wright a replacement theologian? Wright himself would think not, but outside observers might not be so sure. The answer might turn on whether the charge is fair when leveled against Calvin. Traditional Calvinists often refer to 'the Church' in the Old Testament, meaning by this 'Israel'. This habit of speaking of an Old Testament 'Church' often strikes others as an unfortunate anachronism.[25] But there is a purpose behind the use of such jarring language: Calvinists want to emphasize the continuity between God's people in the Old Testament and his people in the New Testament, and the Septuagint translation of the Hebrew קהל as ἐκκλησία provides some justification for this practice.

Without doubt Wright believes that God intended all along, beginning with his eternal counsels, to establish a people that would include both Jews and gentiles. Nevertheless, Wright repeatedly

---

[23] Wright, *Climax*, p. 246.

[24] Wright, *Climax*, p. 248.

[25] As an example, consider the following statement from Calvin's *Institutes* (John Calvin, *Institutes of the Christian Religion* [John T. McNeill (ed.); trans. Ford Lewis Battles; Library of Christian Classics 21; Philadelphia: Westminster Press, 1960], II, p. 1048):

> The true Church existed among the Jews and Israelites when they kept the laws of the covenant. That is, by God's beneficence they obtained those things by which the Church is held together. They had the doctrine of truth in the law; its ministry was in the hands of priests and prophets. They were initiated into religion by the sign of circumcision; for the strengthening of their faith they were exercised in the other sacraments. There is no doubt that the titles with which the Lord honored his Church applied to their society.

speaks of Israel's failure. By my count, in his book *Justification*, he uses the word 'failure' or 'failed' ten times in connection with Israel.[26] While this failure may always have been part of God's plan, there is some way in which the career of Jesus counts as a fresh start, the beginning of a new era, in which God's offer of fellowship is not channeled through the Mosaic covenant.

So, in Wright's view does the Church replace Israel? It would probably be more accurate to say that in his view Israel is *transformed* into the Church through Israel's Messiah. But then Calvin's view also might more accurately be described as *transformation of Israel* than replacement of Israel. So Wright's presentation is unlikely to mollify 'dual covenant' theologians. The offence is not so much that Israel has been shown to be unfaithful – even the Hebrew Scriptures proclaim this repeatedly – nor that the Messiah did what Israel had not done. The true scandal – especially for 'dual covenant' theologians – is that the Messiah did what Israel had shown itself to be unable to do. This means that Israel's vocation could not and still cannot be fulfilled apart from Jesus the Messiah.

Wright and Dispensationalism

What is Wright's attitude toward Dispensationalism? It is emphatically and categorically negative, although to my knowledge in his three main books on Paul he nowhere mentions Dispensationalism by name. He is similarly dismissive of Lutheran theology, with its understanding of Law being antithetical to gospel, and of 'dual covenant' theology, which like Dispensationalism maintains that God has two distinct peoples. Wright rejects any system that emphasizes discontinuity between God's purposes for his people under the old covenant and God's purposes for his people under the new covenant.

Although Wright is in many ways critical of Reformation theology, most of his scolding is aimed at Luther, and it becomes clear that Wright understands himself to be a new type of Calvinist, who

---

[26] Wright, *Justification*, pp. 68, 119, 123, 127, 196, 199, 201, 202, 213, 243. Typical is this statement found on page 196: 'The problem with the single-plan-through-Israel-for-the-world was that Israel had failed to deliver. There was nothing wrong with the plan, or with the Torah on which it was based. The problem was in Israel itself.'

basically accepts Calvinism's attendant covenant theology. As he explains:

> There are plenty of theologians who have suggested that God initially gave people a law to see if they could save themselves that way, and then, finding that they could not, decided on a Plan B, namely incarnation and crucifixion and 'justification by faith'. But that is what Calvinism has always rejected, partly because it is a pretty hopeless view of God and partly because it makes little or no sense exegetically. And, within this kind of Calvinism, the point of the law – think of the endless debates over the meaning of *telos* in Romans 10:4 – is not that God has brought it to an end, has put a stop to all that nonsense, but that he has brought it to its glad and proper goal.[27]

While Wright argues persuasively that God's plan to gather a people for himself always included both Israel and the gentile nations, there is a sense in which his presentation of salvation-history mirrors *the rupture implicit in Dispensationalism*. Israel's calling was to be the agent of God's redemptive activity toward the nations of the earth. When Israel proved itself to be unfaithful, God – as in Dispensationalism – refused to allow his plan to be thwarted. He accomplished this by sending his Son, the Messiah of Israel, to fulfill the vocation entrusted to Israel. While Wright's schema does not involve two plans of salvation (as in classical Dispensationalism), it implies two stages in salvation-history divided by a repristination of Israel's vocation in the vocation of Israel's Messiah.

In the preceding paragraph two words are crucial: 'ruptured' and 'thwarted'. Wright would probably be unhappy to learn of anyone saying his presentation mirrors 'the rupture implicit in Dispensationalism'. Wright works hard to present a picture of continuity, not rupture! Nevertheless, for Wright the way in which the Messiah incorporates the vocation of Israel into his own vocation is predicated on the failure of Israel. There is a transition, although not complete discontinuity.[28] God always knew Israel would fail to accomplish

---

[27] Wright, *Justification*, p. 73.

[28] The Gospel of Matthew is not shy about presenting this transition as something of a rupture. In 21.43 Jesus says to the chief priests and the elders of the people: 'Therefore I tell you, the Kingdom of God will be taken away from you

the mission to which it had been called. Moreover, the preordained vocation of the Messiah makes no sense apart from this divine foreknowledge of Israel's failure.

The word 'thwarted' is also important because many believe that, according to Dispensationalism, God changes plans to keep his will from being thwarted. This is thought to reduce God's offer of salvation to the gentiles to a kind of 'Plan B', a 'parenthesis' interrupting his primary purpose, which is to sanctify his chosen people Israel. While there is some truth to this characterization, in part it seems unfair. Dispensationalists believe the Old Testament contains prophecies about the Church as well as prophecies about Israel, suggesting that God's plan for the gentiles was not conceived only as an afterthought following Israel's failure. In fact, God appears to have had the redemption of the gentiles in mind from the beginning of his dealings with humankind. The *Scofield Reference Bible* describes Gen. 3.15, the so-called *protoevangelium*, as 'the first promise of a Redeemer'.[29]

No doubt die-hard Dispensationalists will complain that Wright's program 'spiritualizes' the Old Testament promises of an 'eternal Kingdom' for Israel by applying them to Jesus apart from his rule over a literal earthly kingdom. They will also take offence at his symbolic interpretation of apocalyptic, and the partial preterism and the Amillennialism that flow from it.

Assessment

Wright's program should be recognized as a variation of Calvin's covenant theology, but a variation that achieves substantial improvements over the original. It goes without saying that Wright is critically aware and that he interacts ably with the questions of twenty-first-century biblical scholarship. But the improvement is mainly in how he is able to demonstrate continuity between Old Testament Israel and the New Testament people of God through Israel's Messiah, who takes up Israel's vocation as his own. This is a covenant theology that makes sense.

---

and given to a nation producing the fruits of it'. Most interpreters understand the fruitful 'nation' as an allusion to the Church.

[29] *Scofield Reference Bible* (C.I. Scofield (ed.); Oxford: Oxford University Press, 1906), *ad loc.*

Wright's work also amounts to a devastating critique of Dispensationalism. Judging from the impact Wright is having on America's youngest generation of Pentecostal scholars, it is not hard to predict that challenges to the traditional eschatology that has characterized Pentecostalism may be looming. Rejection of a 'secret rapture' that is separate from God's triumphant judgment over the forces of evil is not so much argued by Wright as assumed. His aversion to bodies flying around at the *parousia* may honestly be based in a judgment as a historian that such theater is unwarranted within the context of first-century Jewish thought, but he never offers an explanation for how the dead rising might happen in a manner that is more normal.

In addition, most Pentecostals will be offended at Wright's suggestion that Jesus never claimed he would return. Equally troubling is Wright's reading of Paul's eschatology. He acknowledges Paul's doctrine of a *parousia* and that Paul wrote of Jesus descending from Heaven to be joined first by 'the dead in Christ' and then by the living 'in the air' (1 Thess. 4.17), but he claims this event was not something Paul expected to see fulfilled literally. While God's triumph will one day become manifest to all of humanity by his raising of the dead to resurrection life, and at the same time Christ will become present to his Church in a new way, Paul does not expect a literal 'meeting in the air' to take place. According to Wright, all this is the symbolic language of apocalyptic, and it was understood to be such by Paul.

Although it remains an open question whether or not this is an adequate understanding of Paul's thought, Wright's analysis should not be viewed simply as a recrudescence of Bultmannian demythologization. Bultmann believed Paul taught a literal descent of Jesus from heaven and a bodily reunion with the saints in the air. He then concluded that modern sensibilities simply could not accept such ideas, so they must be translated into something more palatable to keep them from being dismissed and ignored. Wright, in contrast, concludes that Paul himself did not expect this sort of language to be fulfilled literally. Therefore, the modern reader must not expect a more literal fulfillment than the apostle. For Wright it is not an issue of what the modern mind can accept, but rather an issue of what Paul and the other New Testament authors taught.

One of Wright's most important contributions is his intelligent response to 'dual covenant' theology and its challenge to the uniqueness of salvation in Christ. Although many would like to remove it, there is an irreducible offence associated with the biblical teaching that Israel failed to fulfill her vocation. The good news is that Israel's Messiah has accomplished what Israel could not achieve on its own.

7

FAITH, HOPE, AND LOVE: THE COMMUNION OF SAINTS SEEN FROM N.T. WRIGHT'S ESCHATOLOGICAL PERSPECTIVE

JANET MEYER EVERTS[*]

Introduction – The Communion of Confusion

When I was growing up in the Episcopal Church, my favorite day was the Feast of All Saints. I was a chorister in one of the first Royal School of Church Music (RSCM) programs in the United States and I loved processing around the church singing all eight verses of 'For All the Saints', my all-time favorite hymn, to the stirring tune of *Sine Nomine*. But being in the RSCM was about more than learning Church music. It was also about learning the liturgy, history, and theology of the Anglican Church. So I loved All Saints' Day because I also loved what it represented – the Communion of Saints. When I processed around the sanctuary of St. Stephen's Church I saw myself as part of a great living tradition that stretched around the world and through the ages; I was a part of the Church in heaven and the Church on earth. The words of this hymn formed the foundation of my Christian worldview in profound ways that are still with me today.

---

[*] Janet Meyer Everts (PhD, Duke University) is Associate Professor of New Testament at Hope College (Reformed Church in America), Holland, Michigan. She comes from a long line of Episcopalians, was raised in the Episcopal Church, and was active in the Episcopal charismatic renewal.

So it was quite a shock to me when I joined the Inter-Varsity Christian Fellowship (IVCF) at my college and discovered that most other Protestants did not celebrate All Saints' Day, did not sing 'For All the Saints', and had no clue what the Apostles' Creed meant by the Communion of Saints. Our IVCF group was dominated by the daughters and granddaughters of Calvinist seminary professors. They liked to sing every verse of every hymn, argue about predestination, and have detailed Bible studies. I learned much from them. But I will never forget the day in late October/early November when I and some other Episcopalians in the group suggested singing 'For All the Saints'. We were accused of being Catholic, believing in purgatory, praying to saints, and other 'un-Protestant' behavior. (This was only a few years after the end of Vatican II, so Protestants and Catholics still cherished their differences.) I remember pointing out that we regularly sang the last verse of 'The Church's One Foundation', which mentions 'mystic sweet communion with those whose rest is won' and asking the Calvinists what they meant when they said the Apostles' Creed. I was told that the Communion of Saints referred to the worldwide communion of Christians and that Protestants celebrated Reformation Sunday. I do not remember singing the last verse of 'The Church's One Foundation' in IVCF again. At the inter-denominational Evangelical seminary I attended this same confusion about the doctrine dominated – there was no point arguing about it with people whose minds were already made up.

I was equally surprised when I moved into the Bible belt southern United States after seminary and found a living faith in the Communion of Saints, although no one called it that. All my theologically sophisticated East and West Coast friends had made fun of what they saw as the simplistic 'pie in the sky by and by' religion of the rural southern states. The more I lived and worshiped in the South, especially in Baptist and Pentecostal congregations, the more I began to recognize the same type of theological worldview, expressed in less sophisticated ways, that I had known as the Communion of Saints. It was hard to hear choruses like, 'If we never meet again this side of heaven, we will meet on that beautiful shore'[1] or 'If you see my Savior tell him that you saw me, when you saw me I was on my way',[2] and not think of the Communion of Saints, especially when songs like these were sung at funeral services. These southern Evangelical and Pentecostal Christians understood and lived the Communion of Saints even if they never talked about it theologically or said the Apostles' Creed.

So for the last twenty-five years I have wondered if there is any way to explore the doctrine of the Communion of Saints from a Protestant, Pentecostal, and biblical perspective in a way that both creedal and non-creedal churches might find compelling.[3] I was pleasantly surprised when I read N.T. Wright's book, *For All the Saints? Remembering the Christian Departed*.[4] I was impressed to discover that Wright had actually succeeded in clarifying the doctrine of the Communion of Saints I had been taught as a child by placing it within the framework of his biblical eschatology. The result is a historically, theologically, and biblically compelling explication of this doctrine that ought to appeal to most Protestants, including Pentecostals.

In what follows I would like both to summarize what Wright presents in this book and suggest some practical reasons that this might be an important doctrine for Protestants and Pentecostals to incorporate into their theological understanding. Pentecostals love Paul's great chapters on the spiritual gifts in 1 Corinthians 12–14 and his assertion at the end of 1 Corinthians 13 can serve as a guide for forming a clear biblical understanding of the Communion of Saints: 'So faith, hope, love abide, these three; but the greatest of these is love' (13.13). The Christian departed, as our fellow saints, are important to the Church on earth as examples and reminders of faith, hope, and love. They are faithful witnesses to Christ and call us to continue that faithful witness in times of adversity. They are

---

[1] Albert Brumley, 'If We Never Meet Again this Side of Heaven' as recorded by Johnny Cash, *My Mother's Hymnbook* (American Recordings, 2004).

[2] Thomas A. Dorsey, 'If You See My Savior' as recorded in *Say Amen, Somebody* (George Nierenberg, 1982).

[3] I looked at 'A Statement of Catholics and Evangelicals Together: The Communion of Saints', *First Things* 131 (March 2003), pp. 26-32; I found it had little to say about the relationship between believers on earth and the Christian departed beyond the fact that Catholics and Protestants do not agree.

[4] N.T. Wright, *For All the Saints? Remembering the Christian Departed* (Harrisburg, PA: Morehouse, 2003).

reminders of the hope of life with Christ both now and after death. They are bound to us in love as part of the body of Christ, for we remain members of his body together, even as some go on before others to eternal rest.

The Traditional Doctrine of the Communion of Saints

At the Time of the Apostles' Creed

By the fourth century, the phrase 'Communion of Saints' had come to be associated with the view that Christians on earth should be conscious of their fellowship with those who had gone before and were now in the glorious presence of Christ. The martyrs, who had a special place of honor, apostles, angels, and prophets still had a loving communion with God's people on earth and watched over them. Christians on earth gained spiritual benefit from this 'Communion of Saints'. This is the basic doctrine that is affirmed in the Apostles' Creed.[5]

Medieval Development of the Doctrine

But major shifts in the understanding of this doctrine occurred by the time the doctrine of purgatory became official in the Roman Catholic Church of the thirteenth century. (It was never official doctrine in the Eastern Orthodox Church).[6] Before there had been two divisions of the Church: those with Christ in glory and those still on earth. Now there were three: the Church militant consisted of those Christians alive at the present moment who are engaged in the active struggle with sin, the world, the flesh, and the devil.[7] The Church triumphant included those who had made it to heaven and were enjoying the presence and vision of God.[8] But there was now a third group, the Church expectant. This group was formed of Christians who had died but were not yet ready to go directly to heaven. They still needed to be cleansed and complete their satisfaction for sin in purgatory.[9]

---

[5] Wright, *Saints*, pp. 15-16.
[6] Wright, *Saints*, pp. 1-5.
[7] Wright, *Saints*, pp. 1, 13.
[8] Wright, *Saints*, pp. 1-3.
[9] Wright, *Saints*, pp. 4-6.

This new group of Christians gave both the Church militant and the Church triumphant new duties. The saints on earth now needed to pray for those in purgatory.[10] The Church triumphant now functioned like friends at a medieval court. They could petition God and Christ directly on behalf of those on earth and those in purgatory because they were in his presence. They could also be invoked for favors by those on earth.[11] It is this view of the relationship between Christians on earth, saints in heaven, and the departed in purgatory that was the popular view of the Communion of Saints at the time of the Reformation.

At the Time of the Reformation

The Protestant Reformers were unanimous in rejecting the doctrine of purgatory and the abuses attendant upon this doctrine. As Article XXII of *The Articles of Religion* states:

> The Romish Doctrine concerning Purgatory, Pardons, Worshipping and Adoration, as well of Images as of Relics, and also Invocation of Saints, is a fond thing, vainly invented, and grounded upon no warranty of Scripture, but rather repugnant to the Word of God.[12]

For most of the Reformers, the early doctrine of the Communion of Saints had been overshadowed by what they saw as the medieval abuses of the invocation of the Saints. Calvin, in his *Institutes of the Christian Religion*, makes it clear that departed Christians are in repose with Christ and that although

> they yearn for God's Kingdom with a set and immovable will ... their love is contained within the communion of the body of Christ, and is not open wider than the nature of that communion allows ... they do not abandon their own repose so as to be

---

[10] Wright, *Saints*, p. 14.

[11] Wright, *Saints*, p. 3.

[12] *The Book of Common Prayer and Administration of the Sacraments and Other Rites and Ceremonies of the Church According to the Use of the Protestant Episcopal Church of the United States of America* (New York: The Church Pension Fund, 1945), p. 607. Cited hereafter as *BCP*.

drawn into earthly cares ... much less on this account must we always be calling on them!¹³

But not all the Reformers forgot the original purpose of the doctrine of the Communion of Saints or what it meant in the Apostles' Creed. Martin Bucer, a German reformer and contemporary of Luther and Zwingli who finished his career teaching at Oxford, could see that once purgatory was eliminated from the picture, there was really no reason we should not remember and enjoy spiritual communion with the departed saints since we are indeed still one with them in Christ.

> We teach that the blessed saints who lie in the presence of our Lord Christ and of whose lives we have biblical or other trustworthy accounts, ought to be commemorated in such a way, that the congregation is shown what graces and gifts their God and Father and ours conferred upon them through our common Saviour and that we should give thanks to God for them, and rejoice with them as members of the one body over those graces and gifts, so that we may be strongly provoked to place greater confidence in the grace of God for ourselves, and to follow the example of their faith.¹⁴

Bucer's more positive analysis of the Communion of Saints strongly influenced the English Reformers. As Wright points out, this is far more than gratitude for their memory and an effort to follow their example; it is a conscious calling to mind of 'the great cloud of witnesses' of Hebrews 11.39–12.2. By the seventeenth century the great Puritan Richard Baxter, who certainly qualifies as a Protestant, was able to write a hymn in which he celebrates the Communion of Saints and suggests that part of that fellowship is 'jointly petitioning' the Lord in whom all the saints are one.

> We still are centred all in thee,
> Members, though distant, of one Head;
> Within one family we be,
> And by one faith and spirit led.

---

[13] John Calvin, *Institutes of the Christian Religion*, II (ed. John T. McNeill; trans. Ford Lewis Battles; Library of Christian Classics 21; Philadelphia: Westminster Press, 1960), pp. 82-83.

[14] As quoted in Wright, *Saints*, p. 38.

Before thy throne we daily meet
As joint petitioners to thee;
In spirit each the other greet,
And shall again each other see.[15]

The English Reformers retained a view of the Communion of Saints that rejected the idea of purgatory, the invocation of the Saints, and other perceived abuses of the medieval Church, but still valued the doctrine affirmed in the Apostles' Creed. This view was kept alive in the liturgical practice of the Church in the celebration of All Saints' Day and was celebrated in many hymns that have shaped the faith of generations of believers in the Anglican Communion.

N.T. Wright's Rethinking of the Tradition

For All the Saints? Remembering the Christian Departed is far more than a historical review of the development of the doctrine of the Communion of Saints. One of Wright's reasons for writing the book is a chance to rethink the tradition in a way that will clear up some of the confusion that seems to reign in the modern Church. As an Anglican theologian, Wright has identified confusion on several fronts: the liturgical muddle of All Souls' Day, the influence of quasi-Catholic theology about purgatory, and the influence of twentieth-century theology. All these influences have combined to leave many Christians in a state of general confusion about the Christian departed.[16]

Wright's analysis cuts through this confusion with a deceptively simple insight. He bypasses all the Reformation arguments about purgatory and states: 'I begin at the end. The bodily resurrection is still in the future for everyone except Jesus'.[17] In 1 Cor. 15.23, Paul states that Christ has been raised, and at his second coming those who belong to Christ will be raised. Since this second coming has not yet occurred, the Christian dead have not yet been raised. So where are the Christian dead? They are in an intermediate state that is the 'first, and far less important, stage of a two stage process'.

---

[15] As quoted in Wright, *Saints*, p. 37.
[16] Wright, *Saints*, pp. 11-13.
[17] Wright, *Saints*, p. 20.

One can call this intermediate state 'heaven' or 'paradise'. The name is unimportant as long as one remembers that in this intermediate state there are no distinctions between Christians.[18] All are 'saints' because in the New Testament every Christian is referred to as a 'saint', even the confused and sinful. All are in Christ's presence, since Phil. 1.22 asserts that to depart this life is to 'be with Christ'. However, Paul nowhere suggests that this departing to be with Christ is the same thing as the resurrection of the body. This same view of departed Christians is found in Rev. 6.10 where the souls under the altar are awaiting the final redemption. Especially noteworthy are Jesus' words to the dying thief in Lk. 23.43: 'Today you will be with me in Paradise'. If anyone in the New Testament would have needed purgatory, it would have been this thief, but he is promised a place with Christ in paradise immediately upon death.[19]

By beginning 'at the end', Wright is able to rethink the tradition with biblical and theological clarity. Rather than attacking the medieval doctrine of purgatory on its own theological terms, he undercuts its theological underpinnings by approaching the question eschatologically. He does, of course, arrive at the same conclusion as the Reformers, that there is no biblical or theological justification for the doctrine of purgatory. He points out that arguments advanced in support of purgatory do not really come from the Bible, but from the perception that all of us are still sinful when we die and that in order to enter into the presence of a holy God, we need to be cleansed.[20] An example of this sort of argument is found in C.S. Lewis, an Anglican writer who has had tremendous influence in American Evangelical circles. Lewis writes:

> The right view returns magnificently in Newman's *Dream*. There if I remember it rightly, the saved soul, at the foot of the throne, begs to be taken away and cleansed. It cannot bear for a moment longer 'with its darkness to affront that light' ... Our souls *demand* Purgatory, don't they?[21]

---

[18] Wright, *Saints*, pp. 20-21.
[19] Wright, *Saints*, pp. 22-27
[20] Wright, *Saints*, pp. 28-30.
[21] C.S. Lewis, *Letters to Malcolm: Chiefly on Prayer* (New York: Harcourt, Brace, Jovanovich, 1963), p. 108.

Wright's answer to this argument is again based on his insistence that if we forget that the bodily resurrection is still in the future we get it wrong. For the New Testament writers, bodily death actually puts an end to sin.[22] He suggests that the crucial passage is Rom. 6.8-11, especially Rom. 6.7: 'For he who has died is freed from sin'. Although we struggle with sin in this life, 'our remaining propensity to sin is finished, cut off, done with all at once, in physical death'.[23]

Wright concludes this section by summarizing his view and its implications for the Communion of Saints. Because the resurrection is still in the future for all Christians, all the Christian departed are in the same state, that of restful happiness, which can be referred to as either 'paradise' or 'heaven'. This is not their final destiny, which is their bodily resurrection, but is a temporary resting place.[24] There are only two divisions of the Church: the Church militant on earth and the Church both triumphant and expectant in heaven/paradise. There is no purgatory.[25] Since both we in the Church militant and the departed in the Church triumphant/expectant are in Christ, we share in the Communion of Saints. 'Once the false trail of purgatory is erased from our mental map of the *post-mortem* world, there is no reason that we shouldn't pray for them and with them'.[26] Wright does not, however, find any indication in the New Testament that they are praying for us in the present life, nor is there any indication

---

[22] It is here that many Protestants completely misunderstand Wright, probably because they do not understand his Anglican context, and accuse him of being a universalist. Wright makes it clear that he is not a universalist. He does not think universalism takes the problem of evil seriously and is really a variation on the doctrine of purgatory. At this point he clarifies his position on hell and it is worth summarizing here. The New Testament is full of warnings about eternal loss – sinners are left outside the New Jerusalem and thrown in the lake of fire – these are not mere rhetorical devices. There are two positions that take this data seriously: conscious eternal torment for those not saved, annihilation of those not saved (close to the position of the Church of England in *The Mystery of Salvation*). Wright tends toward a form of the annihilationist position in which those who continually chose against God cease to bear the image of God and therefore invoke death and are beyond redemption. He also warns that none of us are in a position to make this ultimate judgment about anyone; only God is judge and his purpose for his creation, according to Romans 5 and Romans 8, is reconciliation (Wright, *Saints*, pp. 42-46).

[23] Wright, *Saints*, pp. 31-32.

[24] Wright, *Saints*, pp. 36-37.

[25] Wright, *Saints*, p. 41.

[26] Wright, *Saints*, p. 37.

that we should ask them to do so. The souls under the altar in Rev. 6.10 are praying for God to bring justice and salvation in the world and may include us in that prayer in a general sense and we may join them in that prayer. We may certainly hold them up in love before God. We should not, however, engage in any practice that would deny by implication our immediacy of access to the Father through the Son in the Spirit. Every Christian is always welcome to come before the throne of the Father with any petition.[27]

Wright's explication of the doctrine of the Communion of Saints is thoroughly biblical and theologically thoughtful. By beginning at the end, and reminding us that everything goes wrong when we forget that the resurrection of the dead is still in the future, Wright introduces clarity to a discussion that is too often marked by confusion.

But is his explication of 'mystic sweet communion with those whose rest is won' able to convince Evangelical Protestants and Pentecostals that this is a doctrine worth reclaiming in traditions that are highly suspicious of anything that suggests Catholicism? Even if it is biblically grounded teaching, do the benefits for believers outweigh the potential dangers?

Faith, Hope, and Love – Abiding in the Communion of Saints

> For now we see in a mirror dimly, but then face to face. So faith, hope and love abide, these three; but the greatest of these is love. (1 Cor. 13.11, 13)

Everyone loves to quote 1 Cor. 13.13: 'So faith, hope and love abide, these three; but the greatest of these is love'. But most forget the context of this verse. Paul is writing about that which will survive when all earthly things have passed away. This is a pretty clear reference to departing this life to 'be with Christ' (Phil. 1.22) when Paul will see Christ 'face to face'. But in the context of all of 1 Corinthians it is also a reference to the 'passing away' of this age (1 Cor. 2.6) and the coming of the end and the final resurrection of the dead (1 Cor. 15.24, 52). Paul is writing about Christian realities

---

[27] Wright, *Saints*, pp. 39-40.

that are so important they transcend earthly existence and become part of life everlasting. It is precisely these Christian virtues that are nourished and supported by the doctrine of the Communion of Saints. They can, of course, be encouraged in other ways, but without the Communion of Saints, the eschatological dimensions of these virtues are too easily lost.

So in the last section of this paper, I would like to follow N.T. Wright's example and rethink the doctrine of the Communion of Saints in light of this great biblical passage and with the help of two great English hymns: 'For All the Saints' and 'The Church's One Foundation'.[28] Although not all Protestants sing 'For All the Saints', this hymn is increasingly appearing in Protestant hymnals. 'The Church's One Foundation' has long been a popular hymn. It is seen as a solidly biblical and Protestant expression of true Christian unity. What most Protestants do not seem to know is the history of this hymn. Samuel Stone wrote it to be included in *Lyra Fidelium: Twelve Hymns of the Twelve Articles of the Apostles Creed*. This hymn was written on the ninth article entitled: 'The Holy Catholic Church; the Communion of Saints. "He is the Head of the Body, the Church".' The original version was seven verses long, but is usually condensed to four or five verses.[29] As N.T. Wright points out, most Christians learn a great deal of their theology from their hymns.[30] In a sense, these two hymns are not just about the Communion of Saints, they are an active expression of the reality of that communion, as those who have departed share their wisdom with the current generation of Christians who continue to worship with them.

The first great reality that Paul says has eternal value is the virtue of *faith*. When we look at faith from an eschatological perspective it looks very different than when we see it from the perspective of most American Protestants. It is very easy to reduce faith to a series of intellectual propositions to be believed if one wants to be a Christian. I would call this the 'catechetical' view of faith. In Protestant circles it is also very common to see it as a 'means' of

---

[28] I have taken the versions of both hymns from *The Hymnal 1940* (New York: The Church Pension Fund, 1940).

[29] Nigel Day, 'The Church's One Foundation', *Claves Regni: The On-line Magazine of St. Peter's Church, Nottingham with All Saints*, <http://www.stpetersnottingham.org/hymns/foundation/html>.

[30] Wright, *Saints*, p. xiv.

salvation – if one is 'justified by faith', one does not have to do much else. Neither of these views does justice to the biblical teaching, but as long as faith is understood as intellectual assent to doctrine, it is easy to read the Bible as supporting these views. But when an eschatological dimension is introduced and the cloud of witnesses that is the Communion of Saints is used to define faith, the picture changes. The first three verses of 'For All the Saints' are all about the faithful departed and their witness to us.

> For all the saints, who from their labours rest,
> Who thee, by faith, before the world confessed,
> Thy name, O Jesus, be for ever blest.
>
> Thou wast their rock, their fortress and their might;
> Thou, Lord, their Captain in the well-fought fight;
> Thou, in the darkness drear, the one true Light.
>
> O may thy soldiers, faithful, true and bold,
> Fight as the saints who noble fought of old,
> And win, with them, the victor's crown of gold.

Here faith is active, a confession of Christ before the world in word and deed. It sounds much more like the faith of those in Hebrews 11 or the Church in Rev. 12.11 who 'have conquered him [Satan] by the blood of the Lamb and by the word of their testimony for they loved not their lives unto death'. Eschatological faith is being faithful to Christ and the gospel; it means trusting God even in the face of certain death. This certainly fits the context of 1 Corinthians better than catechetical faith. In both 1 Corinthians 2 and 1 Corinthians 13, Paul reminds the Corinthians that human wisdom and knowledge, dare we even suggest human theology, will pass away. But radical trust in God and faithfulness to the gospel will endure past the point of death and into the period when we receive our resurrection bodies.

Suggesting that *hope* is an eternal virtue seems a bit odd, especially in light of the definition of hope in Heb. 11.1: 'Now faith is the assurance of things hoped for, the conviction of things not seen'. This seems to suggest that hope will vanish when faith is complete. But in the New Testament, hope is closely related to trust in God, just as faith is, and is therefore foundational to a relationship with Christ. In 1 Cor. 13.13 and in much of Paul's writing, hope is clearly related to the eschatological realities of life after death and the resurrection of the body. Those who have a relationship of trust with God can rest in the sure and certain hope of his promises of life after death and the resurrection of the body (1 Corinthians 15). Remembering the Christian departed certainly helps the Church on earth maintain a vital hope in the promises of God. This is the purpose of the many hymns about heaven found in the Protestant and Pentecostal traditions, however theologically muddled some of them may be. I am eternally grateful to William Walsham How for writing a hymn that taught me the clear distinction between the 'calm of paradise the blest' and 'the yet more glorious day' when 'the saints triumphant rise in bright array' even before I had the benefit of Wright's little book. For those who do not know How's verses on this subject, I quote them below:

> And when the strife is fierce, the warfare long,
> Steals on the ear the distant triumph song,
> And hearts are brave again and arms are strong.
>
> The golden evening brightens in the west;
> Soon, soon to faithful warriors cometh rest;
> Sweet is the calm of paradise the blest.
>
> But lo! There breaks a yet more glorious day;
> The saints triumphant rise in bright array;
> The king of glory passes on his way.
>
> From earth's wide bounds, from oceans farthest coast,
> Through gates of pearl streams in the countless host,
> Singing to Father, Son and Holy Ghost,
>
>   Alleluia!

In these verses the doctrine of the Communion of Saints becomes an occasion for reminding the Church on earth about the 'sure and certain hope of the Resurrection unto eternal life through our Lord Jesus Christ'.[31] It also holds out the hope of heaven in a way that both encourages faith and provides an understanding that it is only a resting place on the way to this glorious resurrection. From a pastoral and catechetical standpoint, this is surely a significant achievement. The example and encouragement of those who have

---

[31] 'The Order for the Burial of the Dead', *BCP*, p. 333.

gone before us can increase our living hope in a living and resurrected Lord.

In 1 Cor. 13.13, Paul writes: 'the greatest of these is *love*'. Yet when it comes to the Communion of Saints, love is by far the most controversial subject of discussion for Protestants. What does it mean for the saints on earth and the departed saints in paradise/heaven to have a relationship of love? Pretty much everyone can agree that all are one in Christ (John 17). But the agreement stops there. Can they still have a care and concern for each other? Can they still pray together before the throne of God? In what sense do they have fellowship in Christ? Even after purgatory is eliminated and all Christians are understood to be in the same state after death the question of how living Christians relate to those who have died remains a difficult question for most Protestants.

Protestant theologians are not much help and give quite contradictory answers to this question. On the one hand, Calvin rather mockingly asks: 'But if any man contend that, since they have been bound with us in one faith, it is impossible for them to cease to keep the same love toward us, who, then, has disclosed that they have ears long enough to reach our voices, or that they have eyes so keen as to watch over our needs?'[32] Calvin is clearly denying not only the medieval idea that the saints can be asked to intercede on behalf of those on earth, but also the traditional understanding of the Communion of Saints in which the saints in heaven surround the Church on earth and watch over it. On the other hand, Richard Baxter, in the hymn quoted above, seems to think that earthly and heavenly saints join in prayer together before the throne of God and even 'in spirit each the other greet'. Commenting on Baxter's hymn, N.T. Wright asserts that since both the living and dead are in Christ and share in the Communion of Saints, there is no reason the living should not pray for and with the departed in Christ,[33] although he sees no indication in the New Testament that the departed pray for the living or that the living should ask them to do so.[34] Here Wright's suggestion that there is no reason 'in principle' that the living should not pray for the dead seems a bit at odds with

---

[32] Calvin, *Institutes*, p. 883.
[33] Wright, *Saints*, p. 37.
[34] Wright, *Saints*, p. 39.

both his eschatological New Testament perspective and the Christian tradition. There is no New Testament evidence that those who are departed to be with Christ in heaven/paradise need the prayers of the living. In fact, the traditional understanding of the Communion of Saints would reverse this claim. From this perspective, which is based on 'the cloud of witnesses' in Hebrews 12 and the prayers of the saints under the altar in Rev. 6.10, the departed are watching over and praying for the Church militant. Wright does acknowledge that there is no reason, again 'in principle', why these saints should not be urging the Father to complete the work of justice and salvation in the world on behalf of the living.[35] But this modest claim is ultimately as far as Wright is prepared to go.

However, when it comes to the doctrine of the Communion of Saints, it appears that Protestants really do get their theology from their hymns and not their theologians. Even Calvinistic Protestants have gradually been adding the hymn 'For All the Saints' to their hymnbooks. They must think the following verse, the only one in the hymn that deals with the fellowship between Christians on earth and Christians in paradise, sufficiently honors Calvin's division between those who 'feebly struggle' and those who 'in glory shine'.

> O blest communion! Fellowship divine!
> We feebly struggle, they in glory shine,
> Yet all are one in thee, for all are thine.

What is very odd is that these same hymnbooks often include the third verse of 'The Church's One Foundation' and leave out the last verse.

> [3] Though with a scornful wonder
> Men see her sore oppressed,
> By schism rent asunder
> By heresies distressed;
> Yet saints their watch are keeping
> Their cry goes up 'How long?'
> And soon the night of weeping
> Shall be the morn of song.

---

[35] Wright, *Saints*, p. 39.

[5] Yet she on earth hath union
     With God, the Three in One
     And mystic sweet communion
     With those whose rest is won
     O happy ones and holy!
     Lord, give us grace that we
     Like them, the meek and lowly,
     On high may dwell with thee.

The reason this is so odd is that the third verse has such a clear picture of the fourth-century view of the Communion of Saints (a view Calvin explicitly repudiates) – they are watching from heaven over the Church on earth as they cry from under the altar (Rev. 6.10) – and the last verse does not differ in any substantive way from verse four of 'For All the Saints'.

But verse three of 'The Church's One Foundation' and Richard Baxter's idea that the saints on earth and the saints in Heaven meet in prayer around the throne of God gives us a way to see love in an eschatological dimension. In Rev. 6.10, the saints under the altar cry out to God for vindication: 'How long, O Lord, holy and true, do you not judge and avenge our blood upon those who dwell upon the earth?' In Lk. 18.1-8, the parable of the widow and the unjust judge is used to encourage God's elect to pray and not lose heart. This parable about prayer is set in an eschatological context by the final verse: 'When the Son of Man comes will he find faith on earth?' The connection of this parable with the saints under the altar in Revelation is not immediately clear unless one knows Greek, but the word used throughout the parable for 'vindication' is the same word used in Rev. 6.10 for 'avenge'. Both the saints on earth and the saints under the altar in heaven are crying out to God for the same thing – vindication – and both must wait until the coming of the Son of Man to see the answer to their prayer. Richard Baxter is certainly right that saints on earth and in heaven meet before the throne of God in prayer. What is interesting is that the New Testament presents this a fellowship of faith rather than a fellowship of love. Or could it be both? If we join with other Christians to pray 'thy will be done on earth as it is in heaven' is this not a fellowship of love and an expression of Christian unity? Maybe this is what eschatological love looks like?

Conclusion

By denying the traditional doctrine of the Communion of Saints, Protestants and Pentecostals may have lost more than they gained. It was certainly important to get rid of the doctrine of purgatory and the abuses associated with that doctrine at the time of the Reformation. But as N.T. Wright has shown, once purgatory is eliminated, and a proper understanding of the relationship between paradise/heaven and the future resurrection of the body is established, the traditional understanding of the Communion of Saints has much to offer both Pentecostals and Protestants.

The first thing it offers us is the reminder that all Christians are 'saints' in the New Testament sense of that word. This is an important point that is too often lost in the Protestant church. We need to remember that we are called to be holy in a world that could not care less about holiness and we need to live that holiness out in ways that matter. The Communion of Saints also gives us clarity about our hope of heaven and the resurrection of the dead. Christians ought to be able to talk about death and heaven and those they love who have departed this life. If more Christians had the sense of a 'cloud of witnesses' surrounding them with love and felt their call to faithful witness before the world, the Church might be transformed. Above all, we need to have a love that will endure beyond this life into the next. This is a love that bears faithful witness and that faithfully prays before the throne of God. This kind of love can pray with and for those we love in this life and with those in heaven for it has a 'mystic sweet communion with those whose rest is won'. The Communion of Saints reminds Protestants and Pentecostals that this is not something to fear, but a foretaste of the time when we will 'depart and be with Christ' (Phil. 1.23) and see God 'face to face' (1 Cor. 13.11).

8

REALIZED ESCHATOLOGY OR ESCHATOLOGY IN THE PROCESS OF REALIZATION?: A PENTECOSTAL ENGAGEMENT WITH N.T. WRIGHT'S VIEW OF THE PRESENT MISSION OF THE CHURCH IN THE WORLD

JEFFREY S. LAMP[*]

Introduction

It is virtually a truism that to speak of N.T. Wright's theology is to speak of eschatology. This is a natural conclusion when one looks at his magisterial project, 'Christian Origins and the Question of God', and the numerous writings in which he teases out the theological framework of the New Testament. According to Wright, sensitive readings of the New Testament that give proper place to the historical and cultural contexts of these writings must deal directly with eschatology, for this was an integral component of the intellectual and theological matrix in which the nascent Christian movement was birthed. Thus virtually everything Wright has to say in scholarly and ecclesiastical contexts eventually comes back to eschatology.

The present discussion will illustrate this tendency as it addresses a topic in which Wright's academic and pastoral concerns come to-

---

[*] Jeffrey Lamp (PhD, Trinity Evangelical Divinity School) is Professor of New Testament at Oral Roberts University, Tulsa, Oklahoma. He has served as a pastor in the United Methodist Church.

gether – the present mission of the Church in the world. Wright's understanding of the current work of the Church draws its rationale, motivation, and substance from a consideration of eschatology. This discussion will proceed in two movements. First, it will examine how eschatology informs Wright's depiction of the Church's mission in the present. It will begin with Wright's depiction of the hope toward which Christian belief and practice aim. It will then focus on the event that brings the future into the purview of the present, the resurrection of Jesus. This section will conclude with an analysis of Wright's conception of the mission of the Church in the present, at which point we will answer the question that forms the title of this essay. The second movement will consist of a Pentecostal engagement with Wright's understanding of the Church's mission. It will necessarily speak in broad generalities. First, it will describe a Pentecostal understanding of the Church's present mission in the world. Finally, it will compare the Pentecostal view of the Church's mission with that of Wright.

Wright's View of the Mission of the Church in the World

The Future Hope according to Wright

We will rely heavily on Wright's volume *Surprised by Hope* in this section, for it represents a recent exposition of his thought on the matter that is both academic and pastoral in substance.[1] Wright begins *Surprised by Hope* with two questions that provide the framework for what follows. First, what is the Christian hope? Second, what hope is there for change, rescue, transformation, or new possibilities within the world at present?[2] For Wright, these two questions are seminal for understanding the Church's mission in the world. If salvation is 'going to heaven' following death to live forever with God, then what happens in the present world is not important. But if God is establishing a new creation with the coming of Jesus, then the Christian hope for the future must have significance for the present.[3] Framing the issue in these terms betrays a fundamental prob-

---

[1] N.T. Wright, *Surprised by Hope: Rethinking Heaven, the Resurrection, and the Mission of the Church* (New York: HarperOne, 2008). Cited hereafter as *SH*.
[2] Wright, *SH*, p. 5.
[3] Wright, *SH*, p. 5.

lem with how Christians view the future – they do not know what the Christian hope is.[4] This is best seen in how Christians assess death: is death a beaten enemy that will be destroyed at the end, or is it a portal from this stage of existence into eternal life?[5] Confusion on this question leads to confusion regarding what God has done in Christ to bring about the Kingdom of God.

This lack of clarity regarding death is coupled with a lack of clarity regarding a Christian understanding of heaven. The popular conception is that heaven is the ultimate destiny for Christians, where they go to spend eternity when they die. Wright attributes this lack of understanding in part to the influence of Platonism via Gnosticism on Christianity.[6] The present order, characterized by evil, is to be escaped. The ideal is a world of pure spiritual existence in which human beings are finally freed from the mortal coil that hindered them on earth. Wright argues that early Christians did not believe that the world was devolving into a chaotic state necessitating escape. Rather, their understanding of Christian hope revolved around three basic assumptions.[7] First, they affirmed the goodness of creation. Human beings were to be God's image reflecting God in worship and stewardship in the world. Second, they believed that evil was not intrinsic to created materiality, but comes from rebelliousness and idolatry. Third, the plan of redemption in Jesus was not scrapping what was created, but rather liberating it from its enslavement to corruption and evil.

So what of heaven? For Wright, the biblical picture is quite clear. In the present, heaven is the hidden dimension of our ordinary life on earth.[8] Revelation 4–5 is cited in support of this picture. Moreover, Revelation 21–22 shows that the destiny of God's creation is for heaven and earth to come together in the consummation of new creation. The picture is not of human beings going to heaven, but of heaven coming to earth.[9] As for how heaven fits into the question of personal eschatology with respect to death, heaven is identi-

---

[4] Wright, *SH*, p. 12.
[5] Wright, *SH*, pp. 13-15.
[6] Wright, *SH*, pp. 88-90.
[7] Wright, *SH*, pp. 94-97.
[8] Wright, *SH*, p. 18.
[9] Wright, *SH*, pp. 19, 104-106.

fied as that place of rest where Christians await their final redemption, the resurrection of their bodies.[10] This construction gives rise to Wright's famous epigram regarding future hope: heaven is life after death, while resurrection is life after life after death.[11] But most important for the present discussion is the line from the Lord's Prayer: 'your will be done, on earth as it is in heaven' (Mt. 6.10). Heaven is to make incursions into the present world.[12]

So what is the Christian hope? For Wright, the future hope is resurrection with bodies fit to inhabit the joined new heaven and new earth.[13] Human beings will be raised with a 'transformed physicality' powered by the Spirit for dwelling in the new heaven and new earth.[14] Here Wright makes a bold move. He ties the redemption of human beings with that of the cosmos (Rom. 8.18-25).[15] The focus here is not simply human beings finding redemption, but the whole creation. The imagery could not be more vivid –'the drastic and dramatic birth of new creation from the womb of the old'.[16] In the end, God will be all in all (1 Cor. 15.28). God's intention is to fill all creation with his own presence and love, implying that the world, created good but enslaved by corruption, will one day attain its destiny. Far from entailing a removal of human beings from the corruption of a world destined for destruction to enjoy a blissful spiritual eternal existence in heaven, the Christian hope is to participate via resurrection in the united new heaven and new earth in which God dwells as all in all.[17]

---

[10] Wright notes that this reality is variously described in the New Testament: 'many dwelling places' (Jn 14.2); 'Paradise' (Lk. 23.43); 'absent from the body, present with the Lord' (Phil. 1.23). Cf. *SH*, pp. 150-51. This reality, however, does not provide, in Wright's estimation, for the Roman Catholic teachings on praying to the saints (cf. *SH*, pp. 171-72) or purgatory (cf. *SH*, pp. 166-67).

[11] Wright, *SH*, p. 151.

[12] Wright, *SH*, p. 18.

[13] Wright, *SH*, pp. 148-49.

[14] Wright, *SH*, p. 160.

[15] Wright, *SH*, pp. 101-104.

[16] Wright, *SH*, p. 104.

[17] As might be deduced from such a construction, Wright has no place in his understanding for 'rapture theology' and subjects this teaching to a substantive and scathing critique (cf. *SH*, pp. 118-34).

Upon what grounds is this hope established? Again, the resurrection of Jesus.[18] In a radical reworking of the traditional Jewish doctrine of resurrection, early Christians believed that God had done for Jesus what he promised to do for Israel at the end of the age, and that Jesus' resurrection anticipates the ultimate resurrection of all.[19] Resurrection becomes of central importance in Christian self-understanding.[20] It is the resurrection of Jesus itself that provides the basis for the Church's understanding of its mission in the present world.

The Resurrection of Jesus in the Church's Mission

Resurrection, though the fundamental basis for Wright's conception of the Church's mission in the world, functions as a synecdoche for a wider complex of considerations germane to this issue. As noted above, the resurrection of Jesus is the grounds for Christian hope. Here we will examine how resurrection and a series of connected notions serve as the ground for the Church's mission.

For Wright, the resurrection of Jesus is an event that is not only a part of history that can be addressed as any other historical event, but is also integral for reshaping the cosmos from that point forward.[21] It is the foundation of new creation. If strands of Jewish eschatology had foreseen that God would work a radical transformation at the end of the age, early Christian eschatology pulled the moment of transformation from the future back into the present. In Jewish thought, resurrection was God's act that would signal not only the salvation of human beings, but also the renewal of the cosmos. By raising Jesus from the dead, God had signaled that the renewal of the cosmos had emerged and taken root in the world. Wright argues that because the resurrection of Jesus happened as an event in history, its implications and effects are to be felt within the

---

[18] In chs. 3, 'Early Christian Hope in Its Historical Setting', and 4, 'The Strange Story of Easter', of *SH*, Wright provides a greatly distilled summary of his monumental study *The Resurrection of the Son of God* (Christian Origins and the Question of God 3; Minneapolis: Fortress, 2003). Cited hereafter as *RSG*. He addresses evidences for the historicity of the resurrection of Jesus, various objections to the resurrection, problems of epistemology related to assessing the evidence, and the historical usage of resurrection and related language in antiquity.

[19] Wright, *SH*, pp. 38-39, 44-45.

[20] Wright, *SH*, pp. 42-43.

[21] Wright, *SH*, pp. 66-67.

present world.[22] The resurrection of Jesus provides a vision of future hope that leads to a vision of present hope, and this vision of present hope is the basis of the Church's mission in the world.

Said another way, God raising Jesus from the dead, in anticipation of the resurrection of all human beings at the end of the age, is God's statement that this project has begun in the present. New creation is here, with history now directed toward the day when God will be all in all. By itself, resurrection need only be a one-time statement that God will do on a large scale what he demonstrated in Jesus on a smaller scale. By itself, it need not imply a present mission, as is evidenced by various strands of Christian tradition that emphasize a wholly future personal salvation in heaven. Here Wright draws on another doctrine in the Christian scheme, one intimately connected with the resurrection of Jesus but frequently misunderstood: the ascension of Jesus.

Wright identifies several caricatures of the ascension that draw away from its place in the logic of God's setting the world to rights.[23] It is frequently collapsed into the resurrection such that they are the same thing. Moreover, the ascension is often interpreted as a way of saying that Jesus has become spiritually present everywhere, especially in the Church. This often leads to the view that the Church itself is the presence of the risen Lord in the world rather than a servant of the Lord. Wright rejects these misunderstandings of the ascension, pointing instead to a couple of realities encapsulated in the doctrine. First, the ascension of Jesus demonstrates that heaven and earth are intrinsically connected in the present.[24] As noted earlier, heaven and earth are not properly seen as two different spatial locations, but as two different but tangentially related dimensions of God's creation. Heaven and earth are in contact; Wright even characterizes heaven as the 'control room' of earth.[25] The ascension of Jesus effects this connection between heaven and earth in two important respects. One, Jesus is a human being who sits enthroned in heaven as the ruling Lord over earth, not just in the future, but now as well. Two, because Jesus has been

---

[22] Wright, *SH*, p. 191.
[23] Wright, *SH*, pp. 109-13.
[24] Wright, *SH*, pp. 115-17.
[25] Wright, *SH*, p. 115.

raised, the Holy Spirit has been poured out on the earth in fulfillment of his promise. The man Jesus reigns in heaven as Lord, and by way of the Holy Spirit effects this lordship on earth through the Church.

Another feature of the ascension crucial for understanding the Church's mission is that it implies the reappearance of Jesus on earth to mark the total renewal of the cosmos (cf. Acts 1.11). But rather than speak of this in terms familiar to popular evangelicalism, namely 'rapture theology', Wright chooses to focus on the Greek term παρουσία, frequently translated as 'coming', but more appropriately, for Wright, as 'presence'.[26] This implies that the absent in body but present in the Spirit Lord will one day be present in body and transform the world, thus becoming its present ruling Lord.

Another key doctrine of this complex flows directly from the doctrines of the ascension and *parousia*: judgment. When Jesus is manifest as the present Lord, he will be present as judge. But according to Wright, an overlooked feature of the biblical doctrine of judgment is that God's coming judgment is seen as the means through which God brings restorative and transformative justice to creation.[27] In the New Testament, Jesus is depicted as the 'son of man' who suffers and is vindicated through resurrection and ascension. This vindicated 'son of man' brings judgment to bear on the world, with the result that Jesus puts the world to rights via his judgment. When Jesus judges as the present Lord, death and decay are overcome and God is established as all in all.[28] What this means

---

[26] Wright, *SH*, pp. 128-30. In one of Wright's more controversial positions, he challenges the popular evangelical interpretations of several biblical passages that speak of Jesus' 'second coming'. He provocatively suggests that Jesus himself never spoke of his return, and that New Testament passages allegedly doing so actually speak of his vindication ('the son of man returning on the clouds'), of his first coming (in the stories Jesus told about kings or servants going away), or of his lordship manifest in bodily presence in the final transformation of the world (cf. 1 Thess. 4.16-17). Cf. *SH*, pp. 125-33. For further discussion, see *Jesus and the Victory of God* (Christian Origins and the Question of God 2; Minneapolis: Fortress, 1996), chs. 8 and 13; and *Paul: In Fresh Perspective* (Minneapolis: Fortress, 2005), ch. 7. Cited hereafter as *JVG* and *Paul* respectively. It is not that Wright denies a future judgment or the presence of Jesus as judge at the end, but that the biblical attestation of such things is not best understood in terms of the popular 'rapture theology'.

[27] Wright, *SH*, pp. 137-39.

[28] Wright, *SH*, pp. 142-43.

for the present mission of the Church is that we stand in history bearing witness to and establishing the future justice of Jesus the judge in anticipation of its culmination in the future.

In summary, the resurrection of Jesus marks the foundation of God's new creation in the course of history. This event stakes God's claim that the present order will finally experience redemption in the future. As such, it is the basis for the ongoing work of the Church in establishing this order. Moreover, this risen Jesus is enthroned in heaven as Lord over the earth in the present via the ascension. The present reigning Lord exercises his lordship through his Spirit-filled people, the Church, whose presence and work attest to and effect the beginnings of the transformation that awaits the cosmos at the manifest presence of the coming judge at the *parousia*. Resurrection, ascension, the Holy Spirit, *parousia*, judgment – the complex of doctrines that inform our understanding of the presence of new creation in the midst of history and the mission of the Church in light of new creation moving toward its fulfillment. It remains to describe the substance of the present mission of the Church in the world.

Wright's Conception of the Church's Present Mission

What does this mission look like? Wright spends the final four chapters of *Surprised by Hope* addressing this issue (chs. 12–15). Here Wright begins by focusing on Jesus' ministry as an integral component of what God was doing in bringing the story of Israel to a climax in the story of Jesus. The miracles, healings, and teachings of Jesus were not simply interesting bits that fill the space before the cross and resurrection; they are paradigmatic for the project God was bringing to realization in the world, pointing forward to the future hope, but also enabling people to begin enjoying that future in the present.[29] The Gospel narratives are not just biography; they are the depiction of what it looks like when God's rule enters the world through new creation.

The mission of the Church largely revolves around what Christians believe about the nature of salvation. Wright believes it is mistaken to see salvation simply in terms of the soul's personal escape from corruption into heavenly bliss. He famously quips on this

---

[29] Wright, *SH*, p. 192.

head, 'We are saved not as souls but as wholes'.[30] Salvation is the hope that we will be raised in God's new creation as genuine human beings in fulfillment of the mandate of Genesis 1 where God gave genuine human beings the task of bringing order to God's world, in short, to bring salvation to the world. And this salvation is 'about whole human beings, not merely souls; about the present, not simply the future; about what God does *through* us, not merely what God does *in and for* us'.[31]

Perhaps Wright's most novel contribution to the understanding of the Church's mission is his insistence that the Church participates with God in 'building for the Kingdom'.[32] This is not the same thing as building the Kingdom itself. Wright argues that 1 Cor. 15.58 confirms that the work of the Church performed in the present accomplishes something that will become in due course part of God's new world.[33] Wright identifies three areas in which the Church builds for the Kingdom in its mission in the world: justice, beauty, and evangelism. The Church's work for justice is in response to the redemptive purpose of God to set creation to rights; creation of beauty through the arts is a response to God's creative beauty and points not only to God but to God's promise for creation; evangelism is the proclamation to every person that God, the creator of the world, is finally becoming the king of the world, and that Jesus, whom God raised from the dead, is the world's true Lord, and that through Jesus, the powers of evil have been defeated and God's new creation has begun.[34] The Church's works of justice, beauty, and evangelism are means by which the future Kingdom is brought into the present, and are mysteriously incorporated into that future Kingdom.[35]

The mission of the Church in the present is not just a matter of works that the Church performs with the world as the object and stage of their performance. Such works are predicated on the Church revisioning itself for mission and life around the story of

---

[30] Wright, *SH*, p. 199.

[31] Wright, *SH*, p. 200.

[32] Wright, *SH*, p. 208.

[33] Wright, *SH*, p. 208. The portion of 1 Cor. 15.58 in view reads, 'you know that in the Lord your labor is not in vain'.

[34] Wright, *SH*, p. 227.

[35] Wright, *SH*, pp. 230-32.

the resurrected Jesus. This reshaping has cosmic and personal dimensions. Resurrection provides for the establishment of new creation in history, and it provides the metaphor for the personal transformation experienced in baptism that is required to become a people shaped for living in God's new creation.[36] Moreover, the Church's corporate life needs revisioning as well. Wright argues that the Church must demonstrate the life of Easter in several ways as it builds for the Kingdom of God. He labels them the redemption of space, time, and matter.[37] Wright further argues that the resurrection informs our practices of spirituality such that the Church's life exhibits signs of new creation.[38]

In summary, Wright has concrete expressions of the work of the Church that accomplish 'building for the Kingdom of God', but these works are predicated on the Church revisioning itself as a people of the resurrection in its life. If God has begun setting the world to rights in the resurrection of Jesus, then the Church must be a community transformed by this new creation reality in order to proclaim this reality in the world.

Is Wright advancing a realized eschatology, or something else? Perhaps the question is misguided. Wright's view is more defined by its point of emphasis than by its taxonomic classification. Its focus on the resurrection of Jesus as that which brings into history the Kingdom of God, and as that which transforms the present order in anticipation of the future hope, betrays an interest in living out eschatology rather than classifying it. So to call it 'eschatology in the process of realization' is not to create a new category, but rather to

---

[36] Wright, *SH*, pp. 250-53.

[37] Wright, *SH*, pp. 259-63. Regarding redeeming space, Wright suggests that the Church must live as a people who see all of God's creation as taken up into God's larger purposes, and who reclaim the idea that worship space is not simply a matter of efficient use of resources, but that it bespeaks of the Church's commitment to the truth that all of creation is valued by God. Regarding time, a reclamation of the liturgical calendar and a long view of Church history as the record of God's future becoming actualized in history serve as defining characteristics of a people who believe God is at work in history. Regarding matter, in the sacraments of Baptism and the Eucharist the Church affirms that the elements of the created order point toward the fulfillment of new creation in the transformation of the present world.

[38] Wright, *SH*, pp. 271-88. Wright lists among these practices Baptism, Eucharist, prayer, use of Scripture, holiness, and love.

place emphasis on the redemption God is currently working in the world through the resurrection- and Spirit-empowered Church.

A Pentecostal Engagement with Wright's Views on the Mission of the Church in the World

Pentecostal Views on the Mission of the Church

Many Pentecostals have identified the evangelization of the world in light of eschatological urgency as the driving force of Pentecostal mission from the inception of the movement.[39] Specifically, adherence to a premillennial dispensational eschatology relegated the missionary focus of the Church to evangelism, a view currently popular with many Pentecostals.[40] In this view, works aimed at social liberation are deemed less important than evangelism, though some of these works may prove preparatory for evangelism.[41] Moreover, the alignment of classical Pentecostals with politically and theologically conservative wings of the Church has further cemented suspicion against a saving role of the Spirit apart from evangelism.[42] Outside of North America, however, Pentecostals have shown more willingness to engage social issues as valid expressions of the Church's mission in the world.[43] Yong and Kärkkäinen highlight numerous non-Western Pentecostal examples of mission beyond evangelism from various two-thirds world contexts.[44] Part of this phenomenon

---

[39] D. William Faupel, *The Everlasting Gospel: The Significance of Eschatology in the Development of Pentecostal Thought* (JPTSup 10; Sheffield: Sheffield Academic Press, 1996); Veli-Matti Kärkkäinen, 'Pentecostal Pneumatology of Religions: The Contribution of Pentecostals to Our Understanding of the Word of God's Spirit in the World', in Veli-Matti Kärkkäinen (ed.), *The Spirit in the World: Emerging Pentecostal Theologies in Global Contexts* (Grand Rapids: Eerdmans, 2009), pp. 155-80.

[40] Frank D. Macchia, *Baptized in the Spirit: A Global Pentecostal Theology* (Grand Rapids: Zondervan, 2006), pp. 272-75.

[41] Macchia, *Baptized in the Spirit*, p. 277; Kärkkäinen, 'Pentecostal Pneumatology of Religions', p. 168.

[42] Kärkkäinen, 'Pentecostal Pneumatology of Religions', p. 170. One interesting historical study of this phenomenon is the movement of the Assemblies of God from an official position of pacifism to one that is more broadly supportive of military means at conflict resolution. See Paul Alexander, *Peace to War: Shifting Allegiances in the Assemblies of God* (C. Henry Smith Series; Telford, PA: Cascadia Publishing House, 2009).

[43] Kärkkäinen, 'Pentecostal Pneumatology of Religions', p. 168.

[44] Cf., Douglas Peterson, 'A Moral Imagination: Pentecostals and Social Concern in Latin America', in Veli-Matti Kärkkäinen (ed.), *The Spirit in the World*

arises from simple demographics. Whereas Pentecostalism has come to enjoy mainstream acceptance in the United States with the concomitant increase of socioeconomic standing among its adherents, Pentecostals in non-Western contexts are truly a church of the 'poor', not simply for the 'poor', living in situations where poverty, sickness, and oppression are part of daily existence.[45]

Given this divergence of opinion, is there a constructive theological rubric for formulating a Pentecostal approach to mission akin to that which Wright has articulated? Frank Macchia has offered one such articulation in his volume, *Baptized in the Spirit*. Macchia seeks to reappropriate the metaphor of Spirit baptism in a way that enables mission within a thoroughgoing pneumatological account of God's saving activity in the world. The result is an account of Spirit baptism that extends beyond individual experience of the Holy Spirit so 'the Spirit is seen as involved in the reach of life toward renewal in all things'.[46] Put succinctly, 'Spirit baptism is a baptism into the love of God that sanctifies, renews, and empowers until Spirit baptism turns all of creation into the final dwelling place of God'.[47]

This definition of Spirit baptism goes well beyond the stereotypical Pentecostal fascination with glossolalia. It is embedded in eschatology, having as its goal the transformation of creation into the dwelling place of God. Critical to the outworking of this goal is the understanding that Jesus is the Spirit baptizer. The one who was anointed with the Spirit to perform his mission in the world was the one who, by the Spirit, 'was to walk the path of the God-forsaken and oppressed and to come into solidarity with them through the

---

(Grand Rapids: Eerdmans, 2009), pp. 53-66; Koo Dong Yun, 'Pentecostalism from Below: Minjung Liberation and Asian Pentecostal Theology', in Veli-Matti Kärkkäinen (ed.), *The Spirit in the World* (Grand Rapids: Eerdmans, 2009), pp. 89-114; Amos Yong, *The Spirit Poured out on All Flesh: Pentecostalism and the Possibility of Global Theology* (Grand Rapids: Baker Academic, 2005), ch. 1. Cf. Samuel Solivan, *The Spirit, Pathos, and Liberation: Towards a Hispanic Pentecostal Theology* (JPTSup 14; Sheffield: Sheffield Academic Press, 1998).

[45] Wonsuk Ma, '"When the Poor are Fired Up": The Role of Pneumatology in Pentecostal/Charismatic Mission', in Veli-Matti Kärkkäinen (ed.), *The Spirit in the World* (Grand Rapids: Eerdmans, 2009), pp. 41-42.

[46] Macchia, *Baptized in the Spirit*, p. 41.

[47] Macchia, *Baptized in the Spirit*, p. 60. Yong articulates a similar view in *Spirit Poured out on All Flesh*, pp. 91, 102.

Spirit on the cross'.[48] In the Spirit-anointed Jesus and his proclamation through the Spirit, the Kingdom of God was present, and by this same Spirit Jesus was raised to break the power of sin and death and in his glorified humanity to impart the Spirit leading to the newness of life.[49] In incarnation, cross, resurrection, and glorification the Son's mission is carried out by the presence and power of the Spirit.

Macchia argues that Spirit baptism is the means by which creation is transformed by the Kingdom to participate in the Kingdom's reign of life.[50] The Spirit poured out on Jesus is the Spirit poured out on all flesh by the resurrected Son in order to liberate creation from within history for new possibilities of eschatological life both in the present and for the future.[51] The Spirit present in Spirit baptism is the same Spirit who groans with the suffering creation in hope of its eventual liberation from corruption, and is the same Spirit with which the Son was anointed on behalf of the Father in response to the cry of creation for redemption, and is the same Spirit poured out by the glorified Son in response to creation's cry for liberation.[52] Spirit baptism is that means by which God redeems the cosmos.

In Macchia's construction, Spirit baptism is God's empathetic, tabernacling presence with his suffering creation as it moves toward redemption.[53] This presence is enfleshed in the world by the Church, the people birthed in the Acts narrative through Spirit baptism for mission in the world.[54] The Church is the Spirit-filled temple of God's dwelling that bears witness in the present of the goal of the Spirit filling all of creation in preparation for its final transformation into the dwelling place of God.[55] It would do so through

---

[48] Macchia, *Baptized in the Spirit*, p. 126.

[49] Macchia, *Baptized in the Spirit*, p. 109.

[50] Macchia draws on Gregory of Nyssa for this insight. Gregory writes, 'The Spirit is a living and a substantial and distinctly subsisting Kingdom with which the only begotten Christ is anointed and is king of all that is' (*On the Lord's Prayer* 3). Quoted in Macchia, *Baptized in the Spirit*, p. 89.

[51] Macchia, *Baptized in the Spirit*, p. 97.

[52] Macchia, *Baptized in the Spirit*, p. 136.

[53] Macchia, *Baptized in the Spirit*, p. 126.

[54] Macchia, *Baptized in the Spirit*, p. 155; cf. Acts 1.8.

[55] Macchia, *Baptized in the Spirit*, pp. 203-204.

a faith oriented toward 'orthopathos', right affections in spirituality and worship, and 'orthodopraxis', right living in holiness, vibrant witness, and participation in social justice.[56]

In summary, for Macchia, Spirit baptism is a metaphor that is elastic enough to provide a framework for understanding God's redemption of the cosmos. It enables Pentecostals to articulate the story of God's salvation in Christ and subsequently through the Church in such a way as to highlight their distinctive participation in the life of the Spirit. It provides a context for the place of the Spirit in the incarnation, crucifixion, resurrection, and glorification of Jesus, in the birth and mission of the Church, and in the eschatological goal of creation becoming the dwelling place of God. In providing such a construction, Macchia is not denying the personal, existential aspects of Spirit baptism, but is expanding the metaphor to explain the place of the Spirit in God's redemption of the cosmos.

A Comparison of Wright's Views with Those of Pentecostals

As is evident by this brief survey, there are many points of similarity and contrast in views of the mission of the Church articulated by Wright and Pentecostals. Broadly speaking, both positions affirm that the Church has a mission in the world. For Wright, it is the Church participating in building for the eschatological Kingdom, whereas historically speaking (at least in Western Pentecostalism) and certainly at a popular level, for Pentecostals it is the evangelistic proclamation of the gospel in light of the imminent return of Jesus. For Wright, the focus is squarely on the redemption of the cosmos, within which the salvation of individuals is included, whereas for Pentecostals evangelism frequently tempers the place of non-evangelistic efforts in the mission of the Church. As we have seen, Wright is openly critical of the dispensational eschatology popular among many Pentecostals that gives rise to its heavy emphasis on evangelism at the expense of social works. In broad strokes, we see that there are many points of divergence within a general consensus that the Church has a mission in the world.

---

[56] Macchia, *Baptized in the Spirit*, p. 112. Gordon D. Fee affirms that the Church is the people of the future in the present who are to continue the proclamation of the Kingdom of God as good news to the poor. See Fee, 'The Kingdom of God and the Church's Global Mission', in Murray W. Dempster, Byron D. Klaus, and Douglas Peterson (eds.), *Called and Empowered: Pentecostal Perspectives on Global Mission* (Peabody, MA: Hendrickson, 1991), pp. 7-21.

Of more interest, however, is a comparison between Wright and what we saw in the reformulation of Spirit baptism by Macchia. At a very significant level, both Wright and Macchia share the view that there is a cosmic understanding of salvation possible that makes sense of God's plan of redemption from creation to new creation. Both authors understand the primary mode of God's work to be transformation of the cosmos such that in the end 'God will be all in all' (Wright) or the cosmos might become 'God's dwelling place' (Macchia). In this regard, eschatology is determinative for how one regards what God is presently doing in the world. Heaven and earth will come together in the end; what takes place now is moving the world toward that goal.

In terms of the mission itself, both Wright and Macchia understand that the whole life of the Church is involved in shaping it for mission. Worship, service, and spirituality must be reshaped in light of the eschatological goal of creation in order to prepare the Church to engage effectively in mission in the world. Mission cannot be relegated to the status of something the Church does simply because it has to do something. It must be the outgrowth of who the Church is in light of its eschatological destiny and how that finds shape in the present.

An interesting point of comparison is how Wright and Macchia understand two important features of God's redemption contributing to the present mission of the Church: the resurrection of Jesus and the giving of the Spirit. Both writers speak of the mission of the Church in light of these topics. However, they differ with respect to which idea is primary. Theologically, one simply cannot separate the two ideas or assign one a higher degree of importance than the other. Jesus is raised by the agency of the Spirit and the risen, glorified Christ pours out the Spirit on all flesh in fulfillment of God's promise and for mission in the world. Yet in terms of emphasis and paradigmatic significance, each writer focuses on one or the other topic. Wright gives special emphasis to the resurrection. Because God has done for Jesus in history what he will do at the end for all human beings, new creation has emerged in history and shapes, through the Spirit-filled Church, how creation moves toward its goal. Resurrection is paradigmatic for understanding the place of the Spirit in God's salvation of the world. For Macchia, Spirit baptism receives emphasis, providing a metaphor for understanding

God's redemption. The Spirit-anointed Jesus proclaims the Kingdom of God in word and deed, is crucified and then raised via the agency of the Spirit in order to be the Spirit baptizer, empowering the Church to engage in the mission of extending the sphere of the Spirit until all creation is transformed into God's dwelling place.

Of course, such difference in emphasis may be nothing more than a consequence of the contexts of Wright and Macchia themselves. Wright approaches his work as a historian, biblical scholar, and bishop, and much of what he says is the direct result of his overarching program 'Christian Origins and the Question of God' mediated through his conviction that such study must engage the Church and the world. Macchia is working as a Pentecostal theologian operating with the conviction that Pentecostals must reclaim an important part of their heritage and rework it in light of a larger understanding of the role of the Spirit in God's redemption of the world. In each case, the interests and academic and ecclesiastical contexts of these writers is largely determinative for how they articulate their visions, and may account for the lack of engagement with each other in the sources that formed the framework for this essay.[57]

Conclusion

This discussion aimed to demonstrate that both Wright and Pentecostals are concerned with the present mission of the Church in the world. One significant outcome of this examination is that perhaps Pentecostals might come to recognize that Wright's emphasis on the importance of eschatology in the definition and motivation of the present mission of the Church might provide a helpful lens

---

[57] This is not to say that Wright has not addressed issues of interest to Pentecostals. As noted earlier, Wright has critiqued a 'rapture theology' that has widespread popular acceptance among many Pentecostals. Moreover, Wright has addressed issues of charismata that are frequently seen as among the distinctives of Pentecostals, but even here, he speaks more to the issues as they appear in Scripture and in the larger ecclesiastical world rather than to Pentecostals themselves. See Wright, *Simply Christian: Why Christianity Makes Sense* (San Francisco: Harper Collins, 2006), p. 110. See also his more pastoral presentation of spiritual gifts in *Paul for Everyone: 1 Corinthians* (Louisville: Westminster John Knox, 2004), pp. 166-70, 179-201. Of course, Macchia has indeed engaged Wright on other fronts, as his essay in this volume attests. See also Macchia, *Justified in the Spirit: Creation, Redemption, and the Triune God* (Grand Rapids: Eerdmans, 2010).

through which they might view their own mission in the world through the power and presence of the Holy Spirit. The Pentecostal emphasis on the role of the Holy Spirit in mission is implicitly an eschatological rationale for mission. A careful engagement with Wright's thought on this point may provide Pentecostals with helpful categories through which they might more fully define their mission in the world and perhaps even expand that vision. Perhaps Wright might find something in Pentecostal formulations that would shape his own thinking as well, particularly in terms of a greater appreciation of the role of the Spirit in mission. It is at least a discussion worth having.

9

THE WORD AND THE WIND: A RESPONSE

N.T. WRIGHT[*]

I am as grateful as I am surprised that a group of Pentecostal theologians would want to engage with my work in this way. I owe particular thanks to Jeffrey Lamp who has been patient beyond the call of duty in waiting for this response. I first read the essays late in 2013, but the fifteen months between then and now (spring 2015) has been swamped with so many urgent tasks that I have been unable to make progress with my comments. I apologise to the contributors, who must have wondered if they had done something to offend me, or if their own work would ever see the light of day. I deeply appreciate the compliment they are paying me, and I shall try in what follows not just to comment but perhaps to move the discussion forwards here and there.

Since these essays were written, as many will be aware, I have published not only my long-awaited large volume on Paul (*Paul and the Faithfulness of God* [London and Minneapolis: SPCK and Fortress Press, 2013]; hereafter *PFG*) but also, with the same publishers and date, *Pauline Perspectives*, a collection of my articles on Paul going back over thirty years. Various other somewhat less academic books

---

[*] N.T. Wright (DPhil, Merton College, Oxford) is Professor of New Testament and Early Christianity at St. Andrews University, Scotland. From 2003–2010 he was Bishop of Durham. Among his numerous publications are the four entries in his series 'Christian Origins and the Question of God'.

have appeared as well, including *How God Became King* (London and San Francisco: SPCK and HarperOne, 2012) and recently *Simply Good News* (London and San Francisco: SPCK and HarperOne, 2015). And there are others in the pipeline. It would be tedious to refer to these frequently as we go along, so let me just agree with the point one of the contributors made, that my work is indeed cumulative: that is to say, though I have had some larger outlines in mind for a long time, I keep on finding more detail within those pictures which seem important to bring out. Often I cannot now remember when I first thought of a particular idea; if it has now made its way comfortably into the centre of my understanding, it is hard to imagine a time when it wasn't there. So I can't blame contributors for not seeing things I hadn't said when they were reading my work, but I shall simply try to show, in dialogue with them, where I now stand.

As well as my own work, readers may like to know that there is a good, clear introduction to my work, showing how it can apply to 'ordinary' Christian life in a parish setting: Stephen Kuhrt, *Tom Wright for Everyone* (London: SPCK, 2011). Like the present book, that one was a surprise, but reading it confirmed my hunch that there are many Christian leaders in many denominations who may be looking for the kind of help that my work is trying to offer. I hope and pray that the present volume may have that effect as well.

As I approach a set of essays from a Pentecostal perspective, my own experience of Pentecostalism, though small, may perhaps be significant. My wife's late parents worshipped for many years in an Elim Pentecostal Church, and to my surprise their minister once invited me to preach. (I can even remember my text: Isaiah 12.) My late father-in-law was the first Dispensationalist I had ever knowingly met, and certainly the only one with whom I had long conversations about the interpretation of Scripture, particularly in relation to the 'Last Days'. He was a well-read student of *The Scofield Reference Bible*, and there were not many gaps in his understanding of how that system worked. I learned a lot from him; sadly, he died too young, before I had really figured out what I wanted to say in dialogue and response. Apart from that, there were the various waves of 'charismatic' movements that arrived in the UK in my student days, some falling into the classic trap of implying that those who didn't speak in tongues were second-rate Christians, some insisting on rebaptism in the name of Jesus only (as in some passages in Acts), and so on. A member of my own close family went to Africa for two years and was gloriously and life-transformingly caught up in one of the East African revivals. In the days when even the most low-church of Anglican services followed the basic liturgy and sang what now seem old-fashioned hymns, the new freedom of charismatic worship was an exciting, edgy opportunity; in more ways than one, it was like going to your first rock concert. My generation of Christian teenagers all read David Wilkerson's famous book *The Cross and the Switchblade*. It may not quite be what its present publicity calls 'The Greatest Inspirational True Story of All Time' (I suspect David Wilkerson would say that was a description of the story of Jesus himself!), but it certainly inspired and energised a lot of us. In part, no doubt, this was because of its vivid descriptions of the dangerous and lurid New York underworld, but it was also because of so many stories of prayers answered, of God acting dramatically in people's lives. So I was always aware of Pentecostalism in one form or another – including, I should say, the Roman and high Anglican charismatic movements, of which my late father-in-law was deeply suspicious.

This is not the place to describe my own Christian pilgrimage, except to say that in my mid-30s, to my own surprise, I began to pray in tongues. This has never been dramatic; I have never used this gift 'out loud' in public. But in pastoral ministry and various other contexts over the last thirty years it has been invaluable as a way of holding before God people and situations whose needs I had not yet understood sufficiently to put into words. I have met people who have prayed in tongues out loud and found that someone present understood the language; but I have never had that experience. As with the gift itself, which I did not seek, I do not ask for more than what I need. I have sometimes prayed for gifts of healing, particularly when ministering to people with serious illness or disability. I suspect there are very good reasons why the answer, so far, has been a gentle 'No'.

Does that make me a 'Pentecostal'? Some would say Yes. I don't much mind. Part of the joy of being Anglican (there are, of course, corresponding sorrows!) is that there is room to move, to grow, to develop, to explore different traditions from a secure 'home base'. For that reason, I have never seen 'Pentecostalism' as a detached tradition, living its own separate life. It shares much, in different directions, with elements of free-church evangelicalism, elements of Plymouth Brethren thinking (particularly on eschatology), and even elements of the Anglican tradition (one of the early British Pentecostals was Alexander Boddy, an Anglican clergyman in Sunderland, one of the main cities in the Diocese of Durham where I ministered as Bishop for seven years; one of the contributors to this volume quotes from the writings of his wife Mary). In particular, it seems to me that the Pentecostal and charismatic movements have made a great contribution to the revival, within an older evangelicalism, of a proper social, cultural, and political concern. Older evangelicalism often lapsed towards a dualism in which God was only interested in souls, not bodies; in evangelism, not politics. However, once the new movements of the Spirit indicated that actually God *was* interested in bodies as well, it was only a short step to recognising – as the great majority of Christians have always done! – that God was interested in the whole world of creation, including society and culture. And with that we arrive back where the Gospels wanted to take us: a vision of God's Kingdom coming on earth as in heaven, a new reality launched by Jesus himself.

That, however, brings us towards one of the central topics which is raised in this volume, and it is high time I turned to the particular essays. Though one might try to be a bit clever here, writing about various key issues while dealing obliquely with the various contributions, I think it's easier for me, and perhaps more helpful for readers, if I respond to the essays one by one.

Jeffrey S. Lamp: Wright or Wrong?

I quite often receive letters and emails from people who have made sketches or diagrams to try to express visually what they find me to be saying about the Bible. It's often difficult to comment on these because all such diagrams are inevitably oversimplifications, and I always want to say 'Yes, but …' However, the sketch which Jeffrey offers is – I say in all frankness – better than many I receive. He has grasped what for me is central to Scripture and indeed to Christian tradition as a whole: that God made creation good, and that the final judgment will not abolish creation but rescue it from its present corruption and decay, putting it to rights once for all – and us with it, in the resurrection. That is indeed absolutely basic, and I'm grateful that it comes out so clearly here.

One element in the picture, however, which Jeffrey mentions late on in his essay, might I think be highlighted much more. This is the fact that humans are made in God's image – which I understand as a *vocation*: to be the 'royal priesthood', reflecting God's wise and gentle stewardship into the world (that's the 'royal' bit) and reflecting the praises and prayers of creation back to God (the 'priestly' bit). This, of course, is highlighted in the book of Revelation (e.g. 1.6; 5.10; 20.6), but it is all over the place in one form or another (e.g. Exod. 19.6; 1 Pet. 2.9). And the point is this: we all too easily see the story of 'creation and fall' in terms of humans being set a moral target, failing to meet it, and then being forgiven. That isn't exactly false, but it isn't the right emphasis. God gave humans a *vocation*, and he made his creation in such a way that it would function properly, and would become what he intended it to become, when the humans were exercising that vocation. The point about sin, therefore, is not just that it incurs moral guilt (though it does), but that it jeopardises the divine plan for creation. The point about redemption, therefore, is not just that it restores us to fellowship with God (though it does) but that it sets us on our feet again, and provides us with the Spirit, so that we can already, here and now, be new-creation people: new creations in ourselves, and the means of new creation in the world.

There are, of course, many issues which arise at that point, and some of them will come up later. For instance: do we, then, bring the Kingdom of God by our own efforts, even our Spirit-driven efforts, here and now? No: only God brings God's Kingdom, in God's own good time; but it has been decisively launched by Jesus and through his Spirit, and we are to be caught up in that. This question of 'inaugurated eschatology' (how much of the ultimate future are we to expect to experience in the present?) has been, I think, a puzzle for many in the Pentecostal and charismatic movements, as it has been, in a different register, within New Testament scholarship. But leaving that for the moment, I move on as Jeffrey Lamp does to the question of Abraham.

Lamp is absolutely right: I have argued that for Paul Abraham is not simply an ancient scriptural example of justification by faith. But I don't think Lamp quite picks up the full import of this, which goes with his later (quite proper) emphasis on biblical narrative as more than simply illustrative. Abraham is the one with whom, in the Old Testament and in Paul's exposition of it, God starts the movement that will eventually get the creation-project (and the human-project as its key central element) back on track. Here we see utter grace at work: God plans a new *family* of humans who will inhabit, and look after, his new *world*; so, to begin this, God calls – a childless nomad! The family and the land are pure gift, and as such they are pointers, not to a future disembodied 'salvation', but to the resurrected humans who will share the Messiah's inheritance of the new creation. All this is spelled out in Romans in particular, where Paul draws together promises not only from Genesis but also from prophets like Isaiah and particularly the Psalms.

So, yes, it is true: Paul, like most second-temple Jews known to us, believed that (as Daniel 9 had indicated) the 'exile' would last, not for 70 years, but for 70 x 7 years. This is not an 'illustration' of something else. It is not simply an 'image' that I 'deploy' in describing God's redemption. It is the this-worldly reality which was the seedbed of hope for what then happened in Jesus, even though that event turned the hope upside down and inside out. In particular, Paul does indeed draw on Deuteronomy 27–30 (and, I would add importantly, 32 as well), not as an illustration but as a long-range prophecy of what he saw happening in the history of Israel and then in its climactic moment in the Messiah. But though the 'curse' of 'exile' is central to that picture, Paul does not say, as Jeffrey Lamp suggests, that God has 'cursed the curse'. In Gal. 3.10-14, the point is that the Torah was absolutely right to pronounce the curse on faithless, idolatrous Israel, and that Jesus took it upon himself as Israel's representative. Paul's use of Deuteronomy 30 in Romans 10 is then his way of saying that now, at last, a new kind of 'doing the law' has emerged, in fulfillment of the prophecy of 'return from exile' and covenant restoration. (Rom. 10.1-13 needs to be read closely with 2.25-29, a much misunderstood, or even ignored, passage).

All that brings us to the resurrection and ascension of Jesus, and the gift of the Spirit. I want to say a bit more than Lamp does in his summary of the ascension in Paul's thinking: here again it is both 'royal' (as in Phil. 2.9-11) and 'priestly' (as in Rom. 8.34). Yes: in the ascended Jesus his people can see their ultimate destiny, to be in the presence of God; but they also see their ultimate *activity and vocation*, to be the 'royal priesthood' – a vocation already launched through the Spirit. And the Jesus who is 'at God's right hand' is not 'absent but reigning'; he is *present* in and with his people, though hidden. Heaven and earth are not, after all, a long way apart. In Jesus, and not least in the Spirit, they come together. Part of the problem, I think, faced by Pentecostals and all of us who have wanted to emphasize the importance of the presence and power of the Spirit is that our conceptions of heaven and earth are wrong. We think of them as a long way apart, as in the ancient (and modern!) philosophy of Epicureanism. Scripture tells a different story; Jesus *embodies* that different story; the Spirit *enables* that different story to become a reality.

The Spirit, then, shapes and energizes the mission of the Church, which as Jeffrey Lamp rightly sees is not simply about 'saving souls' but rather about bringing to birth signs of new creation even within the present old world. However, I'm not sure that the classic Pentecostal emphasis on Acts (as opposed to the Gospels or the epistles) really counts as what I mean by 'narrative'. There is a danger that in telling the stories of Acts we might suppose that all we had to do was to go back and repeat the same narrative over and over again; whereas Acts is all about something being *launched*, a single long-term project being started. Of course, since Pentecostals, like many western Christians, have reacted strongly against traditional denominations, with their formalism and their insistence on the continuity of Church history, it is natural that they would want to say, 'Forget all that dead tradition; we are going back to the beginning'. But the *narrative* of which I have written has to do, not indeed with a dead tradition, but with the extraordinary and Spirit-led story which in one sense began with Abraham, in another sense was re-launched with Jesus, and in another sense again goes right back to the creation and call of Adam – and, wherever it began, continuing into the present time and on to the Second Coming. As I shall be saying in one of the later responses, it is important to go on critiquing all tradition in the light of Scripture; that, despite appearances, is something to which Anglicans are officially committed! But Scripture itself indicates, I believe, that the mission of the Church constitutes, in itself, a new narrative, not a set of random or scattered fragments of sudden spiritual explosions.

So, with all of that as introduction, we come at last to Jesus himself...

Chris Green: Jesus' Self-Understanding

With Chris Green's paper, we uncover a major fault line which runs through much contemporary discussion. The puzzle, however, is that until I read his paper I had not associated this fault line with anything specifically Pentecostal. Indeed, the point I made above, about the way in which the Pentecostal and charismatic emphasis had reintroduced the pietist and evangelical traditions to the fact that God is interested in bodies, in physicality, and therefore also in the real life of social, cultural, and political communities, might have suggested that we would be hearing from Pentecostal or charismatic theologians a ringing endorsement of the necessity of understanding Jesus himself within the historical, cultural, and political context of his times. But no: Dr Green wants to take us away from that dangerous (scriptural) landscape, and into the safe haven of the Church's later tradition. In what sense is this 'Pentecostal'? Has Pentecostalism given up its older belief (shared with most mainline Protestantism) in the authority of Scripture over all traditions? Does it no longer believe in the Word as the authority, and the Wind of the Spirit a blowing fresh air through the dusty corridors of the traditional Church?

Dr Green's remarks about imitating the *faith* of Jesus, and his concluding section about the work of Elisabeth Sisson, do indeed come from the Pentecostal tradition, though these sections then sit (in my view) uncomfortably beside the main thrust of his piece, which seems to me not so much Pentecostal as postliberal (Hauerwas, Jenson, and so forth, in a line going back to Hans Frei). My response is therefore only partly to a specifically 'Pentecostal' emphasis, and more particularly to Dr Green's expression of a strand of modern American thought which has attained considerable popularity in recent years. I welcome the opportunity to engage with this, though I have already done so at more length elsewhere. I draw attention in particular to an article which at one point I thought Dr Green was going to discuss but which he appears to ignore: 'Whence and Whither Historical Jesus Studies in the Life of the Church', pp. 115-58 in the volume *Jesus, Paul and the People of God* edited by Hays and Perrin (2011). Green cites my much briefer 'Response to Richard Hays' in the same volume, but it is in this much longer article where several of his main points are actually addressed head on. I might also cite my recent books *Simply Jesus* (2011) and *How God Became King* (2012), where I restate what I think we can and must say about Jesus, and develop the more positive case I want to make about the way we should read the canonical Gospels. There are many misunderstandings in these areas which it would be good to set to rest, and I hope that that article, and those books, might go some way in this direction. What follows is a brief summary of arguments that really demand much fuller airing.

One initial problem comes in Green's suggestion that I emphasize Jesus' own faith in order to provide a model for us to imitate. As I have said elsewhere, I regard the 'imitation of Jesus' as of only limited value: a bit like my trying to imitate the world's greatest golfer, or pianist. If not actually absurd, that could simply collapse into the 'Jesus-the-great-moral-example' mistake, as though the purpose of the incarnation was simply to show us 'how it's done'. Green, clearly, does not intend that, but I am not quite sure what he does intend instead. Certainly I was not exploring Jesus' own personal faith with that in mind. I do indeed believe that when we read the story of Gethsemane and similar moments in Jesus' life we can find all kinds of echoes in our own life of faith. But the potential analogy between Jesus' sense of vocation and ours was intended to illuminate what we can say about Jesus, not what we can say in reverse. However, that is not really the point.

Green's example of one particular Pentecostal theologian seems to me to cut against what he elsewhere argues. Elisabeth Sisson is indeed creative and interesting, but she seems to me – from what Green cites – to be seriously mishandling both Scripture and tradition. Scripture: her reinterpretation of Gethsemane is at best idiosyncratic and at worst simply distorting the text. Tradition: though she claims to be giving weight to Jesus' humanity, her point seems to negate it, so that the human Jesus has no role to play except that of submission. But in Nicene and Chalcedonian orthodoxy the full humanity of Jesus is affirmed, and unless that is a mere gesture one must enquire what in fact it means, not allow it to be squashed out of sight.

It is the full humanity of Jesus, in fact, which I have done my best to explore over the last thirty years or so. So much of the western tradition, not least in the last two hundred years, has been implicitly docetic ('Jesus wasn't really human; he only seemed to be'). Many, not least within 'evangelical' and 'charismatic' circles, are brought up to believe that Jesus was really 'God in disguise', appearing to be human but actually being more like a 'Superman' figure; indeed, the 'Superman' myth is precisely a Christian heresy. This has then bred a suspicion: supposing he was 'just a man' after all? Faced with that challenge, western Christians have been eager to 'prove that Jesus was divine', mostly using arguments which remain deeply unconvincing (including C.S. Lewis's famous 'Liar, Lunatic, or Lord', which depends [a] on a particular understanding of some sayings of Jesus and [b] on those sayings being accurately reported – both of which are of course regularly questioned). So we have had a stand-off, which falls readily enough into the false either/or of post-Enlightenment thought, owing much here to a revival of Epicureanism. Forced to choose between 'divinity' and 'humanity' the liberal tradition has gone for Jesus-the-Man, and tried to work up from there ('Christology from below'), while the conservative tradition has gone for Jesus-the-God, and tried to include enough humanity to make sense ('Christology from above'). While that debate has rumbled on, many biblical scholars have assumed that the four canonical Gospels are a mixture of trustworthy and untrustworthy traditions, and that they will have to sift out the wheat from the chaff using historical research, sometimes called historical criticism or 'the historical-critical method' (though in fact there is no single such 'method', but rather a variety of approaches). How can we proceed in this confusion? Must we give up historical study of Jesus and, as Dr Green wants us to do, rely entirely on the Nicene and later traditions to tell us what the Gospels are actually saying?

There is no space here to rehearse once more the fuller statement I set out in the rather long article, and indeed the books, I mentioned above. I hope anyone who is attracted by Dr Green's line of argument will study that material carefully, not least the historical preamble in the article (which I shall not repeat here). Let me simply summarize nine main points, of which the fourth subdivides into a further eight.

First, the great early creeds are like the Church's washing line. They tell us where the Church reached agreement on matters that had occasioned fierce controversy and thus necessitated fresh formulation. They were never intended as a complete syllabus of what Christians believed (or ought to believe). I love the creeds, and say them *ex animo* in my daily and weekly prayers. I have not 'rejected' them; I have no intention of being 'unfaithful' to them. But they do not tell me everything that Scripture tells me, and if I thought they did I would be distorting Scripture.

Second, the creeds omit, in particular, what is central to the canonical Gospels: Jesus' launching of God's Kingdom, on earth as in heaven. It is the canon itself, not some dodgy historical reconstruction 'behind' it, that insists on the absolute centrality of Jesus' Kingdom-announcement, in deed and word. It is the canon itself that insists on understanding who Jesus was, what his death accomplished, and what his resurrection and ascension meant, in terms of this Kingdom-inauguration. Words like 'canon' and 'tradition' have become in certain circles mantras to be murmured almost as charms, to ward off the baleful influence of historical scholarship. This will not do. It is the canon itself to which I am appealing. That is why, for instance, Dominic Crossan once called me an 'elegant fundamentalist'. My answer to that has always been that it is a strange kind of 'scientific' historical enquiry which regards as a scholarly virtue the ability to jettison most of the primary evidence.

Third, this emphasis on Jesus' launching of God's Kingdom challenges the large swathe of western Christianity for whom it would be just fine if Jesus had been born of a virgin and died on a cross and never done anything particular in between. If that was true, Matthew, Mark, Luke, and John wasted a lot of time – theirs, and ours. It challenges those who allow the creeds' single mention of the Kingdom ('and his Kingdom will have no end', placed after the promise of the second coming) to imply, which I think it never did, that the Kingdom will *only* be inaugurated at that moment. The canonical Gospels (again, not some shakily reconstructed pseudo-historical theory 'behind' them) insist on this point: read, for instance, Mt. 28.18.

Fourth, drawing this out further: to say all this is not to go 'behind' the four canonical Gospels. It is to insist on *reading the Gospels themselves* and letting *them* tell us the full story of Jesus. To suppose, as Dr Green suggests, that we can only 'identify' Jesus through the creeds, raises several puzzles, including the question of how Christians in the first two or three centuries managed it. (Through the 'regula fidei', perhaps? That, too, omits the Kingdom). Not to make the first three points above is to privilege tradition over Scripture; does Dr Green realise where that would lead? Or, if he wants to privilege *some* traditions over against others (screening out, for instance, the strongly traditional beliefs about Mary), on what basis does he do so? If the answer is, 'by appealing to Scripture', well, yes: let's do that.

This point needs expanding, in nine further sub-points.

> i. Yes, 'historical criticism' (remember, there is no single method or movement of that name) has often tried to go 'behind the text', and to claim that this is the only way to discover the 'real' Jesus. Yes, this supposed 'real Jesus' has often been the cut-down merely-human Jesus of modern liberalism.
>
> ii. But the 'historical-critical method' is not the only way of doing 'history'. It emerged from particular philosophical and theological movements, and was from the first designed to have this truncating effect. We should no more abandon 'history' because of this distortion than we should abandon money because some people are corrupt or sex because some people are perverted. To reject historical study of what the Gospels are actually saying on the grounds that 'historical criticism' goes *behind* the Gospels is a blatant excuse for not paying attention to what the Gospels *in their own context* are actually saying – as opposed to the shrunken, often Kingdom-less reading that has become endemic.
>
> iii. The central theme of the four Gospels is that, in and through Jesus, God's Kingdom was breaking in 'on earth as in heaven'; that the Word was becoming Flesh. *This means that the Gospels themselves insist on historical reality*, not merely abstract theological truth. It also means that we cannot assume in advance that the way the later Church has read the Gospels, both their overall narrative and their particular key phrases, corresponds to what the first

writers meant. As an obvious example of somewhere where the first-century Jewish context is forgotten (as happened fairly early), note how readers understood the phrases 'son of God' and 'son of man' as rough indicators of 'humanity' and 'divinity', forgetting the much more specific meanings which those phrases carried at the time.

iv. If we are not constantly referring back to first-century history, anachronistic distortions will inevitably creep in. Some of these are comparatively harmless: to read Jesus' language about the 'good shepherd' in terms of a romantic pastoral scene will sustain devotion, even if it misses the obvious first-century messianic and political resonances. Some distortions, however, are toxic: that was why Ernst Käsemann insisted on re-starting the 'Quest' in the 1950s, in reaction to the way the picture of 'Jesus' had been manipulated to serve the Third Reich, a process which had been made easier by people saying that we should not try to recover the historical portrait of Jesus! History – proper history, not covert scepticism – is a vital defence against such distortions.

v. The older 'Quest for the Historical Jesus' grew out of the challenge of the Enlightenment: did these things really happen, or was Jesus simply a charismatic young Jewish teacher and/or political leader with no thought of incarnation or atonement? This question has become massive in the last two hundred years, not least in America where *Time* magazine, CNN, and many other media outlets continually ask, 'Did it really happen?' The sceptical position assumes, of course, that 'the Church' made up the 'divine' Jesus in order to sustain and legitimate its own belief and (by the fourth century) its emerging political status. However unhistorical that may be, if we today respond to this challenge simply by saying, 'Never mind about history, this is what our Church tradition teaches', we are simply repeating, and thereby reinforcing, the sneer of the cynic. That's what they assume we are doing: sharing our private fantasies with one another, while they, the sceptics, live in the 'real' world. We might just about get away with that if, and only if, the message of the Gospels had to do with an otherworldly spirituality and a heaven-not-earth hope. Once again, however, the Gospels' language about the Kingdom 'on earth as in heaven' means that the sceptics' questions must be addressed, even if this requires us to think harder about historical method in order to do so.

vi. The canonical Gospels (unlike some elements in the non-canonical ones!) present us with a *vulnerable* Jesus: a Jesus who could be misunderstood, vilified, plotted against, sneered at, and finally spat upon, beaten up, and crucified. This is part of what it meant for him to be genuinely human. That remains the case. *Precisely if we believe in the 'divinity' of the Jesus presented in the canon of Scripture, we must affirm, not as an accident but as a matter of central importance, that God Incarnate was at the mercy of all that abuse.* And, as I shall elaborate presently, Scripture gives us no other God than the God we see embodied in Jesus. If we try to defend Jesus from the sneers and attacks of historical critics, we are in danger of making the same mistake as Peter did when he drew his sword in the garden of Gethsemane. The more strongly we believe (as I do) in Jesus as God Incarnate, and in the central importance of the canon of Scripture as opposed to other things we can reconstruct out of it, the more strongly we must affirm this – and, with it, the necessity of 'doing history', of following the true historical Jesus even when he leads us to places where, like the disciples at the time, we might prefer not to go.

vii. It will not do to appeal to the resurrection, and to the present status of Jesus as the ascended Lord, already reigning (again, as in Mt. 28.18, Phil. 2.10-11, and elsewhere), as though this meant we could now safely leave 'history' behind. Jesus, says Heb. 13.8, is 'the same yesterday, today and for ever'. It is easy, sometimes fatally easy, to imagine a 'Jesus' who will conform to our hopes or fantasies. The only way for faith in the present and future Jesus to be properly anchored is in the 'yesterday' of actual events. The risen and ascended Jesus is precisely *the risen and ascended crucified Kingdom-bringer*, and to make him anything else is to worship an invention of our own.

viii. It is actually the later Church tradition that has 'gone behind' the Gospels, to the supposed dogmatic scheme which it then discerns. Every time someone writes or preaches about Jesus without factoring his Kingdom-announcement into their thinking, understanding that in its first-century historical context, they are doing exactly that. The result – evident in much preaching and teaching – is that most of the material in the Gospels is reduced to the status of stories illustrating incarnation or atonement.

ix. The history of Jesus – the Jesus we find in the four Gospels, whom the Church has often ignored – is therefore a central element in the teaching and preaching, including the apologia, of the Church. Here we meet again the problem that many (not least some in the Barthian tradition) are allergic to any sense of 'apologetics', warning quite rightly against the rationalist danger of supposing we can mount an argument, based on some supposedly 'neutral' foundation, through which we can convince anyone but the stupid or stubborn. The problem comes in the identifying of any 'bridge' between the present creation and the new one launched with Jesus: how (it is asked) can there be anything but Jesus himself from which we can reason forwards? The answer is: precisely so; and in the Church's own canonical Gospels we have exactly that, Jesus himself, launching God's sovereign and saving rule on earth as in heaven, going to the cross to complete that work, and rising again as himself embodying the new creation, free at last from the shackles of sin and death which were defeated on the cross. That new creation is then extended by the Spirit to his followers, who will then go out, still vulnerable and mysterious, into all the world, celebrating and announcing him as its rightful lord. If the Church is not constantly 'doing history' in terms of understanding the Jesus of the Gospels in his own context, the context where the Church's canonical Scriptures themselves place him, we should not be surprised if our language about God, faith, and hope sounds to the rest of the world as though we are simply talking to ourselves in a private little bubble. Indeed, telling the story of Jesus and his launching of the Kingdom was one of the primary tasks of the early Church, as the basis for all that they were now doing. (This shows just how far wrong Bultmann and his whole tradition had gone. The tragedy is how many in evangelical and related traditions have gone that way too).

Fifth, and picking up from this last point, it is central to the Church's canon (for instance, in John 1 or Colossians 1) that we only know who 'God' actually is if we are looking at Jesus. 'No-one has seen God; the only-begotten son has revealed him'; 'He is the image of the invisible God'. In other words, *it is only as we are looking at Jesus that we even know who 'God' is*, and hence of course what the word 'divinity' might even mean. Not to do this is to run the constant risk of Docetism, which as I said has been a besetting sin of many parts of the western Church, not least among evangelicals, charismatics, and others. And looking at Jesus means looking at the real Jesus, not an imaginary one who doesn't quite fit with the historical portrait set out in the Gospels. If Hans Frei really said that God didn't intend us to find him in this way, the canonical Scriptures themselves shout him down. The abstract categories used by later theology, including the Chalcedonian definition, are certainly pointing in the right direction; that is, as Christians we must of course say that Jesus is fully divine and fully human. But we only know what 'divine' and 'human' mean in the light of Jesus himself; we do not 'know' them in advance and then simply insist that they are true of him. And in the Gospels – read, once more, in their historical context – we see, not abstract categories of 'divine' and 'human', but two major strands: first, the return of Israel's God, YHWH, to his people, as long promised; second, Israel's Messiah, confessed as such, though with confusion, by Peter at Caesarea Philippi, hailed as such, though with heavy irony, by Caiaphas and Pilate. What the canonical Gospels offer us is the explosive fusion of these two great biblical strands, which we already see converging in

Daniel and Isaiah: God's promise about his own return, and God's promise to send his Messiah. In Jesus, these parallel lines meet. Those dense phrases, 'son of God' and 'son of Man' do indeed point to this fusion of identities, though not in the ways often assumed. By itself, Chalcedon always looked like a confidence trick, a kind of *credo quia absurdum*. Its Greek categories can be read – and I do so read them – as accurate signposts pointing to the first-century Jewish reality of Jesus as YHWH in person and as Israel's Messiah, and to those two things as being simultaneously true of him.

Sixth, therefore, the 'divinity' of Jesus is affirmed right through all four Gospels (not only in John, as used to be thought). Mark begins by quoting passages in Isaiah and Malachi which are about preparing for the return of YHWH to Zion – and then shows us Jesus. Matthew and Luke have their own ways of saying the same thing. John, of course, introduces us to the Word made Flesh. All these mean what they mean within the world of first-century Judaism, not so easily within the world of third- or fourth-century dogma, though that dogma was doing its best, often rather splendidly, to capture in a different culture and idiom the rich and powerful truth which was already there in Scripture. But, as the Church has moved away from the early and Jewish world of meaning, it has regularly collapsed all this into a fog of misunderstanding: for instance, when the word Χριστός is read either simply as a proper name (as Dr Green sometimes uses it) or as a code for 'the divine one' (as he sometimes seems to be suggesting). But part of my point is that though we might wish – in the post-Enlightenment world, let alone the post-Chalcedon world – that the Gospels were written to affirm, or explain, the 'divinity' of Jesus, that is a distortion. *The 'divinity' of Jesus is the key in which the music is set, but it is not the tune that is being played.* The tune the Gospels are playing is the launching of the Kingdom; and their framing of this, the 'key' for the music, is the belief that Jesus held together in himself the dual identity of Israel's God and Israel's Messiah.

Seventh, then, what can and must we say about Jesus himself in all of this? It is, I suppose, easy to caricature my position by saying that I reject the Church's tradition by declaring it impossible to accept that Jesus 'knew himself to be God'. Anyone who sets out to oppose the powerful latent Docetism in western Christianity is perhaps going to be open to that charge. What I have tried to do, however, is different. I have tried, precisely in faithfulness to Nicaea and Chalcedon, to think historically about what it might have meant for Jesus himself to be the living embodiment of Israel's returning and redeeming God and simultaneously the long-awaited Messiah in whom Israel's destiny was summed up. Some theologians, in earlier times and once again today, have spoken of Jesus having, in effect, two 'minds'. I regard this as the result of a failure to think through the scriptural basis and the Jewish context of what the four Gospels are actually saying. What must we say about Jesus if Chalcedon was a true signpost back to that canonical vision? *That (a) he believed himself to be Israel's Messiah, and (b) he believed himself to be the embodiment of the returning and redeeming God of Israel*, and that he held this double belief as a matter of faith-awareness of his vocation, conceived in the light of his own reading of Israel's Scriptures and his own intimate awareness of the one he called 'Abba'. Why do I not normally call this 'knowledge'? Because that, in my experience, has often gone with the Docetic view in which Jesus ends up not quite being human – and not quite being Jewish! – but being, rather, a 'god' of our imagining, known not in the flesh but despite it. When people hear the word 'knowledge' today, in contemporary western culture, they often collapse it towards a supposedly 'scientific' idea in which one has provable certainty and no doubt. That is, to be sure, a shallow idea of 'knowledge', but if I were to say that 'Jesus knew himself to be God incarnate' that is what many would hear (and it is what many devout Christians, alas, would *want* to hear). I am holding out for a different sort of 'knowledge', the kind that goes with music, and faith, and love. And, yes, vocation. Call it 'vocation-knowledge', if you like; or perhaps 'faith-knowledge'. But the minute that this 'knowledge' fails to leave room for temptation, doubt, or despair – in other words, for Gethsemane and the cry from the cross – it has tipped over into the shallow, over-bright 'knowledge' in which Jesus ceases to be genuinely human; in which, in other words, the great double emphasis precisely of the Church's tradition, which Dr Green accuses me of abandoning, has itself been lost. (I know many people who have been deeply hurt by the pastoral outflow of this kind of teaching, with its implication that we, too, ought to have that kind of 'certainty'). One of the most important things that Jesus reveals to be true of the one creator God, the God of Israel, is that this God consists, through and through, of *love*: the love that humbles itself, the love that reveals its power in weakness, the love that overthrows the power of the world by a different power altogether. This, too, the canonical Gospels say most clearly (e.g. Mk 10.35-45), and Paul of course strongly confirms it (Phil. 2.6-11).

Eighth, what is missing from so many contemporary discussions of Christology is what the New Testament insists on: the Temple. The Temple was the place where heaven and earth met; Jesus himself spoke and acted as though *he* were that place instead, and the early Church picked up and developed this theme. Paul, indeed, sees the Church as that place, indwelt by the Spirit ('indwelling' being itself a 'Temple'-motif). One might suppose that this would be a natural and fruitful theme for Pentecostal theologians to explore.

Ninth, and finally, the whole point about the gospel is that it is public truth. It was not 'done in a corner'. Jesus did not come to set up a private world into which people could escape from the real one. The first article of the great Creeds is belief in God the Father Almighty, *Creator* of heaven and earth. At that point the great tradition is exactly on the same page as the canon of Scripture. What we have in the canonical Gospels – as opposed both to the gnostic so-called gospels on the one hand and to many contemporary readings on the other – is the story of how the creator launched his new creation from within the heart of the old. Jesus' resurrection is the point where this is clearest: his risen body is the same body as the crucified one, only now transformed so as no longer to be subject to corruption and death. The empty tomb is no mere shibboleth guarding a 'supernatural' event. It is the sign that the new creation has begun. And the Spirit is the means by which people are caught up in this, and even become its agents in their turn. Again, this might be a fruitful theme for Pentecostal theology to develop. But it will only mean what it means in the canonical Gospels themselves if they are read with a resolute eye to the first-century history which those Gospels are claiming to describe. Of course, facing that challenge demands hard work, of a kind which some systematic and philosophical theologians seem unwilling even to imagine, let alone undertake. But it is the tradition itself – by speaking of the full humanity as well as full divinity of Jesus – which commands us to undertake it. And it is the canonical Gospels, not some supposed reconstruction 'behind', 'above', or 'beyond' them, that welcome us and offer us the material we need for this task.

I come back where I started. I was, and am, surprised to meet this challenge, so familiar to me in other contexts, within a volume of Pentecostal theology. I associate Pentecostalism with a strong insistence on the word of Scripture as the ultimate authority, and an equally strong insistence on the fresh wind of the Spirit as the energy with which we undertake all our tasks. To appeal (and then selectively) to 'tradition' sounds to me precisely like the sort of thing one would expect from the *enemies* of Pentecostalism, those who were comfortable with the way things were and who didn't want the rushing wind to disturb the papers on the desk or the dust on the Bible. If the Spirit really is given to reveal to us more and more about Jesus (Jn 16.12-15), this cannot be a different Jesus from the one described by Matthew, Mark, Luke, and John, the first-century Jew whom subsequent centuries, and subsequent cultural shifts, have struggled to describe. History matters because the canonical Scriptures matter; the canonical Scriptures matter because Jesus matters. To appeal to 'tradition' over the head of the canonical Scriptures, and the Jesus whom they present in his historical context, is like hoping that the cookery book will provide the meal for you, saving you the time and bother of shopping at the store or standing over the stove. Of course, the book will then help you cook the meal; but a hungry family would prefer to have the food without the book, even if you have to improvise the recipe (a good Pentecostal thing to do?), rather than the book without the food.

Timothy Senapatiratne: Worldview and Hermeneutics

Dr Senapatiratne has provided an interesting angle on hermeneutics, arguing that if I were to include a more thought-out role for the Spirit in my approach it would enable me to avoid problems that I otherwise seem to encounter. That may, in those general terms, be correct. I suspect that all of us, Pentecostals included, could always use more explicit invocation of the Spirit, though as I shall suggest this cannot become a means of avoiding the hard work of history and theology. God can, if he wishes, lift the prophet up by a lock of his hair and take him somewhere else – or, in New Testament terms, 'catch up' a wandering evangelist like Philip and transport him to a different location. But most of us, most of the time, while being equally dependent on the Spirit, somehow find that we nevertheless need to consult a map, pack a lunch, find somewhere to stay, and make the journey mile by mile by whatever means may be available. If, transposing this metaphor to hermeneutics, we suddenly experience a Spirit-given acceleration of the process of understanding the text, that is wonderful; but – and this will be important – we cannot then expect anyone else to follow us. We may be sure we have arrived at our destination, but if we want people to share our joy they may well have to use the map and make the journey in the normal fashion.

But before we get to that point I have a worry about Dr Senapatiratne's discussion of my 'worldview' model. The fact that he can line it up creatively with the Wesleyan quadrilateral, towards the end of his essay, makes me wonder whether he has fully understood what I mean by 'worldview', or what role it was playing in my argument. The Quadrilateral (and its various alternatives in other traditions) is designed to map the way in which *the biblical text becomes authoritative for the Church and the Christian*. That is a much more focused and specific exercise than anything I was envisaging with 'worldview'. The 'worldview' model, as I set it out in *The New Testament and the People of God* (hereafter *NTPG*) and developed it in subsequent books, is designed for a quite different purpose, namely to help us understand cultures and their cultural products – any cultures, any cultural products, of which the first-century Jewish and Christian cultures are two specific examples which I then explore in Parts III and IV of that same book.

The point of the 'worldview' model was to draw on insights from various sources to try to map, in multi-layered detail, the underlying worldview of those Jewish and Christian communities. I need to stress – because this is not always clear in the essay – that a worldview, in my sense, is not what you look *at*, but what you look *through*. It is the network, the grid, of normally unspoken and unexamined assumptions. When Dr Senapatiratne suggests that the 'stories' in a worldview give you advice and insight into ways of creating a system of praxis by which to live, this is precisely *not* what I was talking about. The elements of a worldview – in which 'story' is not privileged, as he suggests, but simply one of the four elements, along with symbol, praxis, and questions (or rather, answers to questions) – interlock in multiple ways, but again this is, so to speak, 'below the radar', not an account of what people are consciously thinking or reasoning. Conscious thinking and reasoning, as I explain at various points, is what happens when they come to articulate their beliefs and their aims, to themselves or to others. But, because cultures other than our own (and sometimes our own as well) are often puzzling, and if we try to guess at 'what's really going on' we regularly guess wrong, the worldview analysis is a way of digging down underneath these explicit and openly stated beliefs and aims to get a more rounded, many-sided picture of why people think, speak, and live in the way they do.

Part of the result of my worldview analysis in *NTPG* was the specific argument that, since most Jews and (so far as we can tell) all early Christians had as part of their worldview the implicit narrative that the one God was the good creator of a good world and that he would one day restore it, their language about God's presence and action in the world was to be taken, at least *prima facie*, as a sign that when they were writing about Jesus they really did intend to refer to events that actually took place. As I suggested in my response to Dr Chris Green, history mattered for them. It may help to point out that I was writing, after several years of teaching in the 1970s and 1980s, in a world where students were regularly bombarded with books and articles pointing out (for instance) that the Sermon on the Mount reflected 'Matthew's theology', or perhaps 'Matthew's community's theology', with the constantly implied conclusion 'therefore this quite likely wasn't what actually happened, what Jesus actually said'. Here is the false either-or to which 'critical realism', in the rather basic form in which I articulated it in 1992, was my attempt at an answer. Against an older positivism which saw a text and deduced a set of 'facts', the mainstream biblical criticism of the postwar years went the other way, seeing a text and deducing a community in which that text was 'really about' their own life and spirituality. It may be hard, now, to realise just how powerful and prevalent that line of thought was (though it still holds sway in some quarters today, of course). That problem was what I was trying to address. Of course, a 'critical realist' reading of, say, the Parable of the Prodigal Son would not result in saying 'Well, perhaps this actually happened': part of the 'critical' bit is to assess the genre of the text or part of the text. But I was addressing a world where people like the late Norman Perrin took it for granted (for instance) that Mark had no intention of writing about 'things that actually happened', and that Luke was odd because, misunderstanding Mark, he wrote as if these things *did* actually happen, and as if this mattered.

In that context, I was specifically and carefully avoiding any collapse back into the positivist trap, and I am surprised that there should be any doubt about that. Of course, those for whom all early Christian literature is 'about' the closed worldview of the community that reads the text may be offended that I think the canonical Gospels intended to describe actual events; but to accuse me of 'positivism' for affirming that they did so is strange, since positivism collapses the hermeneutical distance between knower and object, and that is what I carefully did not do. However, that is incidental to Dr Senapatiratne's main line of thought.

What is more important is to note how history works. Historians really can speak, not as naïve positivists but as critical realists, about things that really did happen. As I said earlier in another context, we really do know that Jerusalem fell in AD 70; that Jesus of Nazareth died by crucifixion; and so on. All kinds of evidence converge at those points. History does not, need not, collapse into a function of the mind of reporters and their communities. When Josephus tells us about the death of Herod the Great, we may question some of his details but we do not say, 'Well, that's just Josephus's idea', or 'that made sense in Josephus's community'. (We presume that this is true as well but not that the whole story was a fiction). The Bultmann school was always anxious about affirming the historical value of the Gospel records, because they were afraid of basing 'faith' on 'history' and so (from their point of view) turning 'faith' into a 'work', something one could build on rather than simply trusting God. This was, and is, a radical mistake. That is what I was getting at. Of course, it is perfectly possible for people to make things up, to write books which look like history but which do not in fact correspond to what actually happened. And of course 'what actually happened' is a loaded phrase: from whose point of view? With whose interpretation? I discussed all those questions in *NTPG*. My point at the moment is simply that history is *possible*. That includes the history of the implied stories, symbols, praxis, and questions that go to make up the worldview of this or that community.

This brings us at last to the question of the interpretation and authority of Scripture, which is more or less a completely different question from the ones I have been discussing. Of course, the question of history does come into this; if the Gospel writers were in fact following 'cunningly devised myths' (2 Pet. 1.16), then anyone who cites the Gospels as evidence about Jesus himself might be deceived. But I do not think that was the question Dr Senapatiratne was addressing; nor do I think that one would be wise to invoke the Holy Spirit in order to bypass the normal process of determining whether a text actually refers to historical events or not. (For instance, it is by recognising the genre of 'parable', not by invoking the Spirit, that one knows that 'the Prodigal Son' is not intended as a description of historical events). However, yes, of course: whenever a church reflects on its teaching and life, and whenever it does so (as it should) in the light of Scripture, it makes all the sense in the world to pray for, and to trust, the guidance of the Holy Spirit – as long as it is clear that, while the Spirit can and does give all sorts of insight, this cannot then be taken as providing the 'correct' answer to the questions, What does the text say?, and What does it mean for us today? I have sat through enough church meetings, Synods, and the like to be wary when someone gets up and declares that the Holy Spirit has revealed to them that such-and-such a text means this, or that. As the First Letter of John indicates, we must test the spirits, and arrive at wise discernment, not invoke the Spirit so we don't have to think.

That throws into sharp relief the question of 'experience' as part of the Wesleyan Quadrilateral. As I have noted in my book on scriptural authority (now in a second edition with extra material, under the title of *Scripture and the Authority of God*), the appeal to 'experience' is a different *kind* of thing from the appeal to 'Scripture', 'tradition', and 'reason'. In fact, they are all different sorts of things, and 'Scripture' is the foundation for the others: 'tradition' is 'what the Church has said as it has read Scripture', and 'reason' is not an independent faculty, but is about thinking clearly, and not talking nonsense, as we read Scripture. 'Experience', however, is different again. There is a sense in which the whole notion of 'authority' is about something which *addresses* 'experience' and calls it to order, not something which arises from it. Every generation of Christians has recognised that some 'experiences' (think of Paul writing to

Corinth!) are misleading if not positively dangerous. Of course, as Christians in every tradition (not only Pentecostals) have recognised, the faith and obedience of the Church as it listens to Scripture is not something which bypasses the feeling, thinking, knowing heart of the Church and of individual Christians. The trouble is that today 'experience' is often invoked to perform tasks which are quite different from Wesley's insistence on a personal heart-knowledge of the gospel. One hears 'experience' invoked constantly, for instance, as the fixed point from which clear scriptural teaching, clear traditional practice, and even clear thinking about both, can be set aside. In my experience, those who have argued most strongly for the inclusion of 'experience' in fresh formulations of 'authority' were hoping thereby, not to reintroduce a Wesleyan sense of the heart being strangely warmed, but the possibility that emotional experiences of various kinds might become self-authenticating even if they appeared to violate Scripture, tradition, and reason. That is not, of course, what Dr Senapatiratne has in mind, but it is widespread, and any fresh integration of 'experience' with a larger model of scriptural interpretation and authority must beware of such a conclusion.

So where does this leave us? I fully agree that we need to work out more explicitly how the Holy Spirit works in relation to the larger interpretative task of the Church as it reads Scripture and tries to live under its authority. And, in giving an account of that work, we might well invoke the worldview-model, not as a kind of shadowy version of the Quadrilateral, but as something quite different: an under-the-microscope study of what the authors of Scripture assumed and took for granted, to make sure that we are interpreting their words in accordance with their overall life, rather than foisting our ideas back on to them in an anachronistic fashion (which has of course been all too common in the Church). And we might also use the worldview-model to uncover the deep, buried assumptions we today hold about all kinds of things, bringing them into consciousness (always a difficult thing to do) so that, if they need radical adjustment in the light of the gospel, we can attempt that task. And, yes, in this work in particular the Church would be foolish not to invoke the powerful, loving, healing presence of the Holy Spirit. To the extent that some of us may not always have made that explicit, the contribution of our Pentecostal friends will always, like the present essay, be most welcome.

Rick Wadholm Jr.: Justification and the Cry of the Spirit

I am grateful to Rick Wadholm for his clear and accurate summary of my work. These matters are of course complex, and from time to time I wanted to nudge him into looking at more exegetical details (see below). But overall he is right: I have tried, throughout my theological writing, to show that the Spirit is necessary for any full Pauline theology of justification. (See, for instance, my early attempt at this in my study of the English reformer John Frith: *The Work of John Frith* [Appleford: Sutton Courtenay Press, 1983].) So I basically agree with more or less everything that has been said here, and welcome the insights from Barth and Bonhoeffer as fully consistent with what I have tried to argue.

I have only two comments to make. First, I am aware in particular that the integration of the Spirit with justification has appeared more natural within the reformed traditions than within the Lutheran traditions. I do not think (though I may be wrong here) that Pentecostalism has a strong link to either, but I suspect that in some Pentecostal thinking at least there may be a bifurcation between an implicitly Lutheran theology of justification, on the one hand, and a quite different theology of Spirit-indwelling on the other. This corresponds very broadly to the way in which the churches have often read the first eight chapters of the letter to the Romans in two quite different halves: chapters 1–4, on justification, and chapters 5–8, on 'sanctification', the Spirit, holiness, and so forth. Since the Spirit is hardly mentioned in Romans 1–4 (and the one exception, 2.25-29, is routinely downplayed), people have imagined that Paul's doctrine of justification, for which those chapters are cited as a *locus classicus*, can be stated without reference to the Spirit. I have argued in many places that this division is a mistake, and that though there is undoubtedly a change of gear at Romans 5 we should take the short passage about the Spirit at the end of ch. 2 as an indication that Paul is already crafting the theology which he will explore in ch. 8. The whole of Romans 1–8 is about justification, and within that the Spirit's role is central and vital.

Second, I am not quite sure that I have fully understood the point being made about the 'cry' of the Spirit in Romans 8 and Galatians 4. Interpreters have sometimes tried to align this with early recitals of the Lord's Prayer, and sometimes – especially with the passage in Romans 8 – with glossolalia. Neither seems to me quite to fit. However, the Spirit-induced recognition and awareness of the creator God as 'father' does seem to be one of the points at which we discern, in the flow of Paul's dense theological argument, a deeply 'personal' and even 'emotional' response: grateful love answering parental love. So many lines of thought in Paul either begin or end with love, that we shouldn't be surprised that justification does as well. And when we speak of love, we speak, of course, of the first element in 'the fruit of the Spirit'. So, yes: justification and the Spirit. Which leads us to the next short paper.

Frank D. Macchia: Justification and the Spirit

Once again, I am grateful for this clear and helpful presentation of my view of what Paul says about justification. I am not surprised at Dr Macchia's protest about my supposed over-constraining of 'justification' itself. In line with Michael Gorman's important work, he notes that I closely correlate what Paul says about justification with more or less all the other major themes in his soteriology. This is a discussion which has been running for some time, and will continue to do so.

However, I do want to register an anxiety with being pushed in this direction. Dr Macchia picks up my image of the car and the steering wheel, and suggests that 'justification' is the whole car seen from one angle. That, in my view, remains to be demonstrated. Yes, Paul's language of justification is closely correlated with more or less everything else he says about the start, the process, and the completion of the work of salvation. Yes, we should not split up 'juridical' and 'participationist' language as though they belong in quite different theological boxes; though I notice that Sanders, though saying that Paul mixes them indiscriminately, nevertheless basically follows Albert Schweitzer in privileging 'participation' as the more fundamental category. (He does, however, indicate that what precisely Paul meant by his participation language is harder to discern than people often think). And yes, we must tease out as carefully as we can how all this relates to the Jewish law (I have written a good deal more on that in *PFG*).

And yet. Part of our problem is the Greek word δικαιοσύνη, which already by Paul's day carried so many meanings that we have no equivalent, not even a somewhat close equivalent, in English or any other modern language known to me. It can obviously carry 'ethical' overtones, and some have tried to reduce it to that (probably in service of an 'imputed righteousness' theology nested within a 'covenant of works' framework, so that 'righteousness' need mean only 'moral goodness' all the way through). This seems to me profoundly wrong in view of Paul's extended lawcourt metaphor in Romans 3 and his extended covenantal discussion in Romans 4 and Galatians 3. (Note, too, Phil. 3.2-11, where many themes which elsewhere in Paul are sketched separately are found together). But when we try, as I have tried, to integrate at least these three – moral, forensic, and covenantal – within Paul's argument about Jews and Gentiles coming together into the single family of Abraham, and when I see the job that argument does in Romans, Galatians, and Philippians alike, I am driven back to affirm that 'justification' still has to do with the quasi-legal and covenantal declaration of the status that believers have in the Messiah.

The question of status is after all not, for Paul, a matter of an abstract legal fiction. It is the ground on which the unity of God's people in the Messiah stands. Ecclesial unity is not based, for Paul, on the transformation of character through the Spirit, vital though that is as we see, for instance, in 1 Corinthians. It is based on the fact that all believers share the same *status*. That is what (for instance) Gal. 2.15-21 is about. Obviously Paul believes that Christian faith itself is the result of the Spirit's work through the gospel, and that 'he who has begun a good work in you will bring it to completion at the day of Messiah Jesus' (Phil. 1.6). Obviously Galatians 2 itself correlates the point about status and unity very closely with the transforming work of gospel and Spirit. But the *status*, as one specific point within that larger soteriology, correlated with everything else yet retaining its own particular meaning and function (the steering wheel in the car!), is the thing upon which Church unity is to be based. There is of course much more to be said about all this, and I and others continue that debate. But this is one important point to note as discussion goes forward.

Glen W. Menzies: The Dispensational Lens

I am grateful for this extraordinarily thoughtful and creative essay. Dr Menzies raises so many issues, in such an interesting manner, that it is hard to know where to break in to the sequence of thought. Let me start with two particular points to clarify.

First, I apologize for any appearance of making 'snide' remarks, in this case in *The Resurrection of the Son of God* (hereafter *RSG*), p. 215. That was not my intention. For most of my life I have heard both preachers and scholars talk about 1 Thessalonians 4 in terms, precisely, of people 'going up in the air', or 'flying up on a cloud', and when these things are discussed in both scholarly and popular circles such language is common. I have argued at length, both in *RSG* and in *Surprised by Hope* (which, by the way, would make a good conversation partner on the topics Dr Menzies is addressing), that the language of 1 Thessalonians 4, and its parallel in content though not expression with 1 Cor. 15.51-57, indicates strongly that Paul is drawing on a variety of biblical language and imagery to say what otherwise would be very difficult to say: that Jesus will 'descend' (like Moses coming down the mountain), that Jesus' people, still alive, will be vindicated (like the 'saints' in Daniel 7), and that there will be a 'meeting' like that which occurs when the citizens of a great city go out to greet their returning emperor – not in order to stay outside the city, but in order to escort him back home.

Of course, all discussion of biblical language and imagery has to proceed step by step. One cannot say 'it's all metaphorical imagery' any more than one can say 'it's all literal'. To assume that because one element is a metaphor none can be literal is simply to mistake how the language works. When Daniel 7 spoke of four monsters coming up out of the sea, his readers knew that he was not predicting literal monsters; these images were obvious and well known code to denote pagan empires and their armies. But when he said that there were four of them, this was not an image; people would expect to be able to identify which four empires he was referring to. As to the point about whether, then, we should take Paul's language of resurrection literally, the answer is, Of course; and Paul makes that abundantly clear in a great many passages, not least Rom. 8.10-11, 1 Corinthians 15 and Phil. 3.20-21. The question 'literal or metaphorical' has to be thought through passage by passage and sometimes word by word. I know how important the 'rapture' theology has been for many movements (not least in America), but I continue, for exegetical and historical reasons first and foremost, to regard it as both mistaken and misleading. But 'resurrection' language, though it can come to be used metaphorically (as in Romans 6 or Colossians 3, applying to ethical behaviour), retains its literal meaning throughout the first century and beyond, as I have argued in detail both in *RSG* and in *Surprised by Hope*.

Another small but significant matter. Dr Menzies attempts to describe my view of Paul's phrase δικαιοσύνη θεοῦ ('the righteousness of God'), but slightly misses the point. God's righteousness, I have argued at length in various places, is not the acquittal itself, not the verdict itself, but the character of God as the covenant God, God as the judge. God's righteousness is on display when he acquits, but righteousness and acquittal are not the same thing. On a similar topic, I do not think that for Paul 'faith' is the way one is incorporated into the messianic family. Faith is the sign *that one has been* incorporated into that family. The means of incorporation is grace, the Spirit, the gospel, and baptism; but that raises, of course, all sorts of other issues.

So to the somewhat larger matters. I do indeed strongly resist the suggestion of 'replacement' theology, for the good reason that in Paul – and in Jesus! – the company of God's people consist of Jesus himself, as Israel's Messiah, and those who are gathered round him, constituted by him. This makes excellent first-century sense. If Israel's Messiah actually shows up, God's Israel will be those who group themselves around him, who hail him as king, and any who decline to recognise him will be seen as self-excluded rebels. Look at the Bar-Kochba movement of 132–135 CE for an example. For Paul, there can be no doubt, as we can see in the great narrative of Rom. 9.6–10.21: the story runs from Abraham, Isaac, and Jacob, through Moses, the Exodus, the period of the monarchy and the prophets, to the exile, and then to the Messiah, in whom the 'new covenant' and 'return from exile' prophecy of Deuteronomy 30 comes true. The result is the puzzle Moses already described in Deuteronomy 32 (widely regarded in Paul's day as a long-range prophecy): Israel in rebellion, God bringing others in to make them jealous.

Obviously this raises vast issues that we cannot address here. I have had another stab at exegeting the relevant passages in chapter 11 of *PFG*, in which I note, just as Dr Menzies has done, that there is an uneasy implicit alliance between the Dispensationalists, on the one hand, who believe that Romans 11 predicts a last-minute conversion of the Jews, and the two-covenant followers of Stendahl, on the other. Each time I work through Romans 9–11 I ask myself again whether there is something there that I have missed; and so far I come back each time to the conclusion that Paul really did see Jesus as Israel's Messiah, the Messiah as Israel-in-person, and Israel as being reconstituted around that Messiah, now incorporating Gentiles as well as Jews. This is not 'replacement'; it is *inclusion*. When Paul said that all God's promises found their 'yes' in him (2 Cor. 1.20) I think he meant what he said. The Dispensationalist idea that some promises were deferred, so that one must now read the Old Testament looking for two different types of prophecy, seems to me profoundly unbiblical, unPauline, unhelpful. And the idea that some of those deferred promises were fulfilled in either 1948 or 1967 strikes me as almost blasphemous nonsense – as it strikes Ultra-Orthodox Jews, for whom any attempt to re-establish the Land until the appearance of the Messiah must be a wicked human invention.

This does *not* mean that the promises have been 'spiritualized'. Paul declares in Rom. 4.13 that God's promise to Abraham was that he would inherit – not 'the Land', but the *world*. This goes back in Jewish tradition to the development of the original Abrahamic promise through such passages as Psalm 2, where the Messiah is given 'the nations' as his 'inheritance', and 'the uttermost parts of the world' as his 'possession'. And it points on to Romans 8, where Paul uses Exodus-language to describe the pilgrimage of the redeemed people on the way to their 'inheritance'; but this 'inheritance' is neither the land of Israel, nor (of course) 'heaven', but is rather *the whole renewed creation*. The entire cosmos is now God's holy land, and to suggest that there are land-related promises still to be fulfilled is to put the new wine of the gospel (new, though promised long before) back into the old wine-skins of the temporary promises. This is exactly cognate with the extension of Abraham's family: not one nation only, but people of all nations (Romans 4, Galatians 3, etc.). The promises have not been spiritualized; they have been universalized. And, yes, the ultimate fulfillment has been postponed, in a way without precedent in other Jewish movements. But Paul believed, like the other early Christians, that Jesus was *already* ruling as Lord (1 Cor. 15.20-28), and that this rule would be consummated, visible, and complete at his 'reappearing' or 'return' (see below).

Of course the post-Holocaust situation has made all this very, very difficult to talk about. Within the postmodern climate, where the only 'argument' is the shrill claim to victimhood, many people are so eager to score political points that they cannot grasp historical arguments which they perceive as an affront to their sensibilities. But that simply makes exegetical debate impossible.

Nevertheless, there is indeed a kind of shadowy parallel between what I take to be the position of the Gospels, of Paul, and of Revelation – to look no further for the moment – and what Dr Menzies calls the 'rupture implied in Dispensationalism'. For the early Christians, the 'rupture' was precisely the crucifixion and resurrection of Israel's Messiah. What could be more of a 'break' than that? But it is a different kind of break, resulting in a very different understanding of the new world opened up by Jesus.

What then about the Parousia? Yes: I do regard Daniel 7, in itself and in its fresh use in Mk 13.26, 14.62 and the parallel passages, as referring not to the *descent* of 'one like a son of man' but to his *vindication*, his being brought to the Ancient of Days in triumphant splendour. That is the natural meaning of the passage in Daniel, and all the signs are that this is how it was taken by Mark – and, I think, by Jesus himself. I think the early Church saw the prophecy as being fulfilled in Jesus' ascension. Like all apocalyptic imagery, it was no doubt capable of fresh interpretation (*4 Ezra* [= *2 Esdras*] 12.12 says exactly that about this very passage). But we have to be careful. So much of the final chapters of Mark, and their parallels in Matthew and Luke, flow directly from Jesus' action in the Temple, and its consequences. The Church has often, sadly, taken passages which apply in one direction and tried to fit them into a scheme which is moving in a different direction. I think that has happened here. From Jesus' point of view, his own coming vindication on the one hand and the destruction of the Temple on the other were two parts of the same event, even though he knew that a generation might have to pass before this double-ended action would be complete. I can see that some would regard this as a 'partial preterite' position; I would prefer, as Dr Menzies rightly notes, to see it as 'inaugurated eschatology'. (I was amused, by the way, to be aligned even slightly with C.H. Dodd. Dodd was a fine Roman historian, and some of his work, notably his book *According to the Scriptures*, is extremely valuable. But throughout my career I have found his famous expositions of the parables, and of Romans, to be seriously deficient. He was, however, the teacher of my teacher George Caird; and, though Caird also disagreed with him, and I in turn with Caird, I owe him a debt particularly in his emphasis on the importance of locating the whole discussion within true first-century history).

Jesus had tried, largely unsuccessfully, to explain to his followers that he was going to have to die as the climax of his Kingdom-inaugurating public career. That was not in their game plan; they were still looking forward to sitting at his right and his left in his Kingdom, any day now. The only way he could speak about any future beyond that, highlighting the destruction of the Temple and his own corresponding vindication, was in the language of Jewish apocalyptic. But once he was risen and ascended (in Luke's account in Acts 1), his followers were told that he would return. They quickly interpreted this in terms of the Old Testament image of the 'day of the Lord'; we can see this already well established in Paul. Nobody had expected this kind of time-lag, with one person being raised from the dead in the middle of history and the world carrying on as before. This was quite new. The teaching about the 'second coming', though it developed from those biblical roots about the return of YHWH to Zion, was quite new as well. For myself, I believe in the Second Coming as firmly, and look forward to it as eagerly, as any Dispensationalist. But I (following Luke!) do not think that this is what Mark 13 is all about.

But the thing about Dispensationalism – if I can put it like that, and remembering many conversations with my late father-in-law – is that at least it was trying to grasp the nuanced and layered way in which, according to the New Testament, the ancient promises were being fulfilled. I think it might be easier for a Dispensationalist to grasp (what I see as) the fully biblical picture of the divine plan than for some non-Dispensational evangelicals who are innocent of any such thing, and have flattened the whole picture out into 'how I can go to heaven'. At least the Dispensationalist is looking at the larger issues: Israel, Church, world, history, promises, land, and so on – which are indeed the elements of this fully biblical picture. It's just that I don't think they line them up the way the New Testament does.

Interestingly, I receive more messages, letters, emails, and so on about my book *Surprised by Hope* than about all my other books put together. Many of those messages are from 'recovering Dispensationalists'. I realise that this will not be welcome news to all readers. But I have tried to argue the case step by step, passage by passage. As with many other controversies, all sides appeal to Scripture, and to Scripture we must go.

Janet Meyer Everts: The Communion of Saints

I much enjoyed Dr Everts' exposition of my little book *For All the Saints*. As I said in the previous response, however, my position is set out much more fully in *Surprised by Hope*, and I would like to think that Dr Everts' discussion could be taken as a signpost to that larger treatment of related issues. Actually, *For All the Saints* grew out of the same original lecture series that also produced *Surprised by Hope*. The treatment of 'saints' was aimed particularly at the strange way in which some Anglican churches have in recent years adopted bits and pieces of early modern Catholic practice for All Souls' Day (November 2), making a clear distinction between the 'saints' who are 'already in heaven' (and who are celebrated on 'All Saints' Day', November 1) and the 'souls' of the great majority – including, by implication, our own loved ones who have gone on before us. This seems to me both completely unbiblical and very bad pastorally. I know that several ministers say it can be helpful to give bereaved people a special day on which they can remember those whom they have loved and lost. My own response to that is that we already have such a day; it is called Easter. To put such memories in the context of a commemoration full of darkness and gloom and the implication (though often not stated explicitly) of Purgatory is hardly a pastorally helpful practice. As Janet Meyer Everts points out, I argue here and elsewhere that the sins of which even the best Christians are conscious right up to the end are done away in death itself.

This is an argument which goes back to the early Reformation, and I think it remains as true today as ever.

I was delighted to see the way in which Dr Everts drew various hymns into her exposition. When it comes to omitting verses of hymns, it may be of passing interest to note that in 'The Church's One Foundation', the verse which begins 'Though with a scornful wonder …' is regularly missed out in St. John's College, Cambridge. The reason is simple. That verse was pointing the finger at Bishop Colenso of Natal, a distinguished graduate of St. John's College, whose views on many topics both theological and ethical were, not without reason, regarded as heretical.

When it comes to praying with and for the departed, I was greatly helped many years ago by listening to Professor Sir Norman Anderson, a leading Anglican layman who was well known as a definite protestant and evangelical. My wife and I were privileged to know Sir Norman in his latter years when we lived in Cambridge. He and his wife had suffered the appalling tragedy of losing all three of their children in early adult life, including his son who, having already been tipped as a future Prime Minister, died of a brain tumour in his early 20s. Sir Norman made it clear that he did not believe in Purgatory. His beloved children were with the Lord. But, having loved them and prayed for them throughout their all too brief lives, was he going to stop holding them in love before God just because they had now died? It was unthinkable. As so often, reaction against a false doctrine and the practice which goes with it can drive out perfectly good and sound practice. I think that is what has happened here.

To be sure, the present state of those who have died remains more mysterious than many Christians allow. The New Testament is not particularly interested in the subject – a point which I often make, and which surprises people. 'My desire is to depart', says Paul, 'and to be with the Messiah, for that is far better'. That, as Dr Everts sees, is not the end: the resurrection is yet to come. 'Heaven', in that sense, is temporary, awaiting the ultimate renewal of heaven and earth and their joining in marriage for ever. But, while the New Testament is remarkably reticent about the exact state and location of the departed, I, like Sir Norman, see no reason why the love which has held them in prayer up to this point ought not to continue to do so. But this is hardly a matter over which Christians should divide.

As with one of the earlier contributions, I was not sure what specifically 'Pentecostal' contribution this essay might bring, except the resonance of the author's own pilgrimage, embracing charismatic elements within an Anglican framework (something I could say about myself). It seems to me that from many points of view God has raised up the Pentecostal churches to remind the rest of us what we might be missing. In these days when many western Christians are not nearly so stuck in one denomination as they used to be, perhaps we can simply celebrate the many gifts we have to share with one another.

Jeffrey Lamp: Mission and Inaugurated Eschatology

I am grateful once more to Jeffrey Lamp for his crystal clear summary of the position I have argued in *Surprised by Hope*, to which I have referred a few times already. The New Testament does indeed offer resources for understanding God's ultimate future plans for his whole creation, focusing on the way in which those plans were decisively inaugurated in Jesus and his resurrection and on the way in which, by the Spirit, we can share not only in the benefits of that achievement but also in the ongoing task of building for the Kingdom. I was especially grateful that Dr Lamp made clear that particular distinction: not 'building the Kingdom', which easily collapses into a kind of socially active Pelagianism, but by the Spirit building *for* the Kingdom, doing things in the present which, to our surprise, will turn out to be part of the eventual new world that God is going to make. This perspective, I have found, can be enormously fruitful not least in helping nervous evangelicals to embrace social, cultural, and political responsibility, while at the same time helping overeager social activists to connect their strong caring impulses with the deep roots of the gospel itself.

I was glad of the final section in which Dr Lamp compares my stated position on these things with that of Dr Frank Macchia. I readily agree that our different emphases ought to complement each other. In particular, in recent years I have often found myself drawn to the picture in Isa. 11.9, Hab. 2.14, and related places: the whole earth is to be filled with the knowledge, and/or the glory, of the

Lord as the waters cover the sea. I line that up with the promise of new creation in Romans 8, and of God being 'all in all' in 1 Corinthians 15. I see it in particular in terms of the entire creation as the true Temple, to which the Temple in Jerusalem always was an advance signpost. Here I have learned much from two valued colleagues: Professor Gregory Beale of Westminster Theological Seminary, in his book *The Temple and the Church's Mission* (Downers Grove: Inter-Varsity, 2004), and Professor John Walton of Wheaton College, in his book *The Lost World of Genesis 1* (Downers Grove: Inter-Varsity, 2009). Between them they pick up the central place of the Temple in biblical theology and demonstrate that from the start it was seen as a pointer to the whole created order, with heaven and earth belonging together. As I explained in an earlier comment, this was then central both to the early Christians' view of Jesus and also to their view of the Spirit. The current popularity of pantheism (or panentheism) in various quarters shows that the somewhat arid modernist worldview, in which heaven and earth are held to be a long way apart, does not do justice to the way many people think and feel. But few realise that what Scripture offers – in the passages already mentioned – is something similar but interestingly different: a kind of eschatological 'the-en-panism', that is, the ultimate goal in which God will be 'all in all', suffusing the entire creation with his presence and love.

I take it that the point made by Dr Macchia, picked up here by Jeffrey Lamp, is that this ultimate goal is anticipated in the indwelling of the Spirit in the Church, and in the mission of the Spirit-led Church in the world. Exactly so. That is, no doubt, a hard truth to hang on to when one is ministering in difficult circumstances, when the Church itself is riven by factions and failing in its calling to holiness. But it is the truth which we grasp by faith and which, from time to time, we are privileged to glimpse. And with that there is, I believe, real convergence. We do not need to aim for *either* 'evangelism' *or* 'social action' as though these were mutually exclusive. Nor do we need to think solely of resurrection and the inauguration of new creation, on the one hand, or of the indwelling of the Spirit, on the other. We need both. All these things go together.

One of the joys of this shared study, for me at least, is in recognising how far we have come in the last generation. It would have been difficult to have this conversation twenty or thirty years ago.

Simply at the level of scholarly awareness of second-temple Judaism, we have learned a huge amount from the researches of the last generation, with the Dead Sea Scrolls being just one example among many. We understand, far better than we did, how the first-century Jewish mind worked, and hence how Jesus' first followers, and then Paul, reacted as they did to his resurrection, reflected as they did upon his death, found themselves caught up as they were in his Kingdom-mission, and went out into the world to put it all into practice, always (as we say in a characteristic Anglican blessing) 'rejoicing in the power of the Holy Spirit'. I thank God for the fellowship exemplified in this book, and in these reflections, and I pray that in the coming days we may continue to learn from one another as we share in the grace of the Lord Jesus, the love of God, and the fellowship of that same Holy Spirit.

BIBLIOGRAPHY

Alexander, Paul, *Peace to War: Shifting Allegiances in the Assemblies of God* (C. Henry Smith Series; Telford, PA: Cascadia Publishing House, 2009).

Anderson, Allan Heaton, *Introduction to Pentecostalism* (Cambridge: Cambridge University Press, 2nd edn, 2014).

Archer, Kenneth J., *A Pentecostal Hermeneutic for the Twenty-First Century* (JPTSup 28; New York: T&T Clark, 2004).

'A Statement of Catholics and Evangelicals Together: The Communion of Saints', *First Things* 131 (March 2003), pp. 26-32.

Barth, Karl, *Church Dogmatics*, III:4 (eds. G.W. Bromiley and T.F. Torrance; trans. A.T. Mackay and T.H.L. Parker; repr.; Peabody, MA: Hendrickson, 2010).

Bartholomew, Craig G., and Michael W. Goheen, *The Drama of Scripture: Finding Our Place in the Biblical Story* (Grand Rapids: Baker, 2004).

Bassett, Paul Merritt, 'The Theological Identity of the North American Holiness Movement: Its Understanding of the Nature and Role of the Bible', in Donald W. Dayton and Robert K. Johnston (eds.), *The Variety of American Evangelicalism* (Knoxville: University of Tennessee Press, 1991), pp. 72-108.

Beale, Gregory, *The Temple and the Church's Mission* (Downers Grove: InterVarsity, 2004).

Betz, Hans Dieter, *Galatians: A Commentary* (Hermeneia; Philadelphia: Fortress, 1979).

Boddy, Mary, 'The Church's One Foundation', *Confidence* 7.9 (June 1915), pp. 110-12.

Bonhoeffer, Dietrich, *Life Together, Prayerbook of the Bible* (ed. Geoffrey B. Kelly; trans. Daniel W. Bloesch and James H. Burtness; Minneapolis: Fortress, 1996).

Brown, Christopher A., 'More than Affirmation: The Incarnation as Judgment', in Ephraim Radner and George Sumner (eds.), *The Rule of Faith: Scripture, Canon, and Creed in a Critical Age* (Harrisburg, PA: Morehouse Publishing, 1998), pp. 77-91.

Calvin, John, *Institutes of the Christian Religion* (ed. John T. McNeill; trans. Ford Lewis Battles; Library of Christian Classics 21; Philadelphia: Westminster Press, 1960).

Carson, D.A., Peter T. O'Brien, and Mark Seifrid (eds.), *Justification and Variegated Nomism* (2 vols.; Grand Rapids: Baker, 2001, 2004).

Childs, Brevard S., 'The Nature of the Christian Bible: One Book, Two Testaments', in Ephraim Radner and George Sumner (eds.), *The Rule of Faith: Scripture, Canon, and Creed in a Critical Age* (Harrisburg, PA: Morehouse Publishing, 1998), pp. 115-25.

Coffey, David M., *Grace: The Gift of the Holy Spirit* (Milwaukee: Marquette University Press, 2011).

Cranfield, C.E.B., *A Critical and Exegetical Commentary on the Epistle to the Romans* (ICC; Edinburgh: T&T Clark, 1975).

Crossan, John Dominic, and Jonathan L. Reed, *In Search of Paul* (New York: HarperCollins, 1994).

Day, Nigel, 'The Church's One Foundation', *Claves Regni: The On-line Magazine of St. Peter's Church, Nottingham with All Saints*, <http://www.stpetersnottingham.org/hymns/foundation/html>.

Dempster, Murray W. *et al.* (eds.), *The Globalization of Pentecostalism: A Religion Made to Travel* (Oxford: Regnum Books, 1999).

Dodd, C.H., *According to the Scriptures: The Sub-structure of New Testament Theology* (London: Nisbet & Co., 1953).

Dunn, James, *Baptism in the Holy Spirit* (London: SCM Press, 1970).

Faupel, D. William, *The Everlasting Gospel: The Significance of Eschatology in the Development of Pentecostal Thought* (JPTSup 10; Sheffield: Sheffield Academic Press, 1996).

Fee, Gordon, 'The Kingdom of God and the Church's Global Mission', in Murray W. Dempster, Byron D. Klaus, and Douglas Peterson (eds.), *Called and Empowered: Pentecostal Perspectives on Global Mission* (Peabody, MA: Hendrickson, 1991), pp. 7-21.

—*God's Empowering Presence: The Holy Spirit in the Letters of Paul* (Peabody, MA: Hendrickson, 1994).

—*Pauline Christology: An Exegetical-Theological Study* (Peabody, MA: Hendrickson, 2007).

Fitzmyer, Joseph A., *Romans: A New Translation with Introduction and Commentary* (Anchor Bible 33; New York: Doubleday, 1993).

Frei, Hans W., *The Identity of Jesus Christ: The Hermeneutical Bases of Dogmatic Theology* (Philadelphia: Fortress Press, 1975).

Galot, Jean, *Who Is Christ?* (Chicago: Franciscan Herald Press, 1989).

Gorman, Michael, 'Effecting the Covenant: A (Not So) New New Testament Model for the Atonement', *Ex Auditu* 26 (2010), pp. 60-74.

Hauerwas, Stanley, *Matthew* (Grand Rapids: Brazos, 2006).

Hays, Richard B., *The Faith of Jesus Christ: The Narrative Substructure of Galatians 3:1–4:11* (Grand Rapids: Eerdmans, 2001).

—'Knowing Jesus: Story, History, and the Question of Truth', in N. Perrin and R.B. Hays (eds.), *Jesus, Paul, and the People of God: a Theological Dialogue with N.T. Wright* (Downers Grove: IVP, 2011), pp. 41-61.

Hollenweger, Walter J., *The Pentecostals* (Peabody, MA: Hendrickson, 2nd edn, 1988).

—'Priorities in Pentecostal Research: Historiography, Missiology, Hermeneutics, and Pneumatology', in J.A.B. Jongeneel (ed.), *Experiences in the Spirit* (Bern: Peter Lang, 1989), pp. 7-22.

—'From Azusa Street to the Toronto Phenomenon', in Jürgen Moltmann and Karl-Josef Kuschel (eds.), *Pentecostal Movements as Ecumenical Challenge* (Concilium 3; London: SCM Press, 1996), pp. 3-14.

Irenaeus, 'Against Heresies', in *The Apostolic Fathers: Justin Martyr and Irenaeus* (ed. A. Roberts and J. Donaldson; trans. A.C. Coxe; Ante-Nicene Fathers I; Peabody, MA: Hendrickson, 1994), pp. 309-576.

Jenson, Robert, *Canon and Creed* (Louisville: Westminster John Knox, 2010).

Jewett, Robert, *Romans: A Commentary* (Hermeneia; Minneapolis: Fortress, 2007).

Kärkkäinen, Veli-Matti, 'Are Pentecostals Oblivious to Social Justice? Theological and Ecumenical Perspectives', *Missionalia* 29 (2001), pp. 387-404.

—'Spirituality as a Resource for Social Justice: Reflections from the Roman Catholic-Pentecostal Dialogue', *Asian Journal of Pentecostal Theology* 6 (2003), pp. 75-88.

—'Pentecostal Pneumatology of Religions: The Contribution of Pentecostals to Our Understanding of the Word of God's Spirit in the World', in Veli-Matti Kärkkäinen (ed.), *The Spirit in the World: Emerging Pentecostal Theologies in Global Contexts* (Grand Rapids: Eerdmans, 2009), pp. 155-80.

Käsemann, Ernst, *Commentary on Romans* (trans. G.W. Bromiley; Grand Rapids: Eerdmans, 1980).

Kuhrt, Stephen, *Tom Wright for Everyone* (London: SPCK, 2011).

Levering, Matthew, *Scripture and Metaphysics: Aquinas and the Renewal of Trinitarian Theology* (Malden, MA: Blackwell, 2004).

Lewis, C.S., *Letters to Malcolm: Chiefly on Prayer* (New York: Harcourt, Brace, Jovanovich, 1963).

Longenecker, Richard N., *Galatians* (WBC 41; Dallas: Word, 1990).

Ma, Wonsuk, '"When the Poor are Fired Up": The Role of Pneumatology in Pentecostal/Charismatic Mission', in Veli-Matti Kärkkäinen (ed.), *The Spirit in the World: Emerging Pentecostal Theologies in Global Contexts* (Grand Rapids: Eerdmans, 2009), pp. 40-52.

Macchia, Frank D., *Baptized in the Spirit: A Global Pentecostal Theology* (Grand Rapids: Zondervan, 2006).
—*Justified in the Spirit: Creation, Redemption, and the Triune God* (Grand Rapids: Eerdmans, 2010).
McCabe, Herbert, *God Matters* (London: Continuum, 1987).
Menzies, Robert, *Empowered for Witness: The Spirit in Luke-Acts* (JPTSup 6; Sheffield: Sheffield Academic Press, 1994).
Moritz, Thorsten, 'Reflecting on N.T. Wright's Tools for the Task', in Craig Bartholomew *et al.* (eds.), *Renewing Biblical Interpretation* (Grand Rapids: Zondervan, 2000), pp. 172-97.
—'Critical Realism', in *Dictionary for Theological Interpretation of the Bible* (ed. Kevin J. Vanhoozer *et al.*; Grand Rapids: Baker Academic, 2005), pp. 147-50.
Newman, Carey C., *Jesus and the Restoration of Israel: A Critical Assessment of N.T. Wright's Jesus and the Victory of God* (Downers Grove: IVP, 1999).
Obeng, E.A., 'Abba Father: The Prayer of the Sons of God', *The Expository Times* 99 (1987–1988), pp. 363-66.
Ocariz, F., L.F. Mateo Seco, and J.A. Riestra, *The Mystery of Jesus Christ* (Portland, OR: Four Courts Press, 1994).
O'Collins, Gerald, *Christology: A Biblical, Historical, and Systematic Study of Jesus* (Oxford: University Press, 2009).
O'Collins, Gerald, and Daniel Kendall, *Focus on Jesus: Essays in Christology and Soteriology* (Herefordshire: Fowler Wright Books, 1996).
Outler, Albert, 'The Wesleyan Quadrilateral – in John Wesley', in Thomas C. Oden and Leicester R. Longden (eds.), *The Wesleyan Theological Heritage* (Grand Rapids: Zondervan, 1991), pp. 21-38.
Pannenberg, Wolfhart, *Systematic Theology, Volume 1* (Grand Rapids: Eerdmans, 1991).
Penney, J.M., *The Missionary Emphasis of Lukan Pneumatology* (JPTSup 12; Sheffield: Sheffield Academic Press, 1997).
Perrin, Nicholas, and Richard B. Hays (eds.), *Jesus, Paul, and the People of God: A Theological Dialogue with N.T. Wright* (Downers Grove: IVP Academic, 2011).
Peterson, Douglas, 'A Moral Imagination: Pentecostals and Social Concern in Latin America', in Veli-Matti Kärkkäinen (ed.), *The Spirit in the World: Emerging Pentecostal Theologies in Global Contexts* (Grand Rapids: Eerdmans, 2009), pp. 53-68.
Piper, John, *The Future of Justification: A Response to N.T. Wright* (Wheaton, IL: Crossway, 2007).

Reno, R.R., 'Biblical Theology and Theological Exegesis', in Craig Bartholomew *et al.* (eds.), *Out of Egypt: Biblical Theology and Biblical Interpretation* (Scripture and Hermeneutics Series vol. 5; Grand Rapids: Zondervan, 2004), pp. 385-408.

Sanders, E.P., *Paul and Palestinian Judaism: A Comparison of Patterns of Religion* (Philadelphia: Fortress, 1977).

Schreiner, Thomas R., *Romans* (Baker Exegetical Commentary on the New Testament 6; Grand Rapids: Baker, 1998).

Scofield Reference Bible (ed. C.I. Scofield; Oxford: Oxford University Press, 1906).

Segwick, Peter, 'Justification by Faith: One Doctrine, Many Debates?', *Theology* 93.751 (1990), pp. 5-13.

Sisson, Elisabeth, 'Resurrection Paper No. 7', *Latter Rain Evangel* 10.3 (July 1911), pp. 18-21.

Solivan, Samuel, *The Spirit, Pathos, and Liberation: Towards a Hispanic Pentecostal Theology* (JPT Sup 14; Sheffield: Sheffield Academic Press, 1998).

Stendahl, Krister, 'Paul and the Introspective Conscience of the West', *Harvard Theological Review* 56 (1963), pp. 199-215.

Stewart, Robert B., *The Quest of the Hermeneutical Jesus: The Impact of Hermeneutics on the Jesus Research of John Dominic Crossan and N.T. Wright* (Lanham: University Press of America, 2008).

Stewart, Robert B., John Dominic Crossan, and N.T. Wright, *The Resurrection of Jesus: John Dominic Crossan and N.T. Wright in Dialogue* (Minneapolis: Fortress, 2006).

The Book of Common Prayer and Administration of the Sacraments and Other Rites and Ceremonies of the Church According to the Use of the Protestant Episcopal Church of the United States of America (New York: The Church Pension Fund, 1945).

Treier, Daniel J., *Introducing Theological Interpretation of Scripture: Recovering a Christian Practice* (Grand Rapids: Baker Academic, 2008).

Wallis, Ian G., *The Faith of Jesus Christ in Early Christian Traditions* (New York: Cambridge University Press, 1995).

Walton, John, *The Lost World of Genesis 1* (Downers Grove: Inter-Varsity, 2009).

Witherington, Ben, III, *Grace in Galatia: A Commentary on Paul's Letter to the Galatians* (Grand Rapids: Eerdmans, 1998).

Witherington, Ben, III, and Darlene Hyatt, *Paul's Letter to the Romans: A Socio-Rhetorical Commentary* (Grand Rapids: Eerdmans, 2004).

Wright, N.T., *Colossians and Philemon* (Tyndale New Testament Commentary; Grand Rapids: Eerdmans, 1986).

—'Jesus', in *New Dictionary of Theology* (ed. David F. Wright *et al.*; Downers Grove: IVP, 1988), pp. 348-51.

—'How Can the Bible Be Authoritative?', *Vox Evangelica* 21 (1991), pp. 7-32.
—*Climax of the Covenant: Christ and the Law in Pauline Theology* (Minneapolis: Fortress, 1992).
—*The New Testament and the People of God* (Christian Origins and the Question of God 1; Minneapolis: Fortress, 1992).
—*The Crown and the Fire: Meditations on the Cross and the Life of the Spirit* (Grand Rapids: Eerdmans, 1995).
—'Romans and the Theology of Paul', in David M. Hay and E. Elizabeth Johnson (eds.), *Romans* (vol. 3 of *Pauline Theology*; Minneapolis: Fortress, 1995), pp. 30-67.
—*Jesus and the Victory of God* (Christian Origins and the Question of God 2; Minneapolis: Fortress, 1996).
—*For All God's Worth: True Worship and the Calling of the Church* (Grand Rapids: Eerdmans, 1997).
—*The Lord and His Prayer* (Grand Rapids: Eerdmans, 1997).
—*What Saint Paul Really Said: Was Paul of Tarsus the Real Founder of Christianity?* (Grand Rapids: Eerdmans, 1997).
—'Jesus and the Identity of God', *Ex Auditu* 14 (1998), pp. 42-56.
—*Reflecting the Glory: Meditations for Living Christ's Life in the World* (Minneapolis: Augsburg Fortress, 1998).
—*The Challenge of Jesus: Rediscovering Who Jesus Was and Is* (Downers Grove: IVP, 1999).
—'New Exodus, New Inheritance: The Narrative Structure of Romans 3–8', in Sven K. Soderlund and N.T. Wright (eds.), *Romans and the People of God: Essays in Honor of Gordon D. Fee on the Occasion of His 65th Birthday* (Grand Rapids: Eerdmans, 1999), pp. 26-35.
—'Jesus' Resurrection and Christian Origins', <http://www.ntwrightpage.com/Wright_Jesus_Resurrection.html>, 2002.
—'Jesus' Self-Understanding', in Stephen T. Davis, Daniel Kendall, and Gerald O'Collins (eds.), *Incarnation: An Interdisciplinary Symposium* (Oxford: Oxford University Press, 2002), pp. 47-61.
—'N.T. Wright Talks About History and Belief: Resurrection Faith', *Christian Century* 119.26 (December 18, 2002), pp. 28-31.
—*Romans* (New Interpreter's Bible 10; Nashville: Abingdon Press, 2002).
—*For All the Saints? Remembering the Christian Departed* (Harrisburg, PA: Morehouse, 2003).
—*The Resurrection of the Son of God* (Christian Origins and the Question of God 3; Minneapolis: Fortress, 2003).
—*Paul for Everyone: 1 Corinthians* (Louisville: Westminster John Knox, 2004).
—'The Holy Spirit in the Church', <http://www.fulcrum-anglican.org.uk/events/2005/inthechurch.cfm>, 2005.

—*The Last Word: Scripture and the Authority of God – Getting Beyond the Bible Wars* (San Francisco: Harper Collins, 2005).
—*Paul: In Fresh Perspective* (Minneapolis: Fortress, 2005).
—'New Perspectives on Paul', in Bruce L. McCormack (ed.), *Justification in Perspective: Historical Developments and Contemporary Challenges* (Grand Rapids: Baker Academic, 2006), pp. 243-64.
—*Simply Christian: Why Christianity Makes Sense* (San Francisco: Harper Collins, 2006).
—'4QMMT and Paul: Justification, "Works", and Eschatology', in Aang-Won (Aaron) Son (ed.), *History and Exegesis: New Testament Essays in Honor of Dr. E. Earle Ellis for His 80th Birthday* (New York: T&T Clark, 2006), pp. 104-32.
—'Wrightsaid Q&A for June 2007', <http://www.ntwrightpage.com/Wrightsaid_June2007.html>, 2007.
—'Reading Paul, Thinking Scripture', in Markus Bockmuehl and Alan J. Torrance (eds.), *Scripture's Doctrine and Theology's Bible: How the New Testament Shapes Christian Dogmatics* (Grand Rapids: Eerdmans, 2008), pp. 59-74.
—*Surprised by Hope: Rethinking Heaven, the Resurrection, and the Mission of the Church* (New York: Harper One, 2008).
—*Justification: God's Plan & Paul's Vision* (Downers Grove: IVP Academic, 2009).
—*After You Believe: Why Christian Character Matters* (San Francisco: Harper Collins, 2010).
—'Response to Richard Hays', in Nicholas Perrin and Richard B. Hays (eds.), *Jesus, Paul, and the People of God: a Theological Dialogue with N.T. Wright* (Downers Grove: IVP, 2011), pp. 62-65.
—*Simply Jesus: A New Vision of Who He Was, What He Did, and Why He Matters* (New York: HarperOne, 2011).
—'Whence and Whither Historical Jesus Studies in the Life of the Church', in Nicholas Perrin and Richard B. Hays (eds.) *Jesus, Paul, and the People of God: A Theological Dialogue with N.T. Wright* (Downers Grove: IVP, 2011), pp. 262-81.
—*How God Became King* (London: SPCK and HarperOne, 2012).
—*Paul and the Faithfulness of God* (London: SPCK and Fortress Press, 2013).
—*Pauline Perspectives* (London: SPCK and Fortress Press, 2013).
—*Simply Good News* (London: SPCK and HarperOne, 2015).
Wright, N.T. (ed.), *The Work of John Frith* (Appleford: Sutton Courtenay Press, 1983).

Yong, Amos, *Spirit-Word-Community: Theological Hermeneutics in Trinitarian Perspective* (Eugene, OR: Wipf & Stock, 2002).

—*The Spirit Poured out on All Flesh: Pentecostalism and the Possibility of Global Theology* (Grand Rapids: Baker Academic, 2005).

Yong, Amos (ed.), *The Spirit Renews the Face of the Earth: Pentecostal Forays in Science and Theology of Creation* (Eugene, OR: Pickwick, 2009).

Yun, Koo Dong, 'Pentecostalism from Below: Minjung Liberation and Asian Pentecostal Theology', in Veli-Matti Kärkkäinen (ed.), *The Spirit in the World: Emerging Pentecostal Theologies in Global Contexts* (Grand Rapids: Eerdmans, 2009), pp. 89-114.

Index of Biblical (and Other Ancient) References

Old Testament

Genesis
1	10, 59, 132
1.26	10
1.28	92
3.15	104
12.1-3	12
15	12

Exodus
| 19.6 | 145 |

Deuteronomy
27-30	146
27-29	91-92
28-30	77
29.10-30.6	14
30	16, 146, 170
30.16	83
32	146, 170

2 Samuel
| 7 | 88 |

Ezra
| 3.13 | 91 |
| 9.9 | 91 |

Psalms
2	171
19	11
74	11

Proverbs
| 3.19 | 10 |

Isaiah
11.9	176-77
12	142
18.19-21	42
32.14-16	81
33.5	92
42.6	92
49.6	92
52.5	92
52.13-53.12	15

Ezekiel
| 36.22 | 92 |

Daniel
| 7 | 95, 97, 169, 172 |
| 9 | 146 |

Hosea
| 10.12 | 81 |

Habakkuk
| 2.14 | 176-77 |

Haggai
| 2.3 | 91 |

New Testament

Matthew
6.10	127
21.43	103-4
24.30	95
24.31	97
24.36-44	96-97
24.40-41	97
26.28	79-80
28.18	151, 154

Mark
10.35-45	159
13	173
13.26	95, 172
14.24	79-80
14.62	172

Luke
18.1-8	122
21.23-24	96
21.24	89
21.27	95
22.20	79-80
23.43	114, 127

John
1	156
5.30	41-42
12.24	79-80
14.2	127
16.12-15	160
17	120

Acts
1	173
1.8	136
1.11	96, 130
2.17	xii

Romans
1-11	11
1-8	100, 166
1-4	166
1.4	83
1.17	83
1.18-23	92
2	166
2.6	99
2.24	92
2.25-29	146, 166
2.25	100
2.26	100
3	168
3.20	99
3.21	83
3.23-24	79
4	12, 78-79, 168, 171
4.3	98

Romans, cont'd		11.25	89, 100-1	3.13	15
4.9	98	11.26	90, 99-100	3.14	80, 81
4.13	171	11.32	79	3.16	15
4.17	83			3.21	14, 83
4.23	83	*1 Corinthians*		4	66, 167
4.25	83	2	118	4.4-7	66, 67
5-8	166	2.6	116	4.6	61, 66, 69-72
5	115, 166	4.8	93	5.19-21	93, 99
5.12-21	92	6.9-11	93	6.16	90, 100
5.12	11	6.9-10	99		
5.18	83	8.6	10	*Ephesians*	
5.21	83	12-14	109	2.10	99
6-8	16	12.2	100	4.17	100
6	16, 19, 170	12.3	66		
6.7	115	12.30	25	*Philippians*	
6.8-11	115	13	109, 118	1.6	66, 168
7.1-8.11	16	13.11	116, 123	1.22	114, 116
7.7-12	92	13.13	109, 116,	1.23	94, 123, 127
7.7	14		118-19, 120	2.5-11	92
7.8b-9	14	15	11, 119, 169,	2.6-11	159
7.9-11	14		177	2.9-11	146
7.13	14	15.20-28	172	2.10-11	154
8	19, 66, 115,	15.23	113	3.2-11	168
	166, 167,	15.24	93, 116	3.2	100
	171, 177	15.28	127	3.20-21	169
8.3	15	15.45	20, 92		
8.4	72	15.51-57	169	*Colossians*	
8.9	66	15.52	116	1	156
8.10-11	169	15.58	132	1.15-20	11
8.12-30	16			1.15	92
8.12-17	66	*2 Corinthians*		1.16	10
8.12-16	66	1.20	171	1.20	11
8.15	61, 69-72	3.6	83	3	170
8.18-25	21, 127	5.17	19, 22		
8.34	146			*1 Thessalonians*	
9-11	79, 171	*Galatians*		2.12	93
9-10	100	2	168	4	169
9.6-10.21	170	2.15-21	168	4.5	100
10	146	2.17-20	81	4.13-5.11	21
10.1-13	146	2.17	80	4.16-17	97, 130
10.4	103	3	78-79, 168,	4.17	105
10.5-13	16		171		
11	100, 171	3.1-5	80	*2 Timothy*	
11.11	89	3.3	60	2.15	88
11.13-14	101	3.6-18	12		
11.25-27	100-1	3.8	80, 81	*Hebrews*	
11.25-26	90 100-1	3.10-14	146	1.3	42

Hebrews, cont'd		*2 Peter*		20.6	145
5.8	38	1.16	164	20.11	89
11	118			21-22	21, 126
11.1	118	*Revelation*			
11.39-12.2	112	1.6	145	Apocrypha /	
12	121	4-5	126	Pseudepigrapha	
12.2	37	5.10	145		
13.8	154	6.10	114, 116, 121, 122	*Wisdom of Solomon*	
				7.22-8.1	10
1 Peter		12.11	118		
2.9	145	20	95	*4 Ezra* [= *2 Esdras*]	
		20.1-6	88	12.12	172

Index of Authors

Alexander, P.   134
Anderson, A.H.   5
Anderson, N.   175
Archer, K.J.   51
Augustine   62, 70, 77
Barth, K.   53-54, 73-74, 166
Bartholomew, C.G.   23
Bassett, P.M.   52-53
Baxter, R.   112, 120, 122
Beale, G.   177
Betz, H.D.   70
Blaising, C.   87
Bock, D.   87
Boddy, A.   38, 144
Boddy, M.   38
Bonhoeffer, D.   73-75, 166
Borg, M.   94
Breshears, G.   87
Brown, C.A.   40
Bucer, M.   112
Bultmann, R.   96, 105, 156, 163
Caird, G.   173
Calvin, J.   33, 87-88, 90, 101-4, 111-12, 120-22
Carson, D.A.   19
Chafer, L.S.   87
Childs, B.S.   40
Coffey, D.M.   53
Cranfield, C.E.B.   71-72
Crossan, J.D.   21-22, 151
Darby, J.N.   87, 88
Day, N.   117
Dempster, M.W.   3
Dodd, C.H.   93, 173
Dunn, J.D.G.   80
Everts, J.M.   xi, xiv, 5, 174-76
Faupel, D.W.   134
Fee, G.   70-71, 74-75, 137
Fitzmyer, J.A.   71
Franklin, B.   1
Frei, H.W.   39, 148, 156
Frith, J.   166

Fuller, T.   1
Galot, J.   38
Goheen, M.W.   23
Gorman, M.   79-80, 167
Green, C.   x-xi, 4, 148-60
Gregory of Nyssa   136
Hauerwas, S.   40, 148
Hays, R.B.   1, 18, 32, 40-41, 63, 148-49
Hollenweger, W.J.   23
Hyatt, D.   69
Irenaeus   39, 84
Jenson, R.   40-41, 148
Jewett, R.   69
Josephus   163
Kärkkäinen, V-M   24, 134-35
Käsemann, E.   71, 153
Kendall, D.   38
Kuhrt, S.   142
Lamp, J.S.   xi, xii, xiv, 1, 2, 4, 5, 6, 144-48, 176-77
Land, S.   3
Levering, M.   33
Lewis, C.S.   114, 150
Longenecker, R.N.   70
Luther, M.   74-75, 90, 98-99, 102, 112
Ma, W.   135
Macchia, F.D.   ix, 4-5, 23, 60-61, 73, 134-39, 167-68, 176-77
Martin, L.R.   2, 6
McCabe, H.   37
McGrath, A.   62
Menzies, G.W.   x, xi, 5, 169-74
Menzies, R.   23
Moritz, T.   45, 47-48
Newman, C.C.   34
Obeng, E.A.   69
O'Brien, P.T.   19
Ocariz, F.   38
O'Collins, G.   27, 37-39
Outler, A.   55

Index of Authors

Pannenberg, W. 41, 53
Penney, J.M. 23
Pentecost, D. 87
Perrin, Nicholas 1
Perrin, Norman 163
Peterson, D. 134
Piper, J. 1-2, 4, 19, 61, 85
Reed, J. 21
Reno, R.R. 39
Riestra, J.A. 38
Ryrie, C. 87
Sanders, E.P. 80, 167
Saucy, R. 87
Schäfer, P. 90
Schreiner, T.R. 71
Schweitzer, A. 94, 167
Scofield, C.I. 87, 88, 104
Seco, L.F.M. 38
Segwick, P. 76
Seifrid, M. 19
Senapatiratne, T. xiii, 4, 160-66
Sisson, E. 41-43, 148-49
Solivan, S. 135
Stendahl, K. 76-77, 87, 90, 171
Stewart, R.B. 22, 28, 34
Stone, S. 117
Thomas, J.C. 6
Treier, D.J. 54
Wadholm, R. ix, 4, 166-67
Wallis, I.G. 37-38
Walton, J. 177
Walvoord, J. 87
Wesley, J. 53, 55, 57, 165
Wilkerson, D. 143
Witherington, B. 69-70
Yong, A. 2, 23, 25, 53, 134-35
Yun, K.D. 134-35